NEW WOMEN,
NEW NOVELS

ANN L. ARDIS

NEW WOMEN, NEW NOVELS

Feminism and Early Modernism

RUTGERS UNIVERSITY PRESS
NEW BRUNSWICK *and* LONDON

Copyright © 1990 by Ann L. Ardis
All rights reserved
Manufactured in the United States of America

Library of Congress Cataloging-in-Publication Data

Ardis, Ann L., 1957–
    New women, new novels: Feminism and early modernism / Ann L.
Ardis.
        p.   cm.
    Includes bibliographical references (p.   )
    ISBN 0-8135-1581-5 (cloth)   ISBN 0-8135-1582-3 (pbk.)
    1. English fiction—19th century—History and criticism.
    2. English fiction—20th century—History and criticism.
    3. Feminism and literature—Great Britain.   4. Modernism
(Literature)—Great Britain.   5. Women and literature—Great
Britain.   6. Feminism in literature.   7. Women in literature.
    I. Title.
PR878.F45A74   1990
823'.089352042—dc20   90-35039
                                                                          CIP

British Cataloging-in-Publication information available

For

Ethel Layer Ardis

and

Phillip David Mink

CONTENTS

ACKNOWLEDGMENTS

I TAKE THIS opportunity to thank, first, the Education Foundation of the American Association of University Women. Under the auspices of an A.A.U.W. dissertation fellowship, I began this project. *Because* of that fellowship, I gained the confidence I needed to finish it.

I also thank Michael Chase-Levenson and Holly Laird, whose comments on early versions of this study guided my work well beyond the dissertation. Michael in particular was willing to read drafts long before I should have given them to him, and for that I am both embarrassed and grateful. Margaret Stetz not only engaged me in conversation about New Women and New Woman novels, she and Mark Samuels Lasner gave me the run of their library, introduced me to the look and feel of the 1890s. And the men and women who participated in the University of Virginia's Feminist Theory Reading Group between 1984 and 1987 have been an imagined audience for this work.

Thanks also go to Janice Harris, Leslie Mitchner, and my colleagues who read more recent versions of this project: Barry Chabot, Barbara Gates, Kerry Powell, Judith Roof, Jim Sosnoski, and Kristina Straub. A Miami University Summer Research Grant enabled me to make a second research trip to England. Dale Bauer was generous enough to read parts of the manuscript more than once or twice, each time regaling me with witty, insightful marginalia.

Finally, I thank the friends and family who have sustained me: Deborah Booth, Michael Williams, and the rest of the gang at Williams Corner Bookstore filled my time away from the dissertation with laughter. Wally Parchment, Trudy Rush, and the Rush family gave me weekends to look forward to after long days in the British Library. Anne Djokic kept track of both my progress on this project and the elk migrations in Jackson, Wyoming. My family has humored me and, I hope, forgives me for being the last to arrive and the first to leave family gatherings for the past five years. And Phillip Mink has lived with and talked me through all of this. My thanks go always to him.

NEW WOMEN,
NEW NOVELS

INTRODUCTION

Attending to Marginality:
The New Woman,
the New Woman Novel,
and the History of Modernism

S HE WAS CALLED "Novissima": the New Woman, the Odd Woman, the Wild Woman, and the Superfluous Woman in English novels and periodicals of the 1880s and 1890s. A tremendous amount of polemic was wielded against her for choosing not to pursue the conventional bourgeois woman's career of marriage and motherhood. Indeed, for her transgressions against the sex, gender, and class distinctions of Victorian England, she was accused of instigating the second fall of man. The anonymous author of an 1889 *Westminster Review* article, for example, claims that the New Woman's attempts to transform herself from a relative creature into a woman of independent means are "intimately connected" with "the stirrings and rumblings now perceivable in the social and industrial world, the 'Bitter Cries' of the disinherited classes, the 'Social Wreckage' which is becoming able to make itself unpleasantly prominent, the 'Problems of Great Cities,' the spread of Socialism and Nihilism."[1] Having noted that social change, once instigated, cannot be revoked, this author ends his essay by reminding his readers of an ancient fable with a modern moral. When the Fisherman liberated the genii in Hans Christian Andersen's fairy tale, the genii "promptly rewarded him by proposing to annihilate

him." As with the Fisherman, "so it will fare with the modern emanci-
pators." Though the world has decided that the "Ego [of Woman] shall
have the apple . . . the world cannot foresee the changes which its
liberality will bring about." "The Ego [of Woman] is a mighty Gen[ii],
and the acrid smoke of its ascent may disintegrate many precious superorganic structures" (382).

Rewriting the Andersen fairy tale as Genesis and characterizing the
New Woman as Eve in her bid for emancipation from the Victorian cult
of true womanhood, this critic accomplishes several things. He naturalizes the cultural status quo; he figures social change as violation of a
God-given order. And he domesticates the problems associated with or
produced by Victorian England's transitional industrial economy by
characterizing them as part and parcel of "The Woman Question." To
put this another way, he subordinates other social concerns to this
particular one, thereby presuming to solve them all when he offers his
moral: keep "the Ego" from getting the apple, and you might still
convince yourself that Victorian England is a prelapsarian state. Liberate her and you will bring about the "disintegration" of patriarchal
bourgeois culture. Liberate her and all else will be lost, for this will be
no fortunate fall.

In spite of such dire predictions, English culture survived the turning of the new century. If certain "precious superorganic structures"
like the novel "disintegrated" in the process, however, we might well
wonder how the "Ego of Woman" contributed to that transformation.
In addressing this general issue, my study organizes itself around two
more specific questions: namely, why were so many apocalyptic stories
written about the New Woman at the turn of the century? And why is
she so conspicuously absent from modernism's stories about its own
genesis? Why, in other words, was the uproar in the 1880s and 1890s
about the New Woman followed by such a resounding silence?

This book differs most importantly from previous research on the
New Woman and the fiction written about her at the turn of the
century in terms of the claims made about the place of this fiction in
modern literary and cultural history. With the notable exceptions of
Tess of the D'Urbervilles, *Jude the Obscure*, and *The Odd Women*, most
critics have excluded New Woman novels from genealogies of modern-

ism. In the handful of studies written about them to date, these novels have often been characterized as a literary subcultural backwater, rank with hysterical feminist fervor.[2] The female writers among this company have been described even by some feminist critics as a pool of mediocre talents out of which the great female modernists emerged.[3] The first approach treats the novels as evidence of the final failure of nineteenth-century English realism. The second, while establishing their importance for later writers, limits their sphere of influence unnecessarily to women writers—and defines such influence in relatively negative terms.

In contrast, I will argue that the New Woman novelists anticipate the reappraisal of realism we usually credit to early-twentieth-century writers. Most obviously, the "natural" inevitability of the marriage plot is challenged as New Woman novelists "replace" "the pure woman," the Victorian angel in the house, with a heroine who either is sexually active outside of marriage or abstains from sex for political rather than moral reasons. In more subtle ways, the Victorian conceptualization of "character" or identity as something seamless, unified, and consistent over time is also shattered as these novelists demystify the ideology of "womanliness," an ideology that gives middle-class women "no life but in the affections."[4] In some of these novels the convention of omniscience is also dismantled by female characters who assert their autonomy from a male narrator—thereby turning what Mikhail Bakhtin terms the "monologic" structuring of realistic narrative into a polyphonic form. And in still others, the epistemology of representation is itself questioned, as New Woman novelists reject the reality principle governing the tradition of literary realism. Instead of assuming that art imitates reality and re-presents something both external and prior to the work of fiction, these authors figure desires that have never been realized before; they imagine worlds quite different from the bourgeois patriarchy in which unmarried women are deemed odd and superfluous "side character[s] in modern life."[5]

Three aspects of this fiction that previously have been taken as signs of its aesthetic deficiency will be highlighted here: its ideological self-consciousness, its intertextuality, and its disruption of the conventional distinction between popular culture and high art. The intertextual dynamic, the increasingly diversified "conversation" among what I term naturalistic, antinaturalistic, and utopian narratives about the New Woman, means that these novels defy formalist assumptions about the "unity" of a literary work. Insofar as they make frequent reference to extratextual circumstances, they resist a reader's efforts to extricate the literary artifact from history, and thereby from politics. Because their authors choose *not* to view art as a sphere of cultural activity separate from the realm of politics and history, these narratives refuse to be discrete. They do not want to be read singly or separately; moreover, they choose not to be silent about the intertextual debate in which they participate.

Because these narratives also resist classification as either popular or high art fiction, their commercial success was very threatening to the critical establishment at the turn of the century. Over a hundred novels were written about the New Woman between 1883 and 1900.[6] A few are by authors like Thomas Hardy and George Gissing. A handful of others are by well-known popular writers of the period—writers such as Ouida, Rhoda Broughton, Mrs. Elizabeth Lynn Linton, and John Strange Winter, all of whom were well established in their novel-writing careers before they contributed to the debate over the New Woman. Still other New Woman novels are by writers known at the time for their work in nonliterary fields. Grant Allen, for example, was known as a popular science writer when *The Woman Who Did*, one of the most hotly contested New Woman novels, appeared in 1895. But by far the majority of these narratives, many of which went through numerous editions in quick succession, are by writers who were as unfamiliar to the Victorian reading public as they are to most Victorian specialists today. And the critical establishment responded hostilely to the success of these unknown writers in particular. Demanding in true Arnoldian fashion that the public recognize a distinction in kind between "classics" and these "racy" new novels, conservative critics depoliticized "Literature" as they sought to disenfranchise the New Woman novel. They began to valorize the kind of formalist aesthetic we associate with high modernism as they tried to steer readers away from these highly politicized and controversial works.

Anglo-American modernism is usually said to have begun as a literary movement after the turn of the century. It "explains" itself as a formalism, an aesthetic centered on neutrality and apolitical objectivity. Why might it have been important for modernists *not* to acknowledge either turn-of-the-century New Woman writers' experimentations with the form of the novel or the "gate-keeping" stance of these writers' harshest critics? Gayatri Spivak's reflections on the politics of cultural explanations suggest that there is reason to interrogate the modernists' silence on the subject of the New Woman and the New Woman novel. In her essay, "Explanation and Culture: Marginalia," Spivak invites us to "displace the distinction between margin and center" in the explanations that constitute our culture.[7] When we attend to marginality, she suggests, we begin to suspect "that what is at the center [of our cultural narratives] often hides a repression" (104). More specifically, what is repressed are "the practical politics of cultural explanations" (104). And the only way to avoid reinforcing or contributing to this kind of repression is by "narrating the relation of center and margin" as a "shifting limit" (102).

Spivak's observations are provocative in thinking about the relations between margins and centers that come into play in juxtaposing the turn-of-the-century New Woman novel with the "masterworks" of high modernism. To attend to marginality, to narrate a shifting limit between the New Woman novel and high modernism, means challenging the familiar periodization of modern literary history.[8] Still more importantly, it means addressing the politics repressed by the modernists' "explanations" of early-twentieth-century literary and cultural history. It means exposing the reactionary conservatism that is so often occluded by the modernist valorization of style over content.

There is another margin-center dynamic I want to interrogate in this study, however: the marginalization of the New Woman novel in revisionary histories of this period written by contemporary feminist critics. As both Sheila Jeffreys and David Rubenstein have noted, the suffragettes have tended to overshadow other women and other aspects of women's history at the turn of the century.[9] While Rubenstein argues that this neglect has been redressed in current work on the 1890s, he does not try to account for the negative tenor of recent "revisionings" of this history. Two studies are worth mentioning in this context, both of which "reclaim" this period—but reproduce earlier critics' condemnations of the New Woman novel in particular.

In the introduction to her pioneering work of feminist criticism, *A Literature of Their Own* (1977), Elaine Showalter writes quite movingly of the way "the lost continent of the female tradition [rises] like Atlantis from the sea of English literature" as the "works of dozens of women writers [are] rescued from . . . 'the enormous condescension of posterity.' "[10] Yet, she herself treats the work of late-nineteenth-century women writers with enormous condescension. In her study, the novels of Olive Schreiner, George Egerton, and Sarah Grand resurface—only to be sunk again, more deeply, more irretrievably. In spite of her commitment to the lost Atlantis of a female literary tradition, and in spite of her interest in what she more recently has termed "gyno-criticism," Showalter finds nothing to value in these "minor" works by "minor" women writers.[11] Criticizing Olive Schreiner's interest in rejecting "the biological yoke of femininity," characterizing Schreiner, Egerton, and Grand as women "disgusted by sex and terrified by childbirth," Showalter argues that these writers had nothing to offer the twentieth-century women writers she turns to next in her study (190). Identifying three stages in the British women's literary tradition (feminine, feminist, female), Showalter characterizes the movement from the second to the third as a complete reversal of program; turn-of-the-century feminist writers, she claims, had only one story to tell, and exhausted themselves in telling it (215).

Patricia Stubbs is equally dismissive of the New Woman novel in *Feminism and the Novel: Women and Fiction, 1880–1920* (1979). Nineteenth-century women writers, she argues, never "discarded the traditional association in fiction between women and private feeling."[12] Because of this, "far from being a radical departure from tradition," the "new but ultimately disproportionate emphasis placed on female sexuality" in the New Woman novel at the turn of the century cannot be considered a "genuinely feminist" development in the history of the novel (xiii). Turn-of-the-century feminists, she goes on to argue, were "blind to the revolutionary possibilities of their movement" (132). Such blindness then leads Stubbs to locate, as if by default, all innovations in the treatment of female character at the turn of the century in the work of

Henry James, Arnold Bennett, and D. H. Lawrence. If, as Stubbs argues, the "virgin heroine" disappeared from English fiction between 1880 and 1920, she seems determined not to lay credit for this at the feet of the woman writers of the period (225).

Why, given their commitment to "gynocriticism," do Showalter and Stubbs reproduce the condescension of posterity toward the New Woman novel, even as they "rescue" a canon of women's writing from the Sargasso Sea of uncanonized literature? Why do certain segments of women's history still remain hidden from history? And what connections can be made between the modernists' silence and the condescension or silence of feminist literary and cultural historians on the subject of the New Woman?

Several things need to be taken into account in answering such questions. I would begin by noting that *A Literature of Their Own* and *Feminism and the Novel* were both written at a point in time when feminist criticism was making its first inroads into the academy. Notwithstanding my objections to Showalter's and Stubbs's characterizations of late nineteenth-century feminist writing, I think that both of these studies have to be recognized as landmarks in the history of feminist criticism: works that both legitimized the study of women's writing and brought feminist criticism onto the center stage of debate in the discipline of English studies. But I also think Barbara Herrnstein Smith's criticism of feminist work in general pertains to these studies in particular: namely, a "non-canonical theory of value" is not developed in these studies.[13] The literary canon is attacked—but we are not disabused of the idea that we need a set of "masterworks." A new canon, a female countercanon, is promulgated, but the production of literary value has not been demystified. In short, these critics continue to practice a "magisterial mode" of evaluation as they rain praises on Doris Lessing and Monique Wittig, respectively, while confirming traditional views of the New Woman novel as a "topos of disvalue."[14]

If such studies are not as revisionary or as revolutionary as they claim to be, there are at least two reasons for this that Herrnstein Smith does not acknowledge. First, feminist criticism's marginality within the discipline of English studies even in the late 1970s would have made a different strategy of argument implausible. In other words, instead of simply criticizing Showalter and Stubbs for failing to produce a noncanonical theory of value, I take the defensiveness of their arguments about the New Woman novel as a sign of feminist criticism's marginality in the academy in the 1970s. These early feminist arguments need to be recognized as compromise formations. The endorsement of traditional standards of literary value was the price these critics paid for getting the academy to take women's literature seriously.

It should come as no surprise that the standard of literary value that Showalter and Stubbs reproduce is the aesthetic of high modernism. Others have told the story of how this aesthetic was first institutionalized in the 1930s, 1940s, and 1950s with the advent of New Criticism.[15] Together with the marginality of feminist criticism in the 1970s, the fact that the modernist aesthetic is still dominant today begins to explain, I think, why Showalter and Stubbs reinforced a New Critic like Lloyd Fernando's evaluation of the New Woman novel. Notwithstanding the differences in their methodologies, feminists and New Critics alike have agreed that these novels are disfigured by their feminist politics. And the echo of the modernists' judgments of this material is easy enough to hear in recent revaluations of these narratives, revaluations that still see these narratives as bemired in history, never aspiring to be Yeatsian "monuments of unaging intellect."

The past ten years have seen considerable changes in the discipline of English studies: postmodern literary theory continues to challenge the traditional humanistic orientation of literary studies. Anglo-American feminists—white women as well as women of color—have joined what Barbara Christian terms the race for theory, trading their sensible shoes and their willingness to do the dirty work of literary historical housekeeping for the more glamourously abstract interests of French-inspired theory.[16] And third-world and multicultural scholars have begun demanding further revisions of the canons that were revised in the 1970s and early 1980s.

Why, then, write a study of the New Woman novel now? First, because the practical politics of modernism are revealed when we attend to its margins, centering our attention on the works it excludes from its "explanation" of modern literary and cultural history. And second, because the New Woman novel gives us an opportunity to reflect on the history of feminist criticism: gives us reason to interrogate our own omissions and exclusions. In *Nostalgia and Sexual Difference*, Janice Doane and Devon Hodges analyze male American writers' responses to contemporary feminism. According to Doane and Hodges, the writers they term "nostalgic" "construct visions of a golden past," a prelapsarian or natural patriarchal social order.[17] Denying the differences within feminism, these nostalgic writers also create a monolithic Medusa-like figure of The Feminist, against whom they do combat. In defeating her, they can then claim to have protected the fatherland from the Enemy. In view of feminists' own surprisingly unsympathetic interpretations of the New Woman, one might well ask whether a similar nostalgia has informed contemporary feminists' searchs in our mothers' gardens. Have we in fact contributed to the labeling of the feminist as Other by marginalizing certain portions of our history? Because the naming of the feminist is such an interesting process, I devote Chapter One to this subject. A discussion of the fiction written about the New Woman cannot be undertaken until we have considered the violent rhetoric with which she herself was greeted at the turn of the century.

1

Preliminaries:
Naming the New Woman

GIVEN THAT THE New Woman
was so many things to so many people at the turn of the century, the
name we have remembered her by is oddly singular. Two issues concern
me here: how the New Woman acquired her name, and why the
naming process was so charged for critics such as Mrs. Elizabeth Lynn
Linton—why it was so important to have a label for this agent (and
representative) of social change.

Ellen Jordan tells the "how" part of this story with great spirit in her
essay, "The Christening of the New Woman: May 1894." According to
Jordan, "the first indication that a new breed of feminist was in the
process of being born" came as early as 1883 "with the publication . . . of Olive Schreiner's novel, *The Story of an African Farm*."[1] But
the New Woman was not actually christened as such until Ouida, in
May of 1894, responded to Sarah Grand's essay, "The New Aspects of
the Woman Question," which had been published two months earlier
in the March 1894 issue of *North American Review*. Prior to 1894, the
New Woman had been called Novissima, the Odd Woman, the Wild
Woman, and the Superfluous or Redundant Woman.[2] It is Ouida,
Jordan notes, who "selected out" the now-familiar phrase 'the New
Woman' from Grand's title and "supplied the all-important capital
letters" (20). The passage of interest reads as follows:

> It can scarcely be disputed, I think, that in the English language
> there are conspicuous at the present moment two words which

designate two unmitigated bores: The Workingman and the Woman. The Workingman and the Woman, the New Woman, be it remembered, meet us at every page of literature written in the English tongue, and each is convinced that on its own especial W hangs the future of the world.[3]

Naming the New Woman in this manner, Ouida furnished *Punch* and the *Pall Mall Gazette* with both a target for attack and a way to release anxiety about changes in the Victorian social order. The relevance of Freud's theories about the psychological functions of the joke should be obvious: rather than consider seriously either the New Woman or any of the "old" aspects of the "Woman Question," critics who followed Ouida's example subsequently singled out the New Woman for ridicule.[4]

If Jordan is right and the New Woman was not labeled as such until 1894, nevertheless her account fails to explain how the name itself was a means of controlling the phenomenon: a way of undermining the seriousness of real New Women's criticisms of the Victorian social order while at the same time trivializing the "real life" consequences of a literary phenomenon. Jordan, in other words, can explain how *Punch* got the idea for its tomfoolery at the expense of the New Woman in the May 26, 1894 issue:

THE NEW WOMAN

("OUIDA" says "the New Woman" is an unmitigated bore. "SARAH GRAND" declares that Man, morally, "is in his infancy" and that "now Woman holds out a strong hand to the Child-Man, and insists upon helping him" by "spanking proper principles into him in the nursery.")

> *There is a New Woman, and what do you think?*
> *She lives upon nothing but Foolscap and ink!*
> *But though Foolscap and Ink are the whole of her diet,*
> *This nagging New Woman can never be quiet!*[5]

Jordan cannot, however, explain the plethora of highly charged rhetoric that predates Ouida's naming of the New Woman. Significantly, such rhetoric was aimed not at characters in novels but at real women, women whose violations of the social code were viewed as a serious threat to bourgeois culture's hegemony. In other words, if naming the New Woman gave the debate about "new aspects of the Woman Question" a sharper focus, it also narrowed that debate. In the 1880s and early 1890s, the New Woman was implicated for all manner of "social ills"—from the falling national birthrate to "the 'Problems of Great Cities' " and the "rise of Socialism and Nihilism."[6] After Ouida's essay appeared in May of 1894, however, the New Woman novel, not real New Women, became the center of controversy. Having been a social debate at its inception in the 1860s, what had once been termed the "Woman Question" became a more strictly literary affair following the naming of the New Woman. As more and more New Woman novels were published, as article followed article with titles such as "Reticence in Literature," "Sex in Fiction," and "The Fiction of Sexuality," the expanding controversy focused more and more narrowly on the representation of the New Woman in fiction.[7] Even if Jordan's chronology is correct, then, she slights the significance of this shift in focus. She neglects to mention that this shift, undoubtedly motivated by the publication of two of the three most (in)famous fictional accounts of New Women in 1893 (George Egerton's *Keynotes* and Sarah Grand's *The Heavenly Twins*), is also a means of denying the New Woman's reality.

To label something literary rather than "real" is to quarantine it, in effect: to isolate it in a special corner of life, to box it off as a special kind of phenomenon, not something one encounters in society at large. Thus, for example, Mrs. Eastwood notes with relief in an essay for the *Humanitarian* in 1894, that the New Woman is "amusing as literature" but "thankfully unreal."[8] The New Woman, she claims, has a place "in fiction" but not "in fact." In 1894, Eastwood's view was the exception rather than the rule; at that point in time, most critics were debating the affect fiction about the New Woman might have on "the Young Person," the innocent implied reader of classic Victorian realism. (This debate will be discussed in detail in Chapter Two.) Eastwood's view, however, became increasingly common as the decade wore on. In 1895, for example, a reviewer for the *Athenaeum* argues that "the 'New Woman' is a product oftener met with in the novels of the day than in ordinary life, where, fortunately, she remains so rare as to be seldom seen in the flesh at all."[9] In 1896, Mrs. Morgan-Dockrell follows Eastwood's lead as well, making a distinction between the New Woman as a "figment of the journalistic imagination" and the "genuine New Woman" in her essay, "Is the New Woman a Myth?"[10] And Elizabeth Chapman does the same in *Marriage Questions in Modern Fiction* (1897), contrasting "the interminable flood of gaseous chatter to which the invention of a journalistic myth known as the 'New Woman' has given rise" with "the Best Woman," the "real reformer and friend of her sex and humanity."[11]

Labeling the New Woman a literary rather than a "real" phenomenon, these critics locate all "genuine" change, all "real" reform, in the nonliterary realm. Thus, they curtail the discussion of art's relation to life that is such a large part of the debate on the New Woman in the early 1890s. Moving literature from the center to the margin of culture, they relegate the New Woman novel to the margin of that margin.

But this takes us too far forward, too quickly, in the history of the New Woman and the New Woman novel. We need to return to the 1880s and to consider why the New Woman was lambasted as a "socio-literary portent" of anarchy before she was dismissed as "merely" a literary phenomenon.[12]

As the above might suggest, naming is not an objective activity. We name things in order to reassure ourselves that we know what things are—and that our knowledge gives us some sort of control over them. We name things in order to establish distinctions between the things "we" value and the things "they" value. Typically, when we name something, we are not dealing with an isolated phenomenon; we are working with at least a pair if not a larger set of things that we want to distinguish from each other. Such a model of language use helps explain why turn-of-the-century critics always identified the New Woman by distinguishing her from four other groups of women who either were or were not "revolting" against the Victorian sex, gender, and class system.

First, and most obviously, the New Woman is always distinguished from the "old" woman, the Victorian "angel in the house." As Nancy Cott and others have argued, the ideology of female "passionlessness" empowered women culturally in the high Victorian era because it underwrote the doctrine of separate spheres, the gender-based division of human labor and cultural spaces.[13] So long as women were assumed to be without sexual appetite, they could be recognized as autonomous moral agents in middle-class Victorian culture; they could be credited with having minds that were not controlled by their animal passions. Therefore, they could also be granted autonomy within a limited cultural sphere, the bourgeois household. The title of a single New Woman novel indicates how the New Woman's conceptualization of her sexuality differs from the mid-Victorian angel's. Grant Allen's notorious New Woman, Herminia Barton, is quite literally *The Woman Who Did* what the Victorian angel would not: she has sex outside of marriage, and for pleasure, not for purposes of procreation.[14] The moral agency of a Victorian "lady" is predicated upon the denial of her sexual appetite. In contrast, Allen's Herminia Barton asserts her agency *through* her active pursuit of sexual satisfaction. Much to her lover's surprise, she claims such satisfaction as a natural human need. Moreover, although she will eventually make maternity her calling—rearing her lover's child on her own after his death—she does not do so within a traditional bourgeois household. Instead, living in a London boarding house, she works in the public sector in order to support herself and her child. In this respect, Allen's New Woman challenges not only bourgeois Victorian sexual ideology but also the related ideology of domesticity, the normalization/standardization of both the nuclear family and the independent middle-class household.

In her second important anthology of revisionary historical work on the Victorian period, Martha Vicinus uses the metaphor of a "widening sphere" to gloss Victorian women's challenges to the doctrine of separate spheres between 1860 and 1900.[15] Yet, the metaphor seems misleading, insofar as it suggests a continuum, a smooth and gradual process of cultural change. Because disputes about gender roles entailed reconceptualization of the relation between domestic (female) and public (male) spaces, women in late Victorian England could not simply "widen" their sphere of influence. Depending on what they were trying to accomplish, they offered completely different models of the division of human labor and cultural spheres. In this context, the New Woman was often contrasted not simply with the "old" angel in the house but also with three other groups of women in late Victorian England who struggled to renegotiate the gender-based division of labor. These are, in order of their increasing "deviancy" from the dominant Victorian ideal of femininity and as they have been labeled by recent critics: single-issue social reformers, "Independent Women," and middle-class women who "converted" to socialism in the 1880s and 1890s.

As Judith Walkowitz and Coral Lansbury note, single-issue social reformers—women who advocated extending the vote to propertied women, women who petitioned for the repeal of the Contagious Diseases Acts in the mid-1880s, and the antivivisectionists who perceived cruelty to animals as a crime against women, against the body as a "female" space—presented only local challenges to Victorian social conventions.[16] In the 1880s, the suffragists, for example, rarely questioned either the naturalness of class distinctions or the middle class's right to monopolize the responsibilities of citizenship. As John Goode notes, they questioned the "traditional status and role of women from within the [bourgeois] ideology that insists on [women's subordination]," but they did not contradict "bourgeois theory itself."[17] They demanded the right to vote, but only for themselves, not for all women. Typically, in fact, they were quite outspoken in arguing *against* extending suffrage beyond the ranks of the middle class.

Like the suffragists, the antivivisectionists and the middle-class women who became involved in efforts to repeal the Contagious Diseases Acts in the mid-1880s defied the Victorian social code by speaking out in public. Instead of exerting "influence" over their menfolk—as John Ruskin would have them do—these women took to the streets to support animal rights and to protest the new laws requiring prostitutes to have regular physical examinations (thereby implicating prostitutes, not their male customers, for the increased incidence of sexual diseases). Women appealing the Contagious Diseases Acts broke caste in a second regard by identifying with rather than against their "fallen sisters" as they protested the invasiveness of the new procedures for such examinations (e.g., the use of the newly invented speculum). More often than not, however, these women's political activism was limited quite specifically to the issue of prostitution or animal rights. In other words, having breached the "absolutely

definite and impassable" barrier "separat[ing] the virtuous among
women from the fallen," these women did not inaugurate a new "era
of feminine fellowship and amity" between women of different
classes—as one reviewer will note about New Women.[18] Instead,
single-issue social reformers experienced a primary allegiance to the
"cause of Woman" only temporarily. They challenged the doctrine of
separate spheres—but only briefly. Class allegiances and family allegiances resurfaced immediately after the excitement about the Contagious Diseases Acts died down; activism on this particular issue led to
no further involvement with women of other classes.

If the "Independent Women" Martha Vicinus writes about in her
book by the same title found ways to defy the Victorian social code
more permanently than did single-issue reformers, nevertheless they
avoided a direct challenge to the dominant Victorian ideology of gender by invoking traditional notions of "womanly" behavior as they
created "domestic" or "female" spaces for themselves in the public
domain.[19] The professionalization of nursing and social work; the establishment of women's religious communities, schools and universities;
the development of philanthropical organizations: all were defended by
reference to the "superfluous" middle-class lady's "duty" to "mother
the public" if she had no family of her own. Such single-sex organizations thus represented extensions of the Victorian matriarch's unofficial
social ministry. Eventually, "Independent Women's" unofficial duties
became official paid labor. But, as originally conceived, these new
categories of women's work presented no threat to established "male"
professions and institutions. They simply supplemented existing public services; they provided support service for professions and institutions controlled by men.

What distinguished "Independent Women" from New Women,
then, was the former's endorsement of traditional sex, gender, and class
distinctions. In entering the public sector, in dealing, on a professional
basis, with men and women of other social classes, "Independent
Women" preserved their social class standing as "ladies." Whether
working as nurses, charity workers, settlement house supervisors, or
rent collectors, they used their middle-class status to establish themselves professionally. Like single-issue social reformers, they stopped

far short of obliterating class lines even as they defied the domestication
of middle-class "Womanhood."

But if New Women differed from "Independent Women" insofar as
the former challenged the naturalness of sex, gender, and class distinctions, they also differed from women who became involved in the many
socialist movements of the day because they refused to assume that
distinctions of class were more fundamental than sex or gender distinctions. Socialists in England in the 1880s and 1890s approached the
"Woman Question" in one of two ways.[20] Either, following Marx's
lead, they did not include the family within the framework of their
economic analysis. Thus, for example, the Fabian Society viewed the
"Woman Question" as strictly an individualist concern—not a subject
proper to the collectivists' attention. Or, identifying the "Woman
Question" as one aspect of a more general problem of social organization, they assimilated the former to the latter, the larger, "Cause." Still
regarded as the classic expression of late Victorian Socialist thought,
August Bebel's *Women in the Past, Present, and Future* (1885) exemplifies
this second approach to the "Woman Question." Because there is considerable overlap between Bebel's and the New Women's criticisms of a
bourgeois institution like marriage; and because Bebel's final solution
to these and other social "ills" will not be endorsed by New Women,
the following passage from his study merits inclusion here.

Stating as his premise that the bourgeois world is incapable of either
remodeling marriage or "providing for the unmarried," Bebel predicts
the outcome of "the present folly and unsoundness of our time:"

> I maintain, that within a given time all the evils described will
> have reached a point at which their existence will not only be
> clearly recognized by the vast majority of the population, but will
> also have become unbearable; that a universal irresistible longing
> for radical reformation will then take possession of almost the
> whole community, and make the quickest remedy appear the most
> opportune.[21]

The "quickest," "most opportune," remedy, is, of course, the classic
Marxist solution: "the whole of this private property must be converted

into common property by one great act of expropriation." When "Society assumes all the rights and duties involved in this general expropriation, and regulates and arranges everything in the interests of the community," then and only then will "the interests of the community no longer clash with the interests of the individual" (77).

A passage from an essay about the New Woman published in *Nineteenth Century* in 1894 might serve to highlight the difference between New Women's and Bebel's position on social reform. In "A Reply from the Daughters," Alys Pearsall Smith defends the women who are "revolting" against the ideal of femininity imposed upon them by their elders in the following manner.

> The suffering endured by many a young woman [living as a dependent in her father's household] has never yet been told. Possessing no money in her own right, and obliged to beg, too often from an unwilling father, for all she gets, a girl of character, as she grows into maturity and lives on as a woman in her father's house, suffers from a sense of bitter humiliation that no one who has not experienced it can understand. . . . The revolt of the daughter is not . . . a revolt against any merely surface conventionalities, . . . but it is a revolt against a bondage that enslaves her whole life. In the past she has belonged to other people, now she demands to belong to herself. . . . She asks simply and only for freedom to make out of her own life the highest that can be made, and to develop her own individuality as seems to her the wisest and the best. She claims only the ordinary human rights of a human being, and humbly begs that no one will hinder her.[22]

Like Bebel, Smith claims that the "interests of the community" clash with "the interests of the individual." Mona Caird asserts the same not only in her novels, *The Wing of Azrael* (1889) and *The Daughters of Danaus* (1894), but also in essays like "A Defense of the So-Called Wild Women," where she presents women in general and the New Woman in particular as society's scapegoats, the citizens whose individual needs are sacrificed for the good of both society and their families.[23] Notably, however, Smith, Caird, and other New Women do not endorse Bebel's class-based millenialism. They do not posit the existence of a "universal[,] irresistible longing for radical [social] reformation." While recognizing the need for such radical social change, they question the adequacy of the class-based model of social analysis to explain gender and the history of gender relations. Moreover, they fear that bourgeois society's exploitation of women will be continued under a Socialist regime.

I will discuss the novels that address these issues in detail in Chapters Five and Six. Here I would simply underscore the difference between Bebel's and Caird's or Smith's position on class and gender issues as a preliminary to making a different point altogether: the critics who were most threatened by the prospect of radical social change associated New Women with socialism. They ignored all of the distinctions that New Women and socialists themselves made between the two. They collapsed these two categories, which represented quite different, though equally radical, threats to the bourgeois status quo.

Consider again, for example, Ouida's naming of the New Woman in her response to Sarah Grand: "in the English language there are conspicuous at the present moment two words which designate two unmitigated bores: The Workingman and the Woman. The Workingman and the Woman, the New Woman, be it remembered, meet us at every page of literature written in the English tongue, and each is convinced that on its own especial W hangs the future of the world." Without exactly equating the two "W's," Ouida damns them both by association as "unmitigated bores." In this context, naming the New Woman becomes a way to contain, neutralize, or at the very least delegitimize her radicalism. Such contentious rhetoric obscures the differences between New Women and other antiestablishment movements or interest groups. And yet, that phenomenon is itself of interest. The violence of this rhetoric is revealing not because it tells us much about the New Woman, not because it allows for precise distinctions between the various interest groups putting pressure on the cultural establishment, but because it reveals the anxieties fueling the establishment's need to name her.[24]

Consider, for example, the language of the New Woman's most

vehement critic, Mrs. Elizabeth Lynn Linton. Perhaps best remembered to history for the essays collected in *The Girl of the Period* (originally published by *Saturday Review* in the 1880s), Linton earned a great deal of notoriety in the 1890s for publishing a trilogy of articles on the "Wild Women" in *Nineteenth Century* in 1891 and 1892. In these essays she sets a standard for the kind of high-pitched, self-righteous, apocalyptic rhetoric that will be used subsequently by other critics in the campaign against New Women. Such women, Linton notes, "say they want more to do, and a wider field for their energies than any of those assigned to them by the natural arrangement of personal and social duties;" however reasonable this kind of demand might appear, Linton is convinced that it will be "impossible to satisfy [them] by any means short of changing the whole order of nature and society."[25]

In spite of his reputation for being as conservative as Linton, W. T. Stead, editor of the *Review of Reviews*, supported the New Woman as enthusiastically as Linton disparaged her. Interestingly enough, however, his language is almost identical to Linton's in describing the New Woman's affect on the social order. Comparing the New Woman with John Bunyan's Pilgram, Stead notes:

> having discovered, apparently very much to her own astonishment, that she has really a soul after all . . . [woman] is not going to go back to her old position [as man's dependent]. Through whatever stormy seas and across no matter what burning desert marked by the skeletons and haunted by the ghosts of those who have fallen by the way, she will press on, fleeing from the monogamic [*sic*] prostitution of loveless marriage and the hideous outrage of enforced maternity as Bunyan's Pilgrim fled from the City of Destruction. All social conventions, all religious teachings, and all moral conceptions will have to be reconsidered and readjusted in harmony with this new central factor.[26]

"The Apple and the Ego of Woman" deserves mention again in this context. This anonymous writer for the *Westminster Review* warns his readers that, like the genii in Hans Christian Andersen's fairy tale, the New Woman will reward her liberators "by proposing to annihilate

[them]." Eve is venturing out into the world unchaperoned by a husband, a father, or a brother, he notes. And "the stirrings and rumblings now perceivable in the social and industrial world, the 'Bitter Cries' of the disinherited classes, the 'Social Wreckage' which is becoming able to make itself unpleasantly prominent, the 'Problems of Great Cities,' the spread of Socialism and Nihilism" are all "intimately connected" with the "Ego of Woman's" "ascent."[27]

Was the New Woman indeed a wild woman, a blasphemer against "Nature, God, and Good," as Linton suggests in the first of three essays on "Wild Women" published in *Nineteenth Century*? Or was she simply claiming the "rights, privileges, and responsibilities of a human being," as Stead argues? Was she intent on "sweep[ing] such commonplace virtues as womanliness, wifeliness, and motherliness out of existence?" Was she inordinately curious about sexuality, her own as well as that of "fallen" women? Was she intent on making social progress of the sort that, "if left unchecked, will land [England] in the hospital or lunatic asylum?" Was she the late-nineteenth-century's version of the infamous "Parisian women" of the French Revolution, as both Linton and the anonymous author of "The Strike of a Sex" claim? Or was she merely a woman "whose demands seem ridiculous only because they have been unrecognized," as Mona Caird proposes in her riposte to Linton, "A Defense of the So-Called Wild Women," endorsing a position we have already seen Alys Smith assume in her "Reply of the Daughters"?[28]

Three serious questions fuel such hyperbole. First, what happens to the New Woman herself as she ventures out into the public world? Second, what happens to the nuclear family when women choose careers other than marriage and motherhood? And finally, what happens to the social system as a whole when women enter the workplace in significant numbers for the first time, disrupting further an economic system already struggling with the problems associated with industrialization? As we shall see in Chapter Five, some of the New Woman's most eloquent defenders recognized the connections between these three questions and set themselves the task of refuting the culturally ratified opposition between procreativity and creativity, motherhood and all manner of nonbiological labor. More often than not, however, critics attacking the New Woman built their case against her around one of the three questions outlined above.

Writing for *Fortnightly Review* in 1897, for example, Janet Hogarth finds "few aspects of the Eternal Feminine more disheartening to contemplate than the alarming increase of that monstrous regiment of women which threatens before very long to spread throughout the length and breadth of . . . London."[29] Having introduced the metaphor of a regiment, she quickly withdraws it, choosing instead language that recalls the biblical plagues of Egypt to describe women's increasing membership in the public work force: "it is simply an innumerable host, blindly bent upon forcing its way into professions, many of them already so desperately overcrowded that they are utterly incapable of yielding anything approaching to a comfortable subsistence" (926).

In contrast to Hogarth, Walter Besant focuses on the New Woman's refusal to respect the conventions of monogamy, not her infiltration of the workplace. In his essay, "Candour in English Fiction," he identifies the nuclear family as the "foundation" of the Victorian social system; he does not look beyond the family in his analysis of the New Woman's threat to that system: "the preservation of the family is at the very foundation of our social system. As for the freedom of love [i.e., the expression of sexuality outside of marriage] which you want to treat in your books, it strikes directly at the family. If men and women are free to rove, there can be no family. If there is no fidelity in marriage, the family drops to pieces."[30] Therefore, he concludes quite abruptly, "we will have none of your literature of free and adulterous love" (8).

Linton envisions a similar scenario developing out of society's present permissiveness toward women who defy its dictates. If women "keep swarming out at all doors, running hither and thither among the men"; if they continue to be "anxious to lay aside their tenderness, their modesty, their womanliness [in order to] become hard and fierce and self-asserting like [men]," "there will be no such thing as the old-fashioned home left in England," she warns.[31] And Grant Allen concurs in "Plain Words on the Woman Question," where he reminds his readers that the "self-supporting spinster" is a "deplorable accident" of the social system at present.[32] Given the present population imbalance, our "chivalry" demands that we make it easier for the spinster to earn her living by "remov[ing] all professional barriers," he concedes (455). But he immediately qualifies this: "we ought at the same time to realize that [the spinster] is an abnormality, not the woman of the future. We ought not to erect into an ideal what is in reality a painful necessity of the present transitional age (455–456)." As he had noted previously, women

> ought to be ashamed to say [they have] no desire to become [wives] and mother[s]. . . . Instead of boasting of their sexlessness as a matter of pride, they ought to keep it [in the] dark. . . . They ought to feel they have fallen short of the healthy instincts of their kind, instead of posing as in some sense the cream of the universe, on the strength of what is really a functional aberration. (452)

Significantly, all such rhetoric is informed by the kind of nostalgia that Janice Doane and Devon Hodges analyze in contemporary responses to feminism. Besant's model of the "old-fashioned home;" Linton's insistence upon the maintenance of traditional gender distinctions; Allen's positing of a "healthy" female instinct for motherhood: these ideas are part of a campaign to model high Victorian culture as a "golden past," a prelapsarian state to which the world can be returned—if only women can be kept from "swarming out at all doors."[33] As is clearest in both Linton's and Grant Allen's language, such preservation efforts are best served by the naturalization of the cultural phenomenon these writers value. Thus Allen makes the spinster look "abnormal" by claiming that maternal "instinct" is an essential part of a woman's "nature." Similarly, Linton assumes that "the . . . arrangement of personal and social duties" is natural in explaining why she cannot countenance women's working in the public sphere. "Nature and society," as she goes on to describe them in the following sentence, are one and the same; therefore, all unwanted social change can be deemed "unnatural."

I mentioned earlier but did not discuss in detail the New Woman's association with the "Parisian women" of the French Revolution. This explicitly political rhetoric highlights both the fear of the lower classes and the nationalism that informs nostalgic reactions to the New

Woman at the turn of the century. As Neil Hertz notes in "The Medusa's Head: Male Hysteria Under Political Pressure," French writers both during and immediately after the 1789 revolution figured the revolution as a "hideous, fierce sexual woman," a Medusa who turned the old aristocratic social order to stone and then sent its heads tumbling.[34] To the old aristocracy, the lower class *was* a woman, a woman who could no longer be dominated "sexually," a woman who would no longer submit to domestication. Almost one hundred years later in England, the same logic, the same need to protect the cultural hegemony of the dominant class, fuels comparisons of the New Woman with the sexual "anarchists" of the French Revolution.

Linton, for one, is more explicit about this than the author of "The Strike of a Sex." Having compared the New Women with the Parisian revolutionaries in her first essay for *Nineteenth Century*, "The Wild Women as Politicians," she accuses them in the second, "The Wild Women as Social Insurgents," of lacking all sense of "fitness."[35] By this she means an appreciation for class distinctions. "What is New" about the New Woman, she notes, is "the translation into the cultured classes of certain qualities and practises hitherto confined to the uncultured— and savages:"

> The Wild Women, in their character of social insurgents, are bound by none of the conventions which once regulated society. In them we see the odd social phenomenon of the voluntary descent of the higher to the lower forms of ways and works. "Unladylike" is a term that has ceased to be signficant. . . . Women who, a few years ago, would not have shaken hands with a dressmaker, still less have sat down to table with her, now open shops and set up in business on their own account—not because they are poor . . . but because they are restless, dissatisfied, insurgent, and like nothing so much as to shock established prejudices and make the folk stare. (599)

The point of her association of the New Woman with "the uncultured— and savages" should be clear. Linton equates social progress with social position, then suggests that the New Woman's refusal to practice the mannerisms associated with the latter will bring about racial as well as cultural degeneration.[36]

While her reference to savages suggests a concern for England's status vis à vis non-European cultures, most of her remarks highlight the relationship of English society to the "foreign" components of its own culture—for example, the North-of-England working-class culture she invokes in the following passage as she berates the New Woman for smoking cigarettes.

[The Wild Woman] smokes after dinner with the men; in railway carriages; in public rooms—when she is allowed. She thinks she is thereby vindicating her independence and honouring her emancipated womanhood. Heaven bless her! Down in the North-country villages, and elsewhere, she will find her prototypes calmly smoking their black cutty-pipes, with no sense of shame about them. Why should they not? These ancient dames with "whiskin" beards about their "mou's," withered and unsightly, worn out, and no longer women in desirableness or beauty—why should they not take to the habits of men? . . . When, after dinner, our young married women and husbandless girls, despising the old distinctions and trampling underfoot the time-honoured conventions of former generations, "light up" with the men, they are simply assimilating themselves to this old Sally and that ancient Betty down in the dales and mountain hamlets; or to the stalwart cohort of pitbrow women for whom sex has no aesthetic distinctions. (597)

Interestingly enough, Linton does not recognize sex as a category that cuts across class lines in this passage. She does not object to elderly working women's smoking; she does not view their assumption of this "male" habit a threat to the "natural" distinction between the sexes we have seen her invoke elsewhere—because she does not view working-class women as women. "This old Sally and that ancient Betty" are "withered and unsightly"; therefore, they are "no longer women in desirableness or beauty." They are no longer women, in other words, because their beauty cannot serve as an emblem of

Victorian "Womanhood." The cultural iconography Linton invokes here assumes a distinction in *kind*, not degree, between "the lady" and the "pitbrow" women of the working classes. A lady, Linton stresses, "unsexes" herself—loses both gender and class status—when she refuses to respect "the time-honoured conventions" regarding the relations between the classes as she reaches for a cigarette. A lady stops being a woman when she violates the bourgeois code in this manner.[37]

The gesture of smoking a cigarette may seem ridiculously insignificant, the rhetoric against it mere hyperbole, particularly since we know such gestures now as part of the Virginia Slims advertising campaign.[38] But both the now-clichéd gesture and the rhetoric against such behavior need to be recognized, instead, as evidence of the New Woman's radical threats to the Victorian social order: her simultaneous challenges to the gender-based division of labor, the ideal of the bourgeois home, and the hierarchy of class. As the New Woman questions the naturalness of gender roles through even this small gesture of lighting a cigarette, she questions the naturalness of all of the above. She challenges the cultural ideology that naturalizes the bourgeois patriarchy by appropriating "Woman" as the symbol of its rightful dominance.

Nina Auerbach has argued that "it is virtually impossible to distinguish 'official' from 'subversive' visions of Victorian womanhood."[39] The demon, the old maid, the fallen woman, the New Woman, and the angel in the house: "these are the many faces of a single image," an image of the "dialectic between womanhood and power" that was "so central and general a concern" in the Victorian period (186, 188).

Legally and socially women composed an oppressed class, but whether she was locked in the home, exiled to the colonies, or haunting the banks of the Thames, woman's very aura of exclusion gave her imaginative centrality in a culture increasingly alienated from itself. Powerful images of oppression became images of barely suppressed power, all the more grandly haunting because, unlike the hungry workers, woman ruled both the Palace and the home while hovering simultaneously in the darkness without.

Assuming the power of the ruler as well as the menace of the oppressed, woman was at the center of her age's myth at the same time as she was excluded from its institutions.   (188–189)

While Auerbach offers a subtle and persuasive alternative to simplistic readings of women's victimization in Victorian culture, her model seems misleadingly static. What she misses, I think, is the New Woman's disruption of the symbol system analyzed so carefully in *Woman and the Demon*. Significantly, the New Woman refuses to be assimilated into the iconography of Victorian "Womanhood." As Alys Smith argued, she "demands to belong to herself. . . . She asks . . . for freedom to make out of her own life the highest that can be made, and to develop her own individuality as seems to her the wisest and the best."[40]

On the one hand, the New Woman's program of self-actualization is completely in keeping with the bourgeois ideology of individualism. When Smith claims "only the ordinary rights of a human being" "to develop her own individuality," it is clear she thinks she is merely asking that the self-determination associated with citizenship in a liberal democracy be granted to a class of people previously denied it. But on the other hand, the New Woman's claim to the right of self-definition should be recognized not simply as an expression of but as a challenge to the tradition of liberal humanism. As women articulate specific needs and desires—the desires not of "Woman" but of *women*, of discrete historical agents—they challenge not only the bourgeois Victorian social order's prescriptive definition of "correct" female behavior but also the pattern of thinking in hierarchically organized binary oppositions that pits men against women, "good" women against "fallen" ones, the middle class against the working class, and European against non-European cultures. This is, I think, the more serious side of what we have remembered as the comic controversy over the New Woman at the turn of the century.

I began this chapter by suggesting that Ellen Jordan explains how but not why the New Woman was named. I have argued that a nostalgic desire to defend "natural" class and gender distinctions informs the attacks of a critic like Elizabeth Linton. I want to suggest in closing that the nostalgia for sexual difference in particular is a second-order phenomenon, a symptom of a more primary and general anxiety about the ability to order the world through the manipulation of language.[41] By labeling her "the Wild Woman," a critic such as Linton would like to be able to bring her into her taxonomy of Victorian character types. She would like to make the New Woman one more entry in her catalog of "the girls of the period." As is clearest in the essay, "The Wild Women as Social Insurgents," she names the New Woman in an attempt to restabilize all of the social hierarchies she sees New Women disrupting. In other words, gender is just one of the many binary oppositions she wants to preserve as she identifies the New Woman as a threat to English middle-class culture—as *the* social phenomenon that threatens most radically the "purity" of that cultural tradition. As I will show in the next chapter, this same dynamic, this same need to identify an Other, informs the literary controversy over the New Woman novel once the latter replaces the New Woman herself as the focus of attention.

2

The Controversy over Realism in Fiction, 1885–1895

As NOTED in Chapter One, critics writing after 1895 attempted to put an end to the debate on the New Woman and the New Woman novel by mocking the whole controversy as an "interminable flood of gaseous chatter."[1] Moving literature from the center to the margin of culture, they relegated the New Woman novel to the margin of that margin. What is worth stressing now is that the cultural work of the novel was seen as both significant and central when the debate over the "new" realism began in the mid-1880s. The term "cultural work" is Jane Tompkins's, and I use it, as she does, to refer to the way works of fiction attempt to "redefine the social order" by offering their readers a "blueprint for survival under a specific set of political, economic, social, or religious conditions."[2] As I will show through a discussion of George Moore's attack on the circulating libraries, literary texts were evaluated in the 1880s and early 1890s as "agents of cultural formation," not as works of art whose formal complexity was to be admired (xi). If, then, critics eventually tried to discredit the cultural work of New Woman novels by focusing on their aesthetic limitations, it is nonetheless worth remembering that what William Frierson has termed "the controversy over realism in English fiction" between 1885 and 1895 was not initially defined as a debate about aesthetics.[3] This controversy had implications for life in

the "real" world, because "books were viewed as powerful and authoritative texts, revelatory of absolute presence and truth."[4]

Frierson's 1928 essay is still the best account of the turnaround in
English attitudes toward French naturalism during this decade. I want
to supplement his argument by discussing the New Woman novel's
contribution to this controversy. Frierson identifies only two parties in
what actually seems to have been a triangulated debate over "candour"
in the English novel. As I will show in this chapter, this debate
ultimately left the New Woman novel in the position French naturalism had held initially as the "decadent" threat to the purity of the
English tradition. I want first to establish what can be termed the
original agenda of the New Woman novel, an agenda that positions
the New Woman novel in opposition to both classic English realism
and French naturalism. I will then consider how changes in the literary
marketplace—specifically, the downfall of the circulating libraries, the
"rise" of small new publishing houses, and the significant increase in
literacy rates after the 1870 Education Act—affected the production of
New Woman fiction. Finally, I will discuss this fiction's reception
among critics in the 1890s, who developed four major arguments
against it. This chapter thus will return us to the point made in
Chapter One about the marginalization of the New Woman novel. But
analysis of the 1890s debate will also suggest an alternative approach
to this fiction: a way that the discussion can proceed in subsequent
chapters so as not to reinforce the negative aesthetic evaluations that
are, at least in part, responsible for posterity's condescension toward
this material.

Literature at Nurse

In his 1895 essay, "Tommyrotics," Hugh Stutfield credits Oscar
Wilde with inventing the New Woman novel—without, however, indicating which of Wilde's works he has in mind. With similar conviction,
Max Beerbohm claims that the New Woman sprang "full-armed from
the brain of Ibsen, who in later years unkindly denied paternity." And

with equal aplomb, W. T. Stead identifies Olive Schreiner's *The Story of an African Farm* (1883) as the first of its kind in "The Novel of the Modern Woman" (1894). Stead claims that Schreiner's novel exemplifies "the fiction of Revolt." Notably, in delineating the parameters of the field, he does not deem any of the other New Woman novels written before 1890—e.g., Mrs. Linton's *The Rebel of the Family* (1880), Annie Edwardes's *A Blue-stocking* (1877) and *A Girton Girl* (1885), Jane Hume Clapperton's *Margaret Dunmore; or, A Socialist Home* (1888), Mona Caird's *The Wing of Azrael* (1889), and Henry Dalton's *Lesbia Newman* (1889)—worthy of inclusion. He presents Schreiner's work as an isolated phenomenon, thereby ensuring its right of primogeniture in the field.[5]

With more self-serving motives, Thomas Hardy attempts a similar feat in the 1912 preface to *Jude the Obscure*, where he refers to, but does not identify by author or title, a German review claiming *Jude* as the Ur-New Woman novel.[6] As Gail Cunningham has it, Hardy "pretends to ignorance" about the dating of "problem-novels" by Grant Allen, Sarah Grand, Menie Muriel Dowie, and George Egerton.[7] His highly selective historical amnesia constitutes a defense of his work's originality. And Cunningham is correct to note that Hardy's own attitude is mirrored by that of his critics: reviewers who credited *Jude* with being original "dissociated it from contemporary movements." Those who attacked it, on the other hand, "saw it as part of the New Woman fiction" (116).

The polemic about the New Woman novel's paternity or maternity is no different from that on the New Woman herself. Given the impossibility of arbitrating such disagreements, it seems more useful to identify not a single point of origin, not an Ur-text, but a set of issues fueling the production of discourse on this subject. George Moore's pamphlet, *Literature at Nurse, or Circulating Morals* (1885), does not predate all New Woman novels. If it therefore should not be viewed as a source for all of the issues considered in this chapter, it can nonetheless function as a point of orientation as we locate the New Woman novel in the controversy over realism in English fiction waged between 1885 and 1895.

As Pierre Coustillas tells the story, Mudie's withdrew George Moore's *A Modern Lover* from circulation in late 1884 when two little

old ladies complained of its vulgarity.[8] Moore retaliated almost immediately by getting Vizetelly—who was later to be jailed for making *Nana*
available to English readers—to publish a three-penny pamphlet. Now
forgotten, Moore's raillery against the circulating libraries' control of
the literary marketplace establishes some of the terms of the debate on
realism to which the New Woman novelists contribute.

Given the dominance of the circulating libraries in the publishing
industry in the mid-1880s, Moore argues, the artist is not "free to go
to nature" in writing fiction because of the "illiterate censorship of a
librarian" (32). This librarian, a mere "tradesman," according to
Moore, nonetheless "considers himself qualified to decide the most
delicate artistic questions that may be raised, and . . . crushes out of
sight any artistic aspiration he deems pernicious" (28). Thus, Moore
complains, the "reading of fiction" is thrown "into the hands of young
girls and widows of sedentary habits." And therefore a "headless,
trunkless, limbless [humanity] is converted into the pulseless, non-
vertebrate, jelly-fish sort of thing which, securely packed in tin-
cornered boxes, is sent from the London depot and scattered through
the drawing rooms of the United Kingdom" under the label of literature (28). Note the claims here: because artists are not "free to go to
nature," nineteenth-century realism is not as realistic as it purports to
be; it is not as realistic as it *needs* to be, if the novel is to inform readers
about all manner of human experience. Moore is blaming the circulating libraries, in other words, for the mimetic bad faith of the three-
decker novel: its avoidance of all controversial or risqué topics and its
facile reproductions of "Mrs. Grundy's" moral platitudes.

Needless to say, Moore's publication of this monograph did not win
him any favors with Mudie's. It did, however, put him at the center of
the controversy over the circulating libraries' control of access to the
literary marketplace. Whether or not the echo is deliberate, in sympo-
siums such as the one on "Candour in English Fiction" published by
the *New Review* in 1890, critics repeat Moore's clarion call for "realer"
realism.[9] Like Moore, writers in this symposium contend that literature does not fulfill its cultural function if it misrepresents life. They
insist that the cultural authority of the novel rests upon its truth-value,
the accuracy of its representations.

Interestingly enough, although she was shortly to make a name for herself as the New Woman's most hostile critic, Elizabeth Linton endorsed Moore's attack on realism in her contribution to this symposium, the first of several offered by the *New Review* in the 1890s.[10] "The result of our present system of uncandid reticence," she argues, "is that, with a few notable exceptions, our fictitious literature is the weakest of all at the present time, the most insincere, the most jejune, the least impressive and the least tragic" (14). "Written for the inclusion of the Young Person among its readers, it does not go beyond the schoolgirl standard" (14). Thus, she concludes, mustering a bit of literary nationalism even as she deploys the sexualized idiom she will soon wield *against* the New Woman novel, "we have the queer anomaly of a strong-headed and masculine nation cherishing a feeble, futile, milk-and-water literature—of a truthful and straightforward race accepting the most transparent humbug as pictures of human life" (14).

The "milk-and-water literature" Linton refers to here is the tradition of nineteenth-century English realism. It will not be long before she establishes a binary opposition between masculine culture and a femininized New Woman novel. In the meantime, this gendered opposition works *against* "classic" realism, works to dislodge it from its position of status in culture, thereby making room for new developments in the literary scene (e.g., the writing of "sincere," "impressive," and "tragic" fiction).

The tone of Thomas Hardy's remarks in the same symposium is more moderate than Linton's, but his message is the same: "the magazine in particular and the circulating library in general do not foster the growth of the novel which reflects and reveals life."[11] As a result of the "censorship of prudery," contemporary fiction cannot rise to the heights of tragedy, "lest we should fright, the ladies out of their wits" with "the crash of broken commandments" (18). This last phrase suggests that Hardy, like Linton, conceives of the relation between literature and culture as a gendered opposition. According to Linton, literature had become feminized in the 1880s; realism, as practiced by the circulating libraries' authors, could no longer satisfy the needs of a "strong-headed and masculine nation." Hardy takes this one step further when he indicates how the novel is to be made "honest" once again. The novel of the future, he predicts, will not end with "the regulation finish that 'they married and were happy ever after' " (17). It will hold the highest place in a "masculine" nation's hierarchy of literary forms only when it portrays "catastrophes based on sexual relationship as it is" (17).

George Moore wanted to break the libraries' moral stranglehold on the production of literature. He wanted the novelist to be able to write without having to worry about readers' moral objections to his "artistic aspirations." Significantly, Hardy's interests are narrower. He focuses his attack exclusively on the representation of sexuality in the nineteenth-century novel. His particular agenda for the "honest" novel of the future includes only one item, the correct representation of "sexual relationship as it is."

This, then, will be the "new" English realism's claim to superiority over the "old" realism: it tells "the truth" about human sexuality. Five years after the symposium on "Candour in English Fiction," for example, Havelock Ellis defends *Jude the Obscure* on precisely this ground. "Wholesome-minded" critics who object to Jude's "waver[ing] between two women" are, Ellis notes playfully,

> as shocked as a farmer would be to find that a hen had views of her own concerning the lord of the harem. If, let us say, you decide that Indian Game and Plymouth Rock make a good cross, you put your cock and hens together, and the matter is settled; and if you decide that a man and woman are in love with each other, you marry them and the matter is likewise settled for the whole term of their natural lives. [12]

"Assuredly," he goes on to mock, the "farmyard view" of human sexual relations "corresponds imperfectly to the facts of human life in our time"—the facts of life in our time being that hens (read New Women) have their own views to express concerning sex and refuse to be dominated by the lords of patriarchal Victorian harems (46).

In a fictional conversation that quite self-consciously reflects the debate on "candour," Eva Clough, a character in W. S. Holnut's novel, *Olympia's Journal* (1895), explains the difference between "old" and "new" realism in very similar terms to a young writer who has come to her for advice. "The writer [used to think that his task was to] keep his company in hand, that is to say, permit them no action or dialogue that would detract from the beforehand rigidly determined characters of each," Clough observes. She then offers a more tentative explanation of the reasons for the perceived shift. "I doubt very much whether we should ever have thoroughly rid ourselves of these restraints—these odious insensate forms [of character]—had not science and psychology come to the rescue and rooted the classics on the one hand and the romanticists on the other, permitting some of us at least to unravel the inconsistencies and marvellous surprises of human nature."[13]

Edmund Gosse goes further still, characterizing the introduction of the New Woman novel, the break with "old" realism, as a fortunate fall.[14] "The public has [now] eaten of the apple of knowledge," Gosse observes, in *Questions at Issue* (1893), "and will not be satisfied with mere marrionettes. Whatever comes next, we cannot return, in serious novels, to the inanities and impossibilities of the old well-made plot, to . . . the madonna-heroine, and the god-like hero, to the impossible virtues and melodramatic vices" (22). Fiction, he announces with satisfaction, "has [finally] taken its place among the arts." And if novelists are to maintain the "hegemony they have garnered over the dramatists and poets over the course of the [nineteenth] century," he warns, they must "contrive to enlarge their borders" still further. They must continue to cultivate fields in the one hundred acre "estate called life" that previously have been left "to the weeds of newspaper police-reports." They must not restrict themselves, as they have in the past, to the two or three-acre plot of the "kitchen-garden of love" (22).

Hardy's assertion that the "honest" novel of the future will be able to depict human sexuality "as it is;" Clough's reference to the way science and psychology have altered the conceptualization of human character; Gosse's argument about both the novel's "hegemony" over poetry and drama and its competition with nonliterary forms of writing: all these remarks need to be recognized as efforts to place the "new" English realism within what Foucault has termed the "general economy of discourses on sex."[15] Recent critics have made much of Freud's acknowledgment in *Dora* that he borrowed the narrative methods of literary realism in developing the form of the case study.[16] This would, of course, be one way in which what Foucault describes as a "confluence" of discourse on sexuality at the turn of the century manifested itself. What interests me here, however, is not psychiatry's borrowings from literature but English fiction writers' borrowings from science, as they sought to ensure the value of their writing as a truth discourse.

Think again about Linton's criticism of the "milk-and-water literature" that tried to pass itself off as realism in the circulating libraries. Such literature offers "the most transparent humbug as pictures of life." As Hardy has it, it does not "revea[l"] life; there is no primal core of truth or reality left after every layer of narrative is stripped away. This will not be the case with the "new" realism, these writers promise. Whereas "old" realism reproduced the moral pablum of polite society, the "new" realism will make nature itself, not social mores, its subject. Using the insights of science and psychology, it will reveal "sexual relationship as it is"—and compete against scientific discourse for recognition as a source of truth on this subject.[17]

If this last point begins to suggest how the "new" English realists were influenced by the "experimental method" of French naturalism (a subject to be considered in more detail in Chapter Four), it also points to the way New Woman novelists distinguish themselves from both French naturalists and English practitioners of "old" realism. An essay by Mrs. Oliphant entitled, "The Anti-Marriage League," articulates these distinctions most clearly. Reacting specifically to the publication of *Jude the Obscure*, but using her review to comment more generally on what she sees as the general trend in contemporary English literature, Oliphant describes "the complete and extraordinary transformation" of the "pure woman" as the "last new development in English fiction."[18] It is, as she goes on to note, "very likely that the original inspiration" for this new development "came from France, as our Art does now. But it has suffered a sea-change on its way." In French naturalism, the "pure woman" is "still a being surrounded with every reverence and respect." In contrast, she notes, the "pure woman" is the "singular captive," the "most prized and precious of prisoners" whom New Woman novelists such as Hardy and Grant Allen have "carried with them out of battle" (137).

Because Oliphant does not make reference to specific texts, it is impossible to know which French novels she has in mind in describing French naturalism as a school of fiction in which the "pure woman" is still "surrounded with every reverence and respect."[19] Certainly, Zola's Nana does not fit the bill. What is important here, however, is her positioning of the New Woman novel in relation to both "old" English realism and French naturalism. Insofar as they set out to correct the false idealization of women in *both* nineteenth-century English realism and French naturalism, New Woman novelists, according to Oliphant, are determined to complete the naturalists' project. They are interested in rewriting an aspect of nineteenth-century realism—the idealized representation of "Womanhood"—which the naturalists neither criticize nor correct, notwithstanding the alleged scientific accuracy of their representations. In this regard, the credit Oliphant gives to French naturalists, the "reverence and respect" they continue to lavish on the "pure woman," becomes a debit: proof that the naturalists did not sustain the rigorous analysis to which they were ostensibly committed; proof that the responsibility will lie with the English New Woman novelists to "defy the censorship of prudery" and present "the truth" about human sexuality.

As I will show in the final section of this chapter, the truth-claims about sexuality made by New Woman novelists did not, in fact, automatically win the New Woman novel the kind of legitimacy its authors desired. Instead, these truth-claims were contested quite fiercely both by critics who objected to particular claims and by those who simply found any explicit mention of sexuality distasteful. These truth-claims were also contested by other New Woman novelists, as a very strong strain of antinaturalism began to develop in the debate on the New Woman. The point I would stress here is that truth-claims about human sexuality were an important part of what can be termed the original agenda of the New Woman novel. Such claims delineated an area of expertise; they made the exploration of "human nature"—and still more specifically, the investigation of female sexuality—the New Woman novel's primary focus. Thus, they provided the grounds upon which, as Edmund Gosse noted, the New Woman novel would establish its "hegemony" not only over poetry and drama but also over the tradition of English realism and French naturalism. Furthermore, these truth-claims represented the basis upon which the New Woman novel would make a bid for authority within the larger "economy" of discourses on sexuality at the turn of the century.

New Publishers, New Novels, New Writers

Most of the writers who responded to Moore's challenge offered to reconstruct the novel from the inside out, so to speak. That is, instead of following up Moore's attack on the circulating libraries for playing nursemaid to English culture, they argued for changes in the conventions of representation, changes in the unwritten rules about what subjects were appropriate for literary treatment. For the most part, they did not complain about circumstances that lay beyond their control; they focused on changes they, as writers, could effect. They saw the "new novel" being produced through changes in content and form, not material format. They emphasized the first two not the last as they promoted their own "realer" realism.

Because the controversy between 1885 and 1895 over realism in fiction looks quite different from a publisher's perspective, I want to discuss several factors external to the self-appointed literary agenda of the New Woman novelists that contributed to the production of this fiction at the turn of the century.

The first of these additional concerns is the establishment of new publishing houses in the early 1890s as the circulating libraries began to lose their moral stranglehold on the literary marketplace. Although he did not go into business for himself until 1897, Grant Richards's comment in his aptly named autobiography, *Author Hunting, by an Old Literary Sports Man*, nicely glosses the sentiment behind the efforts made only a few years earlier by bright young publishers such as William Heinemann and John Lane. "My success would be achieved by audacity," Richards notes with pleasure.[20] The audaciousness of publishers such as Heinemann and Lane lay in the risks they took trying to lure authors and readers alike away from established publishing houses like Smith, Elder, John Murray, George Bentley, and Macmillan's. Such risks were both social and financial: social in that they consciously tried to associate themselves as publishers with the public controversies of the day; financial insofar as they departed from the tried-and-true format of the three-decker novel, issuing single- or two-volume novels that they sold for as little as six shillings each directly to readers (who previously had joined the circulating libraries rather than pay the thirty-one shillings a three-decker novel cost), while also spending more money on advertising than mid-century publishers would have dreamed of frittering away in that manner.[21]

To recognize the link between the social and financial risks associated with publishing novels in the new single- or double-volume format, one need only recall Moore's argument in *Literature at Nurse*. When Victorian readers purchased three memberships to Mudie's (so they could borrow all three volumes of a triple-decker at once), they purchased Mudie's guarantee that they were getting "wholesome" fiction, fit reading for "the Young Person." By contrast, the "new" novels of the 1890s were tainted by sexual and social license. They did not come already stamped with polite society's seal of approval. In this respect, as Elaine Showalter has noted, they inherited the reputation of the sensationalist fiction of the 1860s.[22] There was a certain moral riskiness to the production of these cheap, light volumes, which physically bore a likeness to the "yellowbacks" of the previous generation.

William Heinemann, for one, was not averse, however, to turning a profit on the social controversies of the day. Thus, in his memoir mentioned earlier, Grant Richards notes with both glee and envy that Sarah Grand's *The Heavenly Twins* (1893) was "an abominably printed three-volume novel that no one could read with comfort" before Heinemann "took it over" and "link[ed] it up with the cause of revolting women, an equal moral law for both sexes, social purity, the Contagious Diseases Act and all that kind of stuff" (143).

If Heinemann nonetheless managed to stay on the respectable side of such social scandals, other publishing houses marketed their new fiction by implying it offered illicit pleasures.[23] Any number of publishers used words like "racy," "mischievous," "risky," and "bold" in advertising soon-to-be-published New Woman novels in periodicals and trade magazines such as the *Athenaeum*, the *Academy*, and the *Bookman*. T. Fisher Unwin, for example, used such a strategy to market not single titles but two new series, its "Pseudonym" and "Antonym" collections. Presumably, such anonymity offered protection for authors who might otherwise be hounded for their fictional confessions in novels like *A Game of Consequences* (1895), *A Bachelor Maid* (1895), *A Husband of No Importance* (1894), and *Alleyne: A Story of a Dream and a Failure* (1894). But such anonymity also, of course, might whet readers' appetite for scandal. Certainly the desire to provoke, to tease, the readers' interest lay behind the name of John Lane's new line of fiction. Taking the title of George Egerton's *Keynotes* for his series, John Lane capitalized on the immediate notoriety of Egerton's collection of stories. It was almost as if the most notorious passage in *Keynotes*, Egerton's revelation of female nature, served as advertising copy for the whole series.

> The wisest of [men] can only say we are enigmas; each one of them sets about solving the riddle of the *ewig weibliche*,—and well it is that the workings of our hearts are closed to them, that we are cunning enough or *great* enough to seem to be what they would have us, rather than be what we are. But few of them have had the insight to find out the key to our seeming contradictions—the why a refined, physically fragile woman will mate with a brute, a mere animal with primitive passions, and love him. . . . They have all overlooked the eternal wildness, the untamed primitive savage temperament that lurks in the mildest, best woman. Deep in through ages of convention this primeval trait burns,—an untameable quantity that may be concealed but is never eradicated by culture, the keynote of woman's witchcraft and woman's strength.[24]

While Egerton's protagonist claims to hold the "keynote" of woman's "nature," it was John Lane who turned a neat profit on his "stable" (his term) of women writers.[25]

The above points to two other key factors to be reckoned with here: the existence of new audiences for fiction in the 1880s and 1890s and the democratization/feminization of the literary marketplace. As both Christopher Baldick and Terry Eagleton have noted, the dramatic increase in literacy rates at the turn of the century (pursuant to the Education Act of 1870) increased the market for fiction at the turn of the century.[26] Whether it increased the market for "risky," "mischievous," or "racy" fiction is another matter entirely. But certainly critics saw a connection between these two phenomena, which is why they complained about the impact that the "new one-quarter literate" were having on the production of literature.[27]

Elizabeth Linton, for example, makes the following argument in an essay for *Fortnightly Review* in 1890: "The democratic wave which has spread over all society—and washed down some things which had better have been left standing—has swept through the whole province of literature. The spread of education among the people demands literature cheap enough to at once suit their pockets and meet their wants. This naturally increases the output; and the output necessitates more hands."[28] Linton continues in her now recognizably vehement way to highlight the difference between "Literature: Then and Now":

> Among the hundreds who write where formerly was one, there must of necessity be a larger percentage of the incompetent. So we find it; and so every editor and every publisher and every author of any name at all prove it. . . . In this day of universal disintegration and the supremacy of fads, there are so many who would sacrifice the good of the country—the integrity of the empire—to some impracticable theory that looks like godly justice on paper and would be cruelly wrong in practise.   (527, 529–530)

Notably, she makes no distinction between best sellers and high art. She is not comforted by the idea that the fiction she sees flooding the marketplace is "merely" popular. Rather, she remains deeply distressed that such fiction commands attention at all. Even if these writers are "incompetent"—and Linton is doing her best to prove as much—the commercial success of their work means that the newly expanded reading public is *not* reading texts that sustain "the integrity of the empire" and further "the good of the country."

I take this as evidence that the New Woman novel destablized a familiar conceptualization of the relationship between popular culture and high art. On the one hand, the fact that this fiction sold so well offered proof to its most hostile reviewers that it was a commodity. It did not have value as Art; it was simply faddishly up to date in its portrayal of women rebelling aginst the traditional code of "womanliness." On the other hand, this fiction was gaining pace on high culture; its advocates described it as *the* new fiction, the wave of the future—which only made its unconventional content seem more "dangerous" to someone like Linton.

According to her, all editors, publishers, and "author[s] of any name" are on the side of the cultural establishment. As a collective, they are under siege by "the incompetent," "the hundreds who write where formerly was one." The alliances were not, in fact, quite what Linton imagined. Some editors and publishers disapproved of changes in the literary marketplace, while others, as noted above, sought to benefit by such changes. Similarly, some well-known popular authors (e.g., Iota, Rhoda Broughton, and Rita) seem to have approved of the culture industry's new mass market, while others (e.g., Walter Besant, Henry James, and Linton herself) took a much dimmer view of such developments. If, then, Linton is wrong to suggest that anyone with an established literary reputation opposed the changes in the literary marketplace, she nonetheless captures some of her contemporaries' sense of the dynamic between "insiders" and "outsiders."

This is also where the gender-specific character of what Grant Richards termed "author hunting" becomes important. According to Penny Boumelha, Gaye Tuchman, and Nina Fortin, publishing records extant from the period do not indicate any significant increase in the number of novels by women being published in the late 1880s and early 1890s.[29] Moreover, such records do not suggest that publishers—with the obvious exception of someone like John Lane, who achieved notoriety with and through his "stable" of fillies—were focusing their energies on discovering new female talents. According to Tuchman and

Fortin, as the novel gained cultural prestige in the last third of the nineteenth century, the structures of opportunity in the literary market-place made it increasingly difficult for women to place their fiction with a publishing firm like Macmillan's.

Such empirical evidence to the contrary, the common perception in the 1890s was that women were taking over the literary world. New publishing houses, new audiences for fiction, new publication formats: all were seen to give women writers, particularly previously unpub-lished women writers, a distinct advantage in the literary marketplace. Moreover, in light of what I said earlier about the truth-claims of the New Woman novel, women were seen as the real authorities in this new field of writing. If the project of the "new" novelists was to effect a more accurate representation of women than had been possible in either "classic" English realism or French naturalism, then who—it was argued—could speak with more authority than the New Woman her-self on subjects that the "old" realism neglected to detail? Was not the New Woman herself the best source of information about the sexuality her predecessor, the Victorian angel, had refused to claim? Given the interest in "correcting" realism, in making realistic fiction more "real," was not the New Woman herself in the best position to take up that charge and provide publishers and readers with the "risky," "bold" material they liked?

This, at least, was the argument made by critics who approved of what the new publishers were doing. Taken to its logical limit, this argument led to the characterization of fiction about the New Woman that was also written *by* New Women as a new genre of women's writing, a discourse completely distinct from the tradition of realism in the English novel.

Reviewing the work of six modern writers and artists in 1896, for example, Laura Marholm Hansson claimed that "hitherto, all books, even the best ones, written by women [have been] imitations of men's books with the addition of a single, high-pitched feminine note."[30] For this reason, according to Hansson, women's fiction has been "nothing better than communications received at second hand. Now, however, "the time has come when woman is so keenly alive to her own nature

that she reveals it when she speaks." Thus, the six women whose work
she reviews "feel themselves to be utterly different from what they were
told they were, and which men believe them to be. . . . They are no
longer a reflection which man moulds into an empty form[;] they are
not like Galatea, who became a living woman through Pygmalion's
kiss—they were women before they knew Pygmalion" (70, 72). Contrasting George Egerton's work with that of the "other Georges," Eliot
and Sand, Hansson then concludes: "Now that woman is conscious of
her individuality as a woman, she needs an artistic mode of expression,
she flings aside the old forms, and seeks the new. It is with this feeling,
almost Bacchanalian in its intensity, that Mrs. Egerton hurls forth her
playful stories, which the English critics judged harshly, but the public
bought and called for in fresh editions" (78–79).

In *The Ascent of Woman* Margaret Devereux emphasizes the same two
points: women writers in the past imitated male writers rather than
drawing upon their own experience as women in writing about female
characters; hence, a new genre of women's literature is currently being
created as women break with the literary tradition by "correcting" the
representation of women in fiction, by writing about female sexuality
with unprecedented "candour."[31] Hansson had noted that "an entirely
new department of women's literature" is formed when women write
about themselves as they are, "utterly different from what they were
told they were, and which men believe them to be" (70). Similarly,
Devereux claims that "the first loyal, luminous word is still to be
written about woman." Women have not written about women "with
anything like accuracy or profound truth" because they have settled for
"the shroud of convention," she notes (4). Although she then criticizes
New Women writers for turning the pursuit of "candour" into a "cult
of the gutter," she retains hope in a future heralded by the "strange
unloveliness of woman in the present phase:"

> [T]he feminine spirit is still groping in the darkness after a Maya
> of her own invention—an illusion that allures and eludes, a phan-
> tom with no name. . . . Behind her lies the woman of the past,
> prostrate under the weight of her obligations, and before her rises

the first pale promise of her infinite possibility, which may, through the service of beauty and the sceptre thereof, flush with its realization the dawn of a retarded day.   (64, 70–71)

From our perspective, the false stability of both Hansson's and Devereux's vocabulary regarding "Woman" is problematic. Each talks about "the woman writer" in the abstract, then goes on to discuss specific writers, none of whom agrees with any of the others about what W. T. Stead terms "the Standpoint of Woman" might be.[32] But this need not make us dismiss these critics' major contention: that women were writing with new authority about female experience after the downfall of the circulating libraries—and receiving widespread public attention for doing so. Contrary to the model of Victorian women's victimization by publishers proposed by Tuchman and Fortin, then, what the above suggests is that women were edging into, not out of, the literary marketplace in the early 1890s. "Gynocentric" writers may have been pawns in the hands of male publishers like John Lane and William Heinemann, who saw the financial advantages of publishing women's "risky" self-revelations. Morever, the alleged advantage of the novelists who wrote "for" women may quickly have become a disadvantage. Because the "authority of female experience" proved very difficult for some critics and writers to respect, the latter sought ways to debunk it. As I will show in the next section, critics reacted to this material by developing new standards of literary value that delegitimized it. In turn, the novelists that are discussed in Chapter Six wrote cautionary tales about the New Woman, countering other New Woman novelists' "Bacchanalian" efforts to break with literary and social conventions. Furthermore, the public uproar surrounding Wilde's trial in 1895 may also have encouraged publishers *not* to continue affronting Mrs. Grundy with the New Woman's "erotomania."[33] These later events notwithstanding, it can still be said that many writers, women writers in particular, were empowered by the debate on "candour" in English realism between 1885 and 1895. Even if the New Woman novel outlived its usefulness to publishers like Heinemann, T. Fisher Unwin, and John Lane, it nonetheless played a significant role in the revaluation of realism at the turn of the century.

The Critic as Cultural Custodian

Which is more important, changes internal or external to the novel? Experimentation with the format of publication, something over which publishers alone had control? Or experimentation with content and generic form, things for which authors are held responsible? Which kind of innovation contributed more significantly to the success of new authors and the "new" realism in the 1890s? To complicate matters still further, to what extent was production of "new" novels either stimulated or depressed by all of the print being expended upon it across the full spectrum of literary and social journals in the 1890s, from the *Yellow Book* to the *Bookman*, from *Punch* to *Cornhill*, and from the *Lady's Pictorial* to the *Nineteenth Century*? How might critics' arguments about either the feminization of the literary world or the "effeminacy" of the New Woman novel work to disenfranchize it? I use the term "work" again the way Jane Tompkins uses it in *Sensational Designs* to talk about literary texts as agents of cultural formation. Here, however, I want to consider the cultural work not of literature but of literary criticism. I want to survey the arguments made against the New Woman novel in the 1890s in an effort to counterbalance the "topsy-turveyness" it introduced into the cultural scene.

Elizabeth Linton's objection to the "milk-and-water literature" "cherished" by "a strong-headed and masculine nation" is worth mentioning again in this context.[34] In attacking the three-decker novel, Linton set up a binary opposition between a feminized literature and a masculine culture. Mudie's fiction, she argued, cannot do the cultural work it is supposed to do because it offers only "the most transparent humbug as pictures of human life." The "new" realism, by contrast, promises to bring literature back into the cultural fold. It promises readers the "truths" that "a strong-headed and masculine nation" can indeed cherish. In 1890 Linton was in favor of the "new" realism.[35] In subsequent years, however, she and other critics will use the same gendered opposition to discredit not "classic" realism but the New Woman novel. In effect, such critics found a new application for the Victorian doctrine of separate spheres, as they attempted to isolate the New Woman novel, to quarantine it at a safe distance from the cultural mainstream.

Henry James's comments on the popularity of women writers in the 1890s might serve as an example of the first, and most obvious, strategy for devaluing the New Woman novel. In addition to caricaturing George Egerton in "The Death of the Lion," James notes in a letter to William Dean Howells: "a new generation that I know not, and mainly prize not, has taken universal possession" of the literary world.[36] He offers still more explicit objections to the the work of contemporary women writers in his essay, "The Future of the Novel." The following passage is worth quoting in its entirety.

> It is certain that there is no real health for any art—I am not speaking, of course, of any mere industry—that does not move a step in advance of its farthest followers. It would be curious— really a great comedy—if the renewal were to spring from the satiety of readers for whom the sacrifices have hitherto been supposed to be made. It bears on this that nothing is more salient in English life today, to fresh eyes, than the revolution taking place in the position and the outlook of women—and taking place much more deeply in the quiet than even the noise on the surface demonstrates—so we may very well yet see the female elbow itself, kept in increasing activity by the play of the pen, smash with final resonance the window all the time most superstitiously closed. The particular draught that has been most deprecated will in that case take care of the question of freshness. It is the opinion of some observers that when women do obtain a free hand {i.e., as writers, rather than as readers, of fiction] they will not repay their long debt to the precautionary attitude of men by unlimited consideration for the natural delicacy of the latter.[37]

What James proposes here is a kind of literary eugenics. Like the writers for the *New Review* symposium, he posits the need for a "renewal" in the literary world. But in his inimically evasive way, he also seems to question whether women writers' pursuit of "candour" will produce a positive kind of change in the novel. To use a Jamesian metaphor, the house of fiction has many windows; and, he warns, if certain windows are opened, or broken by an overly active female elbow, the health of all its occupants might be at risk.

But James should not be credited with originating this kind of argument. The first such attack on the New Woman novel is to be found in Arthur Waugh's 1894 essay, "Reticence in Literature." Published in the first issue of the *Yellow Book*, this essay merits attention because Waugh is the first critic to practice what he terms "the hale and hearty" school of literary criticism.[38] In the following passage he uses Linton's notion of a gendered opposition between culture and literature to attack the New Woman novel for its generic "effeminacy."

> There is all the difference in the world between drawing life as we find it, sternly and relentlessly, surveying it all the while from outside with the calm, unflinching gaze of criticism, and, on the other hand, yielding ourselves to the warmth and colour of its excesses, losing our judgment in the ecstasies of the joy of life, becoming, in a word, effeminate. . . . The man lives by ideas; the woman by sensations; and while the man remains an artist so long as he holds true to his view of life, the woman becomes one as soon as she throws off the habit of her sex, and learns to rely on her judgment, and not on her senses. It is only when we regard life with the untrammelled view of the impartial spectator, when we pierce below the substance for its animating idea, that we approximate the artistic temperament. *It is unmanly, it is effeminate, it is inartistic to gloat over pleasure, to revel in immoderation, to become passion's slave; and literature demands as much calmness of judgment, as much reticence, as life itself.*   (209, emphasis added)

As he had noted earlier in this essay, Waugh is worried that the novel as a literary form will "mel[t] into mere report, mere journalistic detail," in the hands of the novelists who present controversial ideas "without the restraint and tutelage of art and beauty" (204). According to

Waugh, the New Woman novel puts more at risk than the generic distinction between journalism and fiction. It also threatens to make the novel indistinguishable from either photography or pornography. For, if left unchecked, Waugh insists, the "natural inclination of frankness" "would blunder on resolutely, with an indomitable and damning sincerity, till all is said that can be said, and art is lost in photography" (204).

Such photographic realism, Waugh insists, is indistinguishable from pornography, insofar as it domesticates "the refinements of lust" and "permeates marriage with the ardours of promiscuous intercourse" (258). "We are told," he notes with dismay, "that this is part of the revolt of woman, and certainly our women-writers are chiefly to blame." But "how is art served by all this?" he asks in conclusion. What will be the end result of the present-day "cry for realism, naked and unashamed?" And how will the "unsuspecting Young Person" be affected by the "unpalatab[ly] detail[ed]" accounts of pregnancy she reads in the "new" realism (218, 219)? This last question points to what other reviewers will refer to as the "sex mania," "erotomania," or "tommyrotics" of the New Woman novel. Because James Ashcroft Noble addresses this topic in more detail than Waugh does, I want to consider Noble's essay, "The Fiction of Sexuality," before pursuing a discussion of the other two objections Waugh makes to the New Woman novel.

What is of primary concern to Noble—and critics such as Hugh Stutfield, B. A. Crackanthorpe, D. F. Hannigan, and Janet Hogarth, in essays titled, respectively, "Tommyrotics," "Sex in Modern Literature," "Sex in Fiction," and "Literary Degenerates"—is not the New Woman novel's generic effeminacy but its reconceptualization of the relation between sexuality and human "character" or personality.[39] As Noble argues,

The new fiction of sexuality presents to us a series of pictures painted from reflections in convex mirrors, the colossal nose which dominates the face being represented by one colossal appetite which dominates life. Sometimes it is made as inoffensive as deformity can ever be made; sometimes it is unspeakably revolting; occasionally, as in that ridiculously over-praised book, "The Heavenly Twins," it is allied with moralising as aggressive as that of a Sunday-school story-book; but everywhere it *is a flagrant violation of the obvious proportion of life.* Be the prominent people in this new fiction young or old, married or unmarried, voluptuaries or ascetics, *the sexual passion provides the main-spring of their action*, and within its range lies their whole gamut of emotion. . . . Is this persistent presentation of the most morbid symptoms of erotomania a seeing of life steadily and wholly? Is it even a clear, truthful seeing of *that part of life which it unnaturally isolates?* (493, emphasis added)

The question of where sexuality figures into the whole of human character is, I think, one of the most significant issues to emerge in the debate on realism and representation in the New Woman novel. As I tried to suggest in the previous section, it also takes this fiction out of a strictly literary context and places it in the context of a growing interdisciplinary discourse on sexuality. It is obvious from this extract that Noble would like to curtail the production of such discourse. He tries to accomplish this by invoking not only the Arnoldian principles of steadiness and wholeness but also a notion of "the obvious proportion of life." Positing the existence of "normally constituted human beings" who would object to the views of human sexuality presented in this fiction, he goes on to argue that sex is not supposed to be " 'the end of speech,' " the subject of conversation. "The just action of the appetites is secured by keeping them inattentive to themselves." " 'Not rules of quantity, but habits of forgetfulness, constitute our emancipation from the animal nature,' " he argues, citing a medical authority to substantiate his point (495). Arnoldian steadiness and wholeness of vision can only be achieved by curtailing the representation of the appetites, by "breaking every mirror in which their face may be beheld."

Noble's suggestion that mimesis should be marshaled in support of self-control brings us back to Waugh's question: what will be the end result of the present-day "cry for realism, naked and unashamed"? As noted earlier, Waugh remains obsessed with the generic degeneration of the novel. Picking up Noble's rhetoric about mirroring and representation, other critics answer Waugh's question by arguing that the New Woman novel models "dangerous," sexually degenerate, behavior for its readers. Reactions to Grant Allen's *The Woman Who Did* provide a particularly striking instance of this.

Grant Allen's 1895 novel is about a woman who travels with her lover to Italy, gives birth to their illegitimate daughter after his death from a sudden illness, and then returns to England as a single parent. Years later, when her daughter turns against her, accusing her mother of ruining her chances to make a society marriage, Herminia Barton begins to regret her New Womanly violations of the social code. Thinking that her death will relieve her daughter's embarrassment and free her to marry as she wishes, she commits suicide at the end of the novel.

Critics writing about Allen's novel recently have made much of Herminia's self-destructiveness.[40] They have commented extensively on the irony of Allen's title: Allen's New Woman "did," that is, she dared to have a sexual relationship outside of marriage and raised an illegitimate child. But she finally kills herself for doing it. Thus, they argue, her story confirms rather than defies the power of the Victorian social code. Her New Womanly gesture of defiance is just that—a gesture, an action effectively countered by her death and by her daughter's aggressive conservatism. Arguing in this manner, recent critics pick up only one of the two issues raised in reviews of *The Woman Who Did* written in the 1890s. They reiterate the point made by W. T. Stead, for example, in calling *The Woman Who Did* a "boomerang of a book."[41] But they do not account for the counterarguments presented by critics such as Mrs. Fawcett.

Writing for *Contemporary Review*, Fawcett argues that Allen wants to weaken the "cramping idea of the family tie."[42]

> He really believes that chastity is "impossibly wicked, and cruel," and so on; he really loathes his own country, cursed as he says it is with the "leprous taint of respectability," and regards patriotism as one of the "lowest of vices," as vicious even as fidelity to marriage vows. England is to him "the shabbiest, sordidest, worst organized of nations." (626)

From Fawcett's perspective, Herminia Barton's suicide is not a suffi-
cient deterrent for the "unsuspecting Young Person." Given readers'
susceptibility to the things they read, Allen's novel ought not to have
been published at all, in her view. For even if Herminia punishes
herself for her infractions of the social code, she lives for a long time in
defiance of it. Fawcett's objection is thus that Herminia provides Allen's readers with the wrong kind of model to emulate in their own
lives.

Such concern for the power of art to affect people's behavior in real
life did not simply fuel critics' outbursts against this fiction; it stimulated the production of New Woman novels as well. At least two novels
were written in 1895 quite explicitly to counter the example of Allen's
Herminia Barton: Lucas Cleeve's [Adelina G. I. Kingscote's] *The
Woman Who Wouldn't* and Victoria Cross's [Vivian Cory's] *The Woman
Who Didn't*.[43] In her preface to *The Woman Who Wouldn't*, Cleeve, for
one, highlights the intertextuality of her work with Allen's. "If one
young girl is kept from a loveless, mistaken marriage, if one frivolous
nature is checked in her career of flirtation by the remembrance of Lady
Morris, I shall perhaps be forgiven by the public for raising my feeble
voice in answer to 'The Woman Who Did.' "[44]

In *The Woman Who Did*, Herminia Barton refuses to marry her lover,
arguing that a legal tie would change the character of their relationship. In *The Woman Who Wouldn't*, a bride initially refuses to sleep with
her husband because she does not want to confuse spiritual love with
animal passion. She has sex with her husband only after she realizes
that her purity has driven him to seek sexual satisfaction elsewhere. In
her preface, Cleeve assumes a kind of Old Testament rigidity in her
thinking about the relation of her own novel to Grant Allen's: an eye
for an eye, a character for a character, Lady Morris for Herminia Barton. Yet, a sense of New Testament grace is conveyed through her
remarks about the desired effect her fiction will have on its readers. If a
fictional life is "lost," a real life will be saved; if a fictional character
compromises herself, a real "frivolous nature" may check her "career of
flirtation." If a fictional character all but loses her husband when she
refuses to sleep with him, the young girl who reads her story will not
need to experiment thus with an unconventional marriage.

I would emphasize the contradiction in Cleeve's thinking. Cleeve does not approve of readers' identification with Grant Allen's Herminia Barton. She would like to curtail the kind of compulsive, hysterical, identification of real women with fictional heroines Oscar Wilde mocks so famously in "The Decay of Lying" through his anecdotes about female readers.[45] Nonetheless, Cleeve is eager to change her own readers' lives. Her fiction, in other words, has the very same "designs upon reality" that she objects to in other New Woman novels.[46]

Did the New Woman novel, in its pursuit of "candour," threaten generic distinctions between the novel and pornography or photography? Did it violate "the obvious proportion of life" by presenting sexuality as "one colossal appetite which dominates life"? And did it thus encourage real-life degenerate behavior in inviting readers to model their actions after the women who did? All three processes, critics argued, make the novel "effeminate." For the novel loses its "potency," its generic "virility," when it cannot be distinguished from other kinds of writing. Moreover, it cannot be considered part of a "strong-headed and masculine nation's" culture if it focuses inappropriately on sexuality and encourages female readers' hysterical identification with women who violate the code of "womanliness."

As powerful as these three arguments are, they yielded to a fourth in the late 1890s: that the New Woman novel did not meet the aesthetic standards of high art. Recall yet another of Arthur Waugh's questions in "Reticence in Literature:" "How is art served by all of this?" Waugh had asked this question, but he put most of his energy into proving the generic impurity of the New Woman novel. In other words, aesthetics were of secondary importance to him. The same is true of other critics writing about the New Woman novel before 1895. For example, a critic reviewing Mary Crommelin's *Dust Before the Wind* for the *Athenaeum* in 1894 simply suggested that it "is not the kind of book that we desire to see multiplied."[47] That same year a reviewer for the same periodical claimed that the references to other New Woman novels in J. Ashby-Sterry's *A Naughty Girl* (1894) are "in distinctly bad taste," because the books named are not "classics or recent books of overwhelming and incontestable excellence."[48] Like Waugh, these critics are uncomfortable with the proliferation of this fiction. But they have

nothing stronger than an inclusive "we" and the bugabear of bad taste
with which to warn readers away from these "socio-literary portents" of
anarchy. They do not articulate a standard of aesthetic value against
which to measure this fiction. Only *after* 1894 will aesthetics be of
primary concern in discussions of this material.

I mentioned the work of Mrs. Eastwood, Mrs. Morgan-Dockrell,
and Elizabeth Chapman in the previous chapter. I will come back to
their work shortly, but first I want to consider a book-length study
published in 1904 that offered its readers an overview of literary production in the 1890s. William Courtney summarizes the New Woman
novel's contribution to literary history in the following way in *The
Feminine Note in Fiction*.

> Recently complaints have been heard that the novel as a work of
> art is disappearing and giving place to monographs on given
> subjects, or else individual studies of character. If the complaint
> be true . . . the reason is that more and more in our modern age
> novels are written by women for women. . . . It is the neutrality
> of the artistic mind which the female novelist seems to find it
> difficult to realize. A great creator like Shakespeare or Dickens has
> a wise impartiality toward all his puppets. Sometimes Thackeray
> shows a personal interest in one rather than another, but he does
> so at the peril of his own success. If a novelist takes sides, he or she
> is lost. Then we get a pamphlet, a didactic exercise, a problem-
> novel—never a work of art.[49]

Critics who followed the example of Mrs. Eastwood in distinguishing
between fictional and real New Women, between the "journalistic
myth" and the "genuine" phenomenon, tried to minimize the interaction between art and life. Denying that art has any effect on life, they
relegated literature to the margin of culture—and the New Woman
novel to the margin of that margin. Significantly, once both the New
Woman novel in particular and literature in general have been pushed
to the margins of culture, a critic such as William Courtney can then
blame the New Woman novel for the poor reputation of literature. In
the above passage, he attempts to reclaim the cultural legitimacy (cen-

trality) of literature by continuing to marginalize the offensive literary detritus of the 1890s: the 1890s fiction "for" women that does not "realize" the "neutrality of the artistic mind."

By feminizing the New Woman novel, Courtney ensures its continued marginality. Feminization justifies marginalization, because "femaleness," as he defines it, is a synonym for aesthetic second-rateness. "Femaleness," moreover, is both metaphorical and literal. That is, Courtney collapses a distinction made earlier by critics in this field: between the alleged feminization of the literary world and the alleged "effeminacy" of the New Woman novel as a form. The former involves the perception that women had the advantage over men in the literary market of the 1890s; the latter, you will recall Arthur Waugh arguing, has to do with how explicitly New Woman novelists—male or female—treat sexuality—male or female. Using the gender of the author to define his field of inquiry, Courtney, however, prefers not to remember how critics had once brought charges of effeminacy against the work of Thomas Hardy and Grant Allen (to name only the men most frequently attacked in tirades against this fiction).[50] Courtney assumes a direct correlation between the sex of the author and the value of the work. Thus, his study confirms what was obvious to him from the start: the "feminine note" in fiction is undoubtedly an aesthetically impoverished one.

Courtney's ploy may seem so ridiculously obvious, and so obviously misogynist, that it is hard for us now to take him seriously. But I think it is important not to belittle the cultural "work" of critics such as Courtney at the turn of the century. He is upset by what was known as the "topsy-turviness" of the literary marketplace in the 1890s. He seeks to control or contain such topsy-turviness through the production of a new, "virile" standard of aesthetic value. Significantly, his interest in aesthetics obscures the difficult questions raised in the debate on the New Woman novel. Namely, what is the "nature" of human sexuality? Does literature reflect or effect social change? Does the novel have a special function in culture? How does it distinguish itself from other modes of writing in a larger discursive "economy?" Courtney's obfuscation of these issues serves him well, insofar as it puts him in a better position to promote a canon of English literature—a canon from which the gynocentric writing of the 1890s will be notably absent.

Consider again Courtney's claims: the artistic mind is "neutral" or objective. Rather than writing about himself or offering a study of individual character, the artist gives us access to something we recognize as universal human experience. Formal control is paramount: the novel that is truly a "work of art" does not reveal its author's "personal interests." Whereas a woman writer always "has a particular doctrine or thesis which she desires to expound," the true artist's work suppresses its temporality; the true artist never uses the novel as a vehicle for expressing his opinions on "local," historically specific and contingent matters (xiii). Courtney wants aesthetic questions to displace the ideological ones that previously had been the center of attention in the debate on the New Woman novel. He wants to close down the substantive controversy surrounding this fiction once and for all by transferring the locus of interest to the formal or structural features of texts.

Barbara Herrnstein Smith's "performative model" of literary evaluation, amended through reference to Christine Froula's notion of "the hysterical cultural script," can help us understand the impact of this shift in the terms of debate on the New Woman novel.[51] In "Contingencies of Value," Smith describes how characterizations of literature's universal and atemporal appeal have been used to defend a canon of literature that serves establishment interests through the reproduction of an ongoing and unchanging cultural tradition. At the risk of oversimplifying Smith's complex argument, I extrapolate the following remark, which bears directly upon Courtney's development of a distinction between novels that are "works of art" and "the feminine note in fiction" that serves as his topos of disvalue. Works that get labeled as "classics," Smith claims,

> tend to be those that appear to reflect and reinforce establishment
> ideologies. However much canonical works may be seen to "question" secular vanities such as wealth, social position, and political
> power, "remind" their readers of more elevated values and virtues,
> and oblige them to "confront" such hard truths and harsh realities
> as their own mortality and the hidden griefs of obscure people,

they would not be found to please long and well if they were seen to undercut establishment interests *radically* or to subvert the ideologies that support them *effectively*. (30, emphasis in original)

Earlier in her essay, Smith described the dynamic of standardization and "pathologization" whereby texts are valued or devalued for their performance of cultural functions. Subtle as her analysis is, Smith ignores the role gender can play in such dynamics. As noted above, when Courtney wants to devalue the New Woman novel, he does not simply "pathologize" it, he feminizes it. In other words, he begins to inscribe something that Smith's analysis does not gloss but that Christine Froula has termed " 'the hysterical cultural script': the cultural text that dictates to males and females alike the necessity of silencing woman's speech when it threatens the father's power" (141). As Froula argues in "The Daughter's Seduction: Sexual Violence and Literary History," such a script "insures that the cultural daughter remains a daughter, her power suppressed and muted; while the father, his power protected, makes culture and history in his own image" (141).

Courtney did not, of course, actually silence the women writers of the 1890s. Nor am I trying to suggest that he is to be credited for single-handedly devaluing their work so effectively that no one has bothered to read it since then.[52] I am arguing that, through their writing about the New Woman novel, critics like Courtney produced a male image of culture and history. Recall Eastwood's claim that the New Woman has a place "in fiction" but not "in fact." According to her, the New Woman is "merely" literature. According to Courtney, however, she is not even that—she is featured in the second-rate "problem-novels" of the 1890s, none of which will be part of an enduring literary canon. Courtney's new, "virile," standard of aesthetic value thus serves to inoculate the English literary tradition against contamination by the "didactic exercises" of the New Woman writers. Courtney's "male" (read "human") and allegedly transhistorical and universal standard of aesthetic value will protect and reinforce establishment ideology by discrediting the subjective and historically contingent writings either by or about New Women.

As I turn now from the criticism written about the New Woman

novel at the turn of the century to the novels themselves, I should note
that I shall not be offering aesthetic evaluations of them. As is so
clearly the case in Courtney's work, all too often such judgments have
been used to shift attention away from other concerns. It is those other
concerns—specifically, the ideological challenges of this fiction to the
bourgeois social and literary tradition—that I wish to highlight in the
next four chapters. In this chapter, I accepted Smith's hypothesis about
the conservative politics of canon formation without question. As I
consider New Woman novelists' objections to the Victorian ideology of
"womanliness" and the experimentation with the form of the novel
they pursue as a result of this interest, I will, in fact, be testing Smith's
hypothesis. Could it be that aesthetic devaluation of New Woman
novels is inversely proportional to their ideological experimentation?
Are these novels "cultural daughters," as Christine Froula has it, whose
power must be muted so that the patriarchy can continue to make
culture and history in the father's image? Such questions can be answered only after we have gained a sense of the thematic as well as the
temporal diversity of New Woman fiction.

3

The Romance Plot:
New Women,
New Plausibilities

Every woman is supposed to have the same set of motives, or
else to be a monster. I am not a monster, but I have not felt
exactly what other women feel—or say they feel, for fear of
being thought unlike others. . . . You are not a woman. You
may try—but you can never imagine what it is to have a man's
force of genius in you, and yet to suffer the slavery of being a
girl. To have a pattern cut out—"this is the Jewish woman;
this is what you must be; this is what you are wanted for; a
woman's heart must be of such a size and no larger, else it must
be pressed small, like Chinese feet; her happiness is to be made
as cakes are, by a fixed receipt."

George Eliot, *Daniel Deronda*[1]

FOUR NOVELS will be discussed in
this chapter: *The Story of an African Farm* (1883), *The Wing of Azrael*
(1889), *Tess of the D'Urbervilles* (1891), and *A Blameless Woman* (1894).
The juxtaposition of Hardy's canonical text with Olive Schreiner's
recently reclaimed feminist "masterpiece" and two long forgotten
works by, respectively, Mona Caird and John Strange Winter [Henri-
etta Stannard] is meant to remind us of something that is easy to
forget: when it was first published, Hardy's text was not spared the

violent rhetoric wielded against other works that long since have been ushered out of the canon. In an essay entitled "Men's Women in Fiction" published in the *Westminster Review* in 1898, for example, Edith Slater blasted Hardy for creating a "repulsive" and "material" heroine. "Does not Mr. Hardy know any 'nice' women?" she queries.[2] "Or is it only the 'nasty' ones that are interesting? They must be beautiful, they must be sensual, they must be selfish." Contrasting them with other male writers' heroines, she despairs of the historical regression she traces in the tradition of Victorian fiction that ends with Hardy. "Have we got no further than this at the end of the 'so-called nineteenth century'?" she asks, raising once again the specter of anarchy and cultural dissolution we have seen other writers raise in connection with both the New Woman and the New Woman novel (575).

My point is this: while current aesthetic evaluations of Hardy's works lift *Tess* above and out of the debate on "candour" in English fiction waged between 1885 and 1895, I want to recontextualize it and the other three novels mentioned above. I want to approach these narratives not as aesthetic objects but as texts with work to do, narratives written to "correct" English realism—and thus to make the novel once again an effective cultural agent. The particular "correction" I want to focus on in this chapter is what Mrs. Oliphant termed "the transformation" of the "pure woman."[3]

As we shall see in Chapter Four, there is more than one way this transformation can be effected. In novels to be discussed subsequently, women's sexual experience will be described more explicitly than would have been possible during the reign of the circulating libraries. In the four works under consideration here, the "pure woman" is "transformed" in the sense that new life stories are made "plausible" for women who would have been rewarded by death at the end of a three-decker novel because they did not live up to the Victorian standard of female purity.[4] As Hardy had predicted, these "honest" novels of the future do not end with "the regulation finish that 'they married and were happy ever after.' " Instead, they portray "catastrophes based on sexual relationship as it is."[5] They are "anti-marriage," to use Oliphant's term, insofar as they reject both the familiar patterning of the marriage plot and the cultural endorsement of marriage as the means by which "patterns of passion and patterns of property" are always "br[ought] into harmonious alignment."[6]

As the epigraph from *Daniel Deronda* might suggest, at least some of these novels are also antimarriage because they attack the totalizing ideology of romance: the will to believe that, as the Princess Halm-Eberstein complains, since all women are fitted to a single social pattern, ambition is "unwomanly" or "monstrous."[7] In *Reading the Romantic Heroine: Text, History, Ideology*, Leslie Rabine describes the "intense contradiction" of romantic love, the contradiction "which can perhaps explain its seduction" in the following way. "As a heterosexual, private, total, exalted love, [romantic love] is supposed to give meaning to an otherwise drab existence, and allow us to transcend daily life to a higher plane."[8] Always characterized as "a total love, combining sexuality, emotional intimacy, and self-reflecting intellect," it serves, in the nineteenth-century novel, as "the central human relation around which all other relations revolve" (vii). On the one hand, Rabine goes on to suggest, "[romantic love] provides one of the few accepted outlets through which women can express their anger and revolt against their situation in a patriarchal order." But on the other hand, it "idealizes and eroticizes women's powerlessness and lack of freedom." This is the contradiction, according to Rabine, that has made the romantic love narrative "so resilient as a literary form and so potent as a cultural myth" (viii).

I will argue in this chapter that New Woman novelists like Olive Schreiner and Mona Caird expose the contradiction of romantic love as they question the plausibilities of the marriage plot. Other narrative conventions associated with "classic" nineteenth-century realism will be challenged as well, as New Woman novelists rethink the orthodox Victorian opposition between the "pure" and the "fallen" woman.

1883: The Story of an African Farm

[Lyndall] was more like a princess, yes, far more like a princess, than the lady who still hung on the wall in Tant 'Sannie's bedroom.

So Em thought. [Lyndall] leaned back in the little armchair; she
wore a gray dressing-gown, and her long hair was come out and
hung to the ground. Em, sitting before her, looked up with mixed
respect and admiration.[9]

"It is not what is done to us, but what is made of us," [Lyndall]
said at last, "that wrongs [women]. No man can be really injured
but by what modifies himself. We all enter the world little plastic
beings, with so much natural force, perhaps, but for the rest—
blank; and the world tells us what we are to be, and shapes us by
the ends it sets before us. To you it says—*Work!* and to us it
says—*Seem!* To you it says—As you approximate to man's highest
ideal of God, as your arm is strong and your knowledge great, and
the power to labour is with you, so you shall gain all that human
heart desires. To us it says—Strength shall not help you, nor
knowledge, nor labour. You shall gain what men gain, but by
other means. And so the world makes men and women." (188)

The first of these passages is the opening paragraph of the chapter
entitled "Lyndall" in Schreiner's *The Story of an African Farm.* The
second appears later in Lyndall's chapter-long tirade about the status of
women in Victorian culture. They are juxtaposed here to emphasize the
"before" and "after" quality. Before Lyndall speaks, before the chapter
"Lyndall" disrupts the course of events in the novel, her childhood
friend Em might well have been justified in mistaking Lyndall for a
princess. For Lyndall looks the part of the Victorian angel in the house:
she is beautiful, well dressed, graceful. From Em's point of view, she is
truly the storybook princess come to life now that she is back home on
this dusty South African farm after four years' absence. Lyndall left
Tant 'Sannie's household an angry young girl. She returns now as a
lady, and Em, the childhood companion who quite literally remained
down on the farm, is now in awe of this dainty little personage who
represents everything she herself is not nor will ever be.

When Lyndall begins to recite her litany of the wrongs women have
suffered under Victorian patriarchy, however, Em begins to feel "re-
buked and ashamed" (184). As she notes silently to herself, "how could

she take Lyndall and show her the white linen, and the wreath, and the embroidery" she is now collecting for her trousseau when Lyndall speaks so disparagingly of men's fickleness and distinguishes herself from "other women [who are] glad of such work" as childrearing? (184). How can Em celebrate the marriage she anticipates as her unique achievement in life when Lyndall sees this as a loss of individuality, assimilation into the anonymity of motherhood?

Em quickly withdraws from their conversation. The bulk of Lyndall's tirade thus falls upon the ears of her other childhood playmate, Waldo, who is addressed in the second of the two passages quoted above and in the following, which contains, as W. T. Stead claims in "The Novel of the Modern Woman," "the germ and essence of all the fiction of the Revolt" to be written over the next fifteen years.[10]

"Look at this little chin of mine, Waldo, with the dimple in it. It is but a small part of my person; but though I had a knowledge of all things under the sun, and the wisdom to use it, and the deep loving heart of an angel, it would not stead me through life like this little chin. I can win money with it, I can win love; I can win power with it, I can win fame. What would knowledge help me? The less a woman has in her head the lighter she is for climbing. I once heard an old man say, that he never saw intellect help a woman so much as a pretty ankle; and it was the truth. They begin to shape us to our cursed end," she said, with her lips drawn in to look as though they smiled, "when we are tiny things in shoes and socks. We sit with our little feet drawn up under us in the window, and look out at the boys in their happy play. We want to go. Then a loving hand is laid on us: 'Little one, you cannot go,' they say; 'your face will burn, and your nice white dress be spoiled.' We feel it must be for our good, it is so lovingly said; but we cannot understand; and we kneel still with one little cheek wistfully pressed against the pane. Afterwards we go and thread blue beads, and make a string for our neck; and we go and stand before the glass. We see the complexion we were not to spoil, and the white frock, and we look into our own great eyes. Then the curse begins to act on us. It finishes its work when we

are grown women, who no more look out wistfully at a more
healthy life; we are contented. We fit our sphere as a Chinese
woman's foot fits her shoe, exactly, as though God had made
both—and yet He knows nothing of either. In some of us the
shaping to our end has been quite completed. The parts we are not
to use have been quite atrophied, and have even dropped off; but
in others, and we are not to be less pitied, they have been weak-
ened and left. We wear the bandages, but our limbs have not
grown to them; we know that we are compressed, and chafe
against them." (188–189)

In her preface to the second edition of *Story*, Schreiner criticizes what
she terms the "stage method" of narration in classic realism, whereby
an omniscient narrator, like a stage director, presents his theater audience, his readers, with a neatly packaged performance.[11] In the novelistic tradition against which her own fiction has been judged wanting,
she notes, "each character is duly marshalled at first, and ticketed; we
know with an immutable certainty that at the right crises each one
will . . . act his part" (27). But if there "is a sense of satisfaction in
this, and of completeness," it is not, Schreiner insists, the "method of
the life we all lead," a life wherein "nothing can be prophesied" (27)
and events are painted in "grey pigments," not in the "brilliant phases
and shapes which the imagination sees in far-off lands" (28). The
conversation between Lyndall and Em epitomizes the difference between Schreiner's "realer" realism and the "stage method" of narration
in the nineteenth-century tradition. Refusing to be Em's storybook
"princess," Lyndall is also refusing to be marshaled into predictability
as a character. In this passage she provides an exhaustive catalog of
reasons for revolting against the Victorian sexual ideology of passionlessness. She quite ruthlessly demythologizes the Victorian patriarchy's
idealization of female beauty by exposing its usefulness in ensuring
women's physical and political powerlessness. Still more notably, her
voice runs rampant in this scene. There is speech and little else here—
no authorial commentary, no attempt on an omniscient narrator's part
to mediate Lyndall's remarks or to package her performance for the
readers' benefit.

Juxtaposed with Lyndall's outburst, Nancy Armstrong's argument in *Desire and Domestic Fiction* can help us appreciate one aspect of both this scene and this novel's divergence from the nineteenth-century tradition of domestic realism. Armstrong claims that the "project" of realism was to distinguish private from public social life and thus to "detac[h] sexuality from political history."[12] Insofar as emotion was presumed to constitute a "female domain of knowledge" in the nineteenth century, the sexual contract (i.e., the marriage plot) that governs the form of the domestic novel authorized the Victorian woman writer. Moreover, insofar as love was assumed to be " 'the most powerful regulating law between two parties,' " the sexual contract overruled the social contract in Victorian domestic realism.[13] Armstrong's interest lies in explaining both the "rise" of the novel, its increasing cultural status in the nineteenth century, and the concomitant "rise" of female authority. Significantly, such female authority was domestic, private, and sexual. Which is precisely why Lyndall characterizes it so mockingly in a passage like the following.

> "And they tell us we have men's chivalrous attention!" she cried. "When we ask to be doctors, lawyers, law-makers, anything but ill-paid drudges, they say,—No; but you have men's chivalrous attention; now think of that and be satisfied! What would you do without it?' " . . . "Power!" she said suddenly, smiting her little hand upon the rail. "Yes, we have power, and since we are not to expend it in tunnelling mountains, nor healing diseases, nor making laws, nor money, nor on any extraneous object, we expend it on [men]." (190, 192)

Lyndall does not want to detach sexuality from political history. She does not want the sexual contract to overrule the social contract. Instead, she refuses to accept the contradiction that fuels the romantic love narrative. She wants Waldo to understand how a Victorian "lady's" sexual "influence" is conjoined with her material, worldly, powerlessness; that is, she wants to explain to him how her erotic ambition is predicated upon the absence of all other ambitions.

But there is another important facet of Lyndall's "revolt." It is significant, I think, that the narrator does not corroborate Lyndall's devastating attack on Victorian women's socialization. Although her comments supplement Schreiner's own attack on the predictability of characterization in "staged" novels, Lyndall's voice stands alone in this scene. Her speech goes on, and on, and on—and it is not endorsed either by the omniscient narrator or by direct authorial commentary. Furthermore, Lyndall's outburst does not just drive Em away in this particular scene; it also alters drastically the trajectory of Schreiner's narrative. I described the two passages cited at the head of this section as the "before" and "after." After this scene, after Lyndall's vocalization of dissent, no one in this novel will stand a chance to enjoy the "private, total, exalted love" Rabine identifies as the cultural myth informing the traditional marriage plot. Gregory Rose leaves Em for Lyndall. Lyndall is attracted neither to Gregory nor to Waldo but to a third man who remains unnamed; she will die giving birth to their illegitimate daughter. The light and dark heroines are not duly rewarded and punished in this novel. The social order is not valorized by a double wedding or the birth of a male heir in the final chapter. The story of an African farm, in other words, cannot be assimilated into that familiar narrative paradigm.

If the above suggests that Schreiner has indeed unraveled the romance plot in *Story*, the objection could still be made that the novel upholds what Nancy Miller terms the conventional "plausibilities" of the marriage plot. Even though Lyndall mounts a formidable thematic assault on the social conventions of "womanliness," her death reinforces the traditional form of the novel. For Lyndall's death epitomizes what Miller terms the "dysphoric" pole of the Victorian heroine's two choices in life (marriage or death). The middle of Schreiner's narrative presents a full-scale critique of the Victorian sex and gender system. But the end of the novel nonetheless deflects that critique because the woman who metaphorically kills the angel in the house dies anyway, leaving the Victorian social order intact.[14]

Such a reading of the ending of *Story* highlights Lydnall's ambivalence about her chosen project of cultural critique. Notwithstanding her damning characterization of the Victorian sexual economy, Lyndall never establishes a different kind of exchange between men and women. Indeed, she never even attempts as much. Long before she resigns herself to death, she mocks her own effort to defy the social order. "But what does it help? A little bitterness, a little longing when we are young, a little futile searching for work, a little passionate striving for room for the exercise of our powers,—and then we go with the drove. A woman must march with her regiment. In the end she must be trodden down or go with it; and if she is wise she goes" (188–189). The day will come, she tells Waldo, "when love is no more bought or sold, when it is not a means of making bread, when each woman's life is filled with earnest, independent labour, love will come to her, a strange sudden sweetness [will] brea[k] in upon her earnest work; not sought for, but found. Then, but not now—" (195). The last phrase in particular reveals Lyndall's inability to believe in herself as a speaker, as someone whose words might have the power to bring about that longed-for future. Waldo senses as much and challenges her in the following manner.

> Waldo waited for her to finish the sentence, but she seemed to have forgotten him.
> "Lyndall," he said, putting his hand upon her—she started "if you think that that new time will be so great, so good, you who speak so easily—"
> She interrupted him.
> "Speak! speak!" she said; "the difficulty is not to speak; the difficulty is to keep silence."
> "But why do you not try to bring that time?" he said with pitiful simplicity. "When you speak I believe all you say; other people would listen to you also."
> "I am not so sure of that," she said with a smile.
> Then over the small face came the weary look it had worn last night as it watched the shadow in the corner.   (195–196)

Thus, in spite of the fact that her words have already had a profound effect on Waldo, Lyndall resigns herself to failure. She claims a voice—and then relinquishes it.

But does not Lyndall's voice continue to be heard, in spite of her relinquishment of it? Lyndall dies, yet the resolution of her life's narrative cannot cancel out the power of her disruptive speech. Notwithstanding her "dysphoric" death at the end of the novel, the chapter "Lyndall" remains as a rich testimony to the power she herself does not believe she has.[15] To put this another way, she speaks "beyond the ending," even if she cannot write or live beyond it. The power and the powerful isolation of Lyndall's voice in *Story* suggests to me that Lyndall's disruption of what Bakhtin terms the "monologic" discourse of classic realism counterbalances the dysphoria of Lyndall's death at the end of the novel.[16]

It might help to note how similar Lyndall's speech is to someone like Alys Smith's claim to the right of self-definition in "The Reply of the Daughters." Lyndall's voice defies traditional narrative strategies of containment. She asserts an agency that is not enclosed or controlled by narrative omniscience. Schreiner's narrator simply gives way to Lyndall in "Lyndall." There will be no contest of wills in *Story* like that Smith describes between Victorian daughters and their parents in her essay for *Nineteenth Century*. As we shall see, however, a female character's "revolt" against the paternalistic authority of an omniscient narrator is not something that every New Woman novelist will be willing to endorse; the shift from monologic discourse to polyphony in the New Woman novel will be as violently contested as so many other issues sparked by the New Woman's "revolt."

1889: The Wing of Azrael

Mona Caird's *The Wing of Azrael* does not present itself as a response to *The Story of an African Farm* in the obvious way that both Lucas Cleeve and Victoria Cross advertised the relation of *The Woman Who Wouldn't* and *The Woman Who Didn't* to Grant Allen's *The Woman Who Did*. But clearly Caird and Schreiner address the same problems: how to win readers' sympathy for a woman who experiences (and acts upon) sexual desire outside of a marriage bond; how to dismantle both the predictability and the "puppetry" of nineteeth-century realism.

Caird echoes the language with which Schreiner criticized the nineteenth-century novelist's "stage method" of narration in the preface to *Story* as she writes her own preface. "If the author preserves his literary fidelity, rebellion among the actors inevitably springs up. Far from being puppets, as they are so often erroneously called, [characters in a novel] are creatures with a will and a stubborn personality who often drive the stage manager [the novelist] to the brink of despair."[17] Thus far, Caird follows Schreiner in objecting to the key assumption underlying the nineteenth-century realist's method of narration: the assumption that characters are completely predictable, that authors have complete control over their characters. At this point, however, Caird alters her terms of analysis, substituting a different modeling of subject-object relations than that implied in the stage metaphor. "The eye only sees that which it brings with it the power of seeing," she goes on to suggest, "whether the 'eye' belongs to one who describes his impression or to him who allows it to be written secretly on his heart. For in the heart of each man lies a recorded drama, sternly without purpose, yet more impressive and inevitable in its teaching than the most purposeful novel ever written" (xi).

Caird achieves two things through this image of the novel as a secret drama recorded on the artist's heart. First, she both anticipates and refutes all objections to its being a vehicle for feminist propaganda. (Recall, by way of contrast, Courtney's characterization of women's fiction as "pamphlets" and "didactic exercises.") Her novel is, she insists, a work of art. It is a work of art, moreover, because—and this is her second important claim—it is authentic. It tells "the truth." Rather than promulgating Mrs. Grundy's social mores, her novel allows readers to recognize what lies below the surface of social convention, the truths inscribed in their own hearts, as well as the artist's.

Presented in her preface as the revelation of an instant, this truth is something Caird's protagonist discovers only after years of living in accordance with society's dictates regarding "womanly" behavior. The youngest daughter of a gentleman with three scapegrace sons, Viola Sedley grows up oblivious to most things but her pleasure in the companionship of a scruffy dog she calls Bill Dawkins. As a girl, she finds a wealthy old landowner's demand for kisses a violation of "her

sense of individual dignity" (1: 8). Even more offensive is his handsome
young son's cruelty toward animals, her own Bill Dawkins included.
But when this same young man offers to marry her several years later,
she realizes she cannot escape his emotional blackmail: if she marries
Philip Dendraith, he will underwrite the upkeep of her father's manor
house; if she does not marry him, and if her parents are forced to move
out of their home, her father's precarious health will be jeopardized,
Philip is quick to remind her. She explains her dilemma to a childhood
friend, only to have him confess that he loves her, although he is in no
position to support her financially. Knowing how her father would
respond to a social faux pas, she does not break her engagement. She
marries Philip, but greets him "at the altar with the words: 'Please do
not forget that I come here against my own wish' " (2: 71).

Although Viola does not love her husband, "her sense of duty holds
firm," the narrator tells us, hinting discreetly at the consummation of
their marriage. "Without the belief that it was *right* to endure all that
she endured, it would have been literally impossible for her to live her
life for another day." And so Viola "struggles on, fighting that desper-
ate fight against her self and her own nature which fills the lives of so
many women with inward storm and wreckage" (2: 114). "Of all forms
of sin, that of loving one man while married to another had [always]
seemed to Viola the farthest removed from the realm of possibility," the
narrator also notes (2: 186). Finding herself attracted to her childhood
friend, Henry Lancaster, however, Viola suddenly understands the Victorian double standard. And her thoughts finally "brea[k] the bounds
of her teaching:" "what was unforgiveable in a woman, a man might do
without ceasing to respect himself or to command respect from others. . . . The line where sin begins and innocence ends did not coin-
cide in the two cases," she now realizes (1: 102, 2: 196–197). Travel-
ing home from a party one evening shortly thereafter, she muses that
the mere touch of Henry's hand has made all "creeds, doctrines, [and]
social laws" suddenly "lose form and substance in [the night's] wild
darkness; they trembled and waned when brought face to face . . .
with the inexorable facts": she is physically and emotionally drawn to a
man who is not her husband (3: 74). Nursing her mother during a fatal
illness, she realizes, too, that the latter gave her life "wholesale, as a

willing sacrifice to God and duty" (3: 75). Watching her mother die, Viola determines not to throw away her life in the same way.

After Viola agrees to elope with Henry Lancaster to France, she impatiently ticks off the days till her departure. When her husband discovers her as she slips out of the house and tries to detain her, she stabs him with a paperknife Henry had given her as a wedding present. At a wedding she had attended shortly before this, Viola had chuckled rather bitterly about the wedding guests who "banished into the vast realm of Impossibility all things which wandered out of the line of their daily pathways" (3: 165). After she murders Philip, after Henry recoils from her in horror when he finds her standing over her husband's body, she herself wanders into "the pitch-black, rayless, impenetrable darkness" of the sea (3: 224).

Caird melodramatically presents Viola's husband as a villainous rake, a wealthy and unethical landowner who toys with his young wife, manipulating her through her (misplaced) loyalty to her parents. Caird does not, however, treat the novel's final scene melodramatically. Instead, readers are encouraged to see how years of subtle psychological abuse have led up to this murder. Moreover, that this gesture sends Viola into "pitch-black, rayless, impenetrable darkness" points up several things. First, it is clear from this plotting that Henry Lancaster did not comprehend until this moment how deeply her marriage to Philip had violated Viola's "sense of individual dignity" (1: 8). "Will you not leave me even a remnant of individuality?" Viola had asked her husband shortly after their wedding (2: 89). "Am I always to be your *wife*, never myself? I have not questioned your authority, but you ask for more than authority. You ask me to surrender my personality." To which Philip had responded: "The world regards and criticizes you as my wife, nothing else. What else are you? You possess no other standing or acknowledged existence" (2: 89). From Viola's perspective, killing Philip is the only way she can prove her independence—both to him and of him. It represents the ultimate rejection of his authority.[18]

Notably, it also represents a rejection of the cultural ideal of female purity, insofar as this ideal of female behavior is an eroticized ideal of female powerlessness and lack of freedom. Henry Lancaster can approve of Viola's rejection of Philip's authority. He is distinctly ambivalent about Viola's rejection of the cultural ideal of Womanhood. His love for Viola, it seems, cannot be sustained in the face of her violent assertion of selfhood. For his love disappears as soon as Viola does something that forces Henry to recognize her not as the object of either Philip's or his own affection but as an independent agent. Thus, when Henry "shrinks" from her as she stands over the dead body of her husband, Viola sees his hesitation and flees, knowing that he cannot forgive her this affront to his conceptualization of female passivity and innate goodness.

In this respect, Viola leaves behind more than Henry Lancaster at the end of *The Wing of Azrael*. She leaves behind the comforting fantasy of a "proper social order" that both the myth of romantic love and the conventions of the marriage plot had sustained in the nineteenth-century novel. As she had noted at the wedding she attended shortly before killing her husband, the cultural mythology surrounding marriage "banish[es] into the vast realm of Impossibility" all things that do not fit its patterning (3: 165). What Viola recognizes here is the public function that romantic love served in the Victorian era. If "Love" was an important part of English culture's ideological apparatus to ensure social stability, such stability will be made unavailable—to everyone, not just to Viola—in the final scene of *The Wing of Azrael*, as readers and characters alike are left in "rayless, impenetrable darkness."[19] To paraphrase Nancy Miller, the end of *The Wing of Azrael* is not merely dysphoric, it is euphorically dysphoric. It cannot be read as Viola's punishment for committing both adultery and murder. Rather, it represents an indictment of the entire social system. For, Samson-like, Viola has pulled down the Victorian temple of marriage on top of her.[20]

1891: Tess of the D'Urbervilles

Because I can assume a reader's familiarity with *Tess of the D'Urbervilles*, let me begin by suggesting how Hardy's remarks in his 1891 essay, "Candour in English Fiction," might help us understand his ambitions for *Tess*.

Life being a physiological fact, its honest portrayal must be largely concerned with, for one thing, the relations of the sexes, and the substitution for such catastrophes as favour the false colouring best expressed by the regulation finish that "they married and were happy ever after," of catastrophes based upon sexual relationship as it is. To this expansion English society opposes a well-nigh insuperable bar. . . . The magazine in particular and the circulating library in general do not foster the growth of the novel which reflects and reveals life. . . . If the true artist ever weeps it is probably then, when he . . . creates a character in a situation which is unprintable.[21]

Without doubt, by Victorian standards Tess's situation is unprintable. Or rather, it is one that would have guaranteed her a very minor part in a classic Victorian novel. A lower-class woman who loses her virginity before she marries; a woman who experiences sexual desire; a woman who bears, and loves, an illegitimate child; a woman who ends a relationship with a man she may never have loved "sincerely," a man she does not love "still:" a woman with this kind of sexual experience would have been a foil for the female protagonist in a novel written earlier in the century, an example to women of what *not* to be and do.[22] Think, for example, of Fanny's role in *Far From the Madding Crowd*—or Esther's in Gaskell's *Mary Barton*. Think of how quickly Hetty Sorrel moves to the margins of the plot in *Adam Bede* once she cannot hide her pregnancy. First and foremost, then, Hardy challenges the middle-class orientation of the nineteenth-century novel by attributing "purity," once the middle-class lady's primary mode of self-identification, to a sexually experienced lower-class woman.

But Hardy does not stop at this, nor does he settle for challenging class-based assumptions about "womanliness" in his presentation of Tess. Instead, he defies the conventions of "formal realism" by letting events as important as Tess's wedding-night confession fall into the white space between chapters.[23] Hardy flaunts the unprintability of Tess's situation. By making Tess's confession of her sexual impurity so vividly present in its absence; by calling attention to what falls outside the bounds of "normal" female sexual (in)experience, as this standard has been established through novelistic representation, Hardy includes in his novel material that neither the *Graphic* nor Macmillan's would have allowed him to represent mimetically. Paradoxically, precisely because Tess's confession is effectively present for the reader, without being represented textually, Hardy is able to depict—without risking a publisher's censure—what he had termed in his essay "Candour in English Fiction" a "catastroph[e] based upon sexual relationship as it is." By making Tess speak so powerfully where she does not speak at all, Hardy defies the "consensual imperative of mimesis," the moral edge of correctness that guides "the Young Person" through the great nineteenth-century tradition of English realism.[24]

This is Hardy's most important challenge to the conventions of nineteenth-century domestic realism, and Tess serves him well in this regard. She is the woman whose life experience reveals the hypocrisy and narrowness of bourgeois society's values. She is the woman whose purity he sets out systematically to prove, thereby doing three things: disproving the validity of Victorian society's judgments of women like her; exposing the xenophobia of the middle classes; and establishing himself as a "true artist" whose novels reflect and reveal life.

And yet, this last goal complicates matters considerably. It significantly affects the way Hardy will go about "correcting" the conventions of nineteenth-century realism. Recall the novel's subtitle: "A Pure Woman, Faithfully Represented by Thomas Hardy." Read in conjunction with the epigraph from Shakespeare, the subtitle establishes the intimacy of Hardy's relationship to his work: "Poor wounded name! My bosom as a bed shall lodge thee." Hardy structures the novel as if it were a Zolaesque experimental novel, as if he were an experimentalist exhibiting his "scientific" knowledge of his characters in all their "phases." But *Tess of the D'Urbervilles* is also a "bosom," a "bed," for Tess to lie in. In other words, it is Hardy's text, not Tess's. In the novel itself Hardy will assume "the dispassionate and omniscient" mode of narration we associate with the nineteenth-century novel.[25] But the subtitle and epigraph establish his very personal investment in the outcome of this narrative.

Proving his "faithfulness" as a narrator, Hardy will thereby establish himself as what he termed in "Candour in English Fiction" a "true artist," an artist who is writing the "honest" novels "of the future." The accuracy of his testimony is meant to ensure his status as one of the "true artists" who are writing "realer" realism. But this also creates a conflict in the narrative, insofar as Hardy's concern for the authority of his testimony leads to his suppression of Tess's. For if Tess's confession were represented in the novel, her words would not simply disrupt the marriage plot Angel Clare set in motion with a single kiss. They would jeopardize the success of Hardy's defense of her purity. "Call me Tess," Tess insists, early on in her relationship with Clare when he lavishes upon her the names of the Greek goddesses like so many posies (186). Though he finds her response puzzling, Angel desists. Yet where in the novel, we might ask, does Tess refute the narrator's naming of her? Where does she insist: "Call me Tess Durbeyfield. My father is a drunk. My mother assumed I might buy my way into the middle classes with my virginity. I have slept with Alec Stoke-d'Urberville. I bore a child by him which I loved until it died. And I am not 'Tess of the D'Urbervilles, A Pure Woman' "?

The fact that Tess's wedding-night confession falls into the white space between chapters indicates that there is no place in a nineteenth-century realistic novel for the text of the New Woman's confession regarding her sexuality. Yet, just as certainly, given what is at stake for *Hardy* in this novel, there will be no place in his text for the New Woman who wants to articulate herself, to create herself, to make a place in the world for herself by speaking. Instead, the only place for the New Woman in *Tess* will be that reserved for her as "a pure woman." Notably, this is a place given to her, a text others inscribe in her.

But perhaps this is a misleading characterization of the novel: an accurate description of the endpoint rather than of the preceding complications in the narrative; a description that ignores the increasing tension in the narrative regarding Tess's status—as both an independent, and increasingly articulate, subject, and as the female object of various males's attention. The competing claims of presentation and self-presentation in a key passage in "Phase the Fourth" foreground the tension in Hardy's narrative between the scripted female self and the speaking subject.

Two pages into "Phase the Fourth, the Consequence," Clare marvels that a "milkmaid's" "mighty personality" can "make the bricks, mortar and whole overhanging sky throb with a burning sensibility." The narrator goes on to note:

> Despite his heterodoxy, faults, and weakness, Clare was a man with a conscience. Tess was not an insignificant creature to toy with and dismiss; but a woman living her precious life—a life which, to herself who endured or enjoyed it, possessed as great a dimension as the life of the mightiest to himself. Upon her sensations the whole world depended, to Tess: through her existence her fellow-creatures existed, to her. The universe itself only came into being for Tess on the particular day in the particular year in which she was born. This consciousness upon which he had intruded was the single opportunity of existence ever vouchsafed to Tess by an unsympathetic first cause; her all; her every and only chance. How then should he look upon her as of less consequence than himself; as a pretty trifle to caress and grow weary of . . . ? (221–222)

Sandwiched between two disclaimers concerning her object-ness is the grand proclamation of Tess's subjectivity, rightly described by Mary Jacobus as the central expression of Hardy's commitment to present Tess as the subject of her own experience.[26] Jacobus's argument needs to be amended, however, by noting that this passage reveals Hardy's ambivalence about his chosen project. It points to the sexual struggle played out in this narrative not only between Tess and Alec, Tess and Angel Clare, but also between Tess and Hardy. Before focusing on the dynamic between character and narrator, we need to consider the interaction between Tess and Angel, the relationship at the level of character that most closely resembles that between Tess and Hardy.

For Angel, recognition of Tess's subjectivity would involve something more than simply ridding himself of his middle-class assumptions about lower-class women. It would involve rejecting the image of her as a "fresh and virginal daughter of nature," which he in fact prefers to her unmaidenly reality (172). "The woman I have been loving is not you," he admits immediately after Tess's first confession. Saying this, he cruelly confirms her earlier suspicion that the "she you love is not my real self, but one in my image" (340, 325). As his dream of burying Tess also might suggest, Angel would like to kill the real Tess for shattering the image of her he has created in his own image. In Bakhtinian terms, he refuses to see her as a subject, an ideologeme, since that would disrupt his monologic view of the world. Fleeing to South America, he flees not only his capacity for violence and his anger at having Tess intrude upon *him*—in contrast to the intrusion upon *her* consciousness acknowledged in the quoted passage from Chapter Twenty-five; he flees also his disempowerment, his inability to make her conform to his idealized image of her.

Of course, Clare's response to Tess's second confession differs radically from his response to the first. In thinking about Tess during his unhappy sojourn in South America, Clare revises his idea of the "moral woman." Reappraising the "old appraisements of morality" (462), he finally acknowledges that "the beauty or ugliness of a character [lies] not only in its achievements, but in its aims and impulses; its true history [lies] not among the things done, but among things willed." On the basis of such a reappraisal of morality, Clare will be willing to forgive Tess and to hold himself culpable for having mistreated her. And yet, his response to Tess's second confession is in fact inconsistent with his reappraisal of morality. Rallying to protect "this deserted wife of his, this passionately fond woman, [who] clings to him now without a suspicion that he would be anything to her but a protector" (525), he lets his "amazement at the strength of her affection for himself" obliterate his initial "horror at her impulse." Thus, to Tess's last, and most nearly graphic, description of the crime she has committed—"He heard me crying about you, and he bitterly taunted me; and called you by a foul name; and then I did it: my heart could not bear it: he had nagged me about you before—and then I dressed myself, and came away to find you" (524)—Clare responds: "I will not desert you; I will protect you by every means in my power, dearest love, whatever you may have done or not have done" (525).

"Whatever you may have done or not have done:" why does Clare add this proviso? Why is it difficult for Clare to acknowledge that Tess exists independently of his sexual desire for her, his need to be needed by her? Why is he unable to understand how she might feel so oppressed by Alec, so "intruded upon" by another person, that she would take that person's life in order to hear her own voice? Why does he view the expression of female sexuality—conceptualized as passive acceptance of male sexual attention—and the expression of female subjectivity as incompatible desires? Given the subtitle and the epigraph to *Tess*, we might ask these same questions of Hardy himself. "A Pure Woman, Faithfully Represented by Thomas Hardy." "Poor wounded name! My bosom as a bed shall lodge thee." The fact that Hardy uses a literary language to describe Angel's difficulty in recognizing Tess's subjectivity exemplifies the extreme self-consciousness of this text.[27] Together with the title and the epigraph, this particular narrative strategy establishes *Tess* as a Barthean "lover's discourse."[28] Significantly, Hardy's interest in knowing Tess—in representing Tess, in being "faithful" to her unique subjectivity—is also, finally, an expression of his interest in *having* Tess. Telling a story that lays bare the sexual imperialism of such a "faithful" discourse—a discourse faithful ultimately not to Tess but to Hardy—Hardy attempts to naturalize his foregone conclusions: that the form of the novel requires the suppression of female subjectivity; that the suppression of female subjectivity is one of the "tragic condition[s]" of "sexual relationship as it is."[29]

In regard to both of these issues, the collusion of Angel and the narrator in the closing sequence is telling. For here Angel and the narrator rally together to "protect" this "passionately fond woman." Both treasure the beauty Tess symbolizes;[30] moreover, both valorize her "passive responsiveness." "I am ready," Tess says in the final moments of her life. Accepting the role Angel Clare and the narrator have given her as "a pure woman," she accepts what Caird's Viola Sedley had not: that the love of men like Henry Lancaster, Angel Clare, and Thomas Hardy himself is predicated upon the denial of female agency.[31] To be the object of their erotic attachment, Tess must remain just that: an object, not a subject. "Angel—I am glad. . . . Now I shall not live for you to despise me," Tess says as she dies in order to become the apotheosis of purity. Tess dies, in other words, so that neither Angel's nor the narrator's love for her will be threatened by anything else she

might say or do. Thus, as Hardy releases the New Woman from the
trap of society's condemnation of women who are sexually active outside of marriage as "impure" or "fallen," he also—unlike Schreiner or
Caird—silences her, obliterates her. He challenges "the censorship of
prudery," but refuses to let the New Woman challenge his own
monologic discourse.

1894: A Blameless Woman

"Contemporary fiction" cannot portray "sexual relationship as it is"
for fear of offending the Grundyites, Hardy complained in 1890. It
cannot "rise to the heights of tragedy," lest "we should fright the ladies
out of their wits" with "the crash of broken commandments." As
Joseph Boone notes, Hardy "corrects" realism by introducing the architectonics of tragedy into the domestic novel.[32] Yet, because he takes
such a tragic view of sexuality, his New Woman novels cover over the
contradictions they expose (129); they "reproduce in form and content
the conservative sexual ideologies against which they seem to rebel"
(130).

What if broken commandments commanded no grand fanfare?
What if a novelist were to "correct" or replace the conventions of
nineteenth-century realism not with the grand architectonics of tragedy but with a more open-ended patterning of plot? The conservative
nature of Hardy's experimentation with the New Woman and the form
of the novel shows up most notably when *Tess* is juxtaposed with John
Strange Winter's [Henrietta Stannard's] *A Blameless Woman* (1894). In
the wake of the uproar surrounding the publication of *Tess*, Winter not
only manages a defense of the New Woman's purity; she also debunks
Hardy's tragic plotting of the New Woman's life.[33] Her protagonist
does not die at Stonehenge. Instead, she lives on—and merely by
living, she refutes Hardy's reimposition of a dysphoric patterning on
the "fallen" woman's life.

Like so many Victorian heroines before her, Winter's protagonist is
introduced to us as a motherless young girl. Margaret lives with her

uncle's family in Blankhampton, flitting from one social engagement
to the next, flirting outrageously with every gentleman she meets. She
flirts with everyone, but she falls in love with a handsome young
Russian prince who asks her to marry him but also explains that, for
reasons having to do with national security, their marriage must be
kept secret for two years. Telling her aunt and uncle she is going to live
with her ex-governess for an indefinite period of time in Germany to
perfect her German, Margaret travels to the continent alone and is
married to Dolgouroff in a private ceremony. Two years later she learns
that the document in Russian she assumed was a marriage license was
in fact an agreement to pay her a thousand pounds a year for life. Her
husband of two years has been married for ten to a Russian princess.

At this point, still quite early in Winter's novel, Margaret returns to
her family "utterly and thoroughly changed" (54). Physically ill and
emotionally demoralized, she is nonetheless determined to keep her
grief private. If her aunt and uncle cannot understand her change in
character, they are nonetheless pleased when, three years later, she
agrees to marry Captain Max Stewart, a man whom she had dismissed
years before in favor of Dolgouroff. "This man," she tells herself, "is
straight and honest and true. He has no past to come between us. No,
it is I who have a past—but not to come between us, because my past is
a past without any tie; my past is a past which does not count" (159).

But, of course, eventually her past does come between them. Margaret and Max move to Scotland to take up residence on the Stewart
family estate. They have two children; at Margaret's insistence they
also adopt Max's cousin, a young girl named Effie who had been living
with the family's "poor relations." Ironically enough, this act of kind-
ness disrupts their marriage. Envious of Max's love for Margaret, and
unhappy at the idea of being in debt to Margaret for letting her live
with them, Effie determines to ferret out any dark secrets this seem-
ingly perfect family might be hiding. Margaret remains ignorant of
Effie's schemes. When her ex-"husband" shows up at their estate as the
guest of another visitor, she even manages a very difficult conversation
with aplomb. "You must know perfectly well," she tells Dolgouroff,
"we can never pretend that the past was not there, or that the present
and the past are absolutely dissociated one from another. What would

be appropriate to our past would not be appropriate to our present, and what is appropriate to our present can have nothing to do with our past," she insists, when he suggests that he still loves her, still maintains a marriage in name only with his Russian wife (273). Margaret does not deny the emotions that now conflict with her loyalty to her spouse and her love for her children. For the sake of the latter, however, she is willing to refrain from acting on these emotions or in any other way upsetting the balance of her ten-year marriage to Max Stewart. Max, on the other hand, cannot forgive Margaret for what he soon learns from Effie. "We Stewarts are an honourable people," he insists, before preceeding with a divorce case against her (338).

The end of the novel finds Margaret living in London, looking forward to nothing more each day than catching a glimpse of her children on their daily carriage ride through the park. When Dolgouroff arrives to tell her that his Russian wife is dead, she refuses to consider reestablishing a relationship with him on any terms. "It was her children's right that she should not deliberately make herself what she had not been and was not then," she feels. "Don't suggest it to me again," she pleads, "a gleam of the mother-light in her eyes." For "it would make *all* the difference to me" (343). Winter's narrative ends on that ambiguous note. Margaret is indeed proved blameless, yet the novel ends with any number of questions unanswered. Does she ever get to see her children? In their final conversation, is she encouraging or discouraging Dolgouroff from asking her again to be his wife? Will she continue to think she must deny her attraction to Dolgouroff for the sake of her children? Will she continue to believe, in other words, that she can be a good mother only if she denies her sexual desire for a man who is not her husband? That these questions remain unanswered in *A Blameless Woman* is, I think, significant. While Hardy would close down discussion of the New Woman's purity, offer a definitive resolution of the New Woman's fate, Winter provides a much more open-ended challenge to the traditional romance plot and the Victorian "pattern" of the good woman that the Princess Halm-Eberstein had criticized so bitterly in *Daniel Deronda*.

The following needs to be emphasized in closing this chapter. Even though the discussion here has followed historical chronology, the

point has not been to model a "progress" in this chapter—a progress
from either the worst to the best novel, in aesthetic terms, or from the
least to the most correct "correction" of nineteenth-century realism.
Rather, I want to suggest that two lines of development are articulated
in these narratives, as their authors define the cultural work of the
"new" realism in one of two ways. On the one hand, Hardy and Caird
sustain the truth-claims associated with the convention of narrative
omniscience in classic realism. Even if they "transform" the "pure
woman" by putting a "fallen" one in her place, they never renounce
their claim to give their readers access to "the truth" about the New
Woman. As I will show in the next chapter, Hardy in particular sets an
important precedent in this regard for other New Woman novelists,
who want to authorize their fiction through their truth-claims.

On the other hand, writers like Schreiner and Winter "transform"
the "pure woman" not by producing the "correct" representation of her
but by transforming the Victorian discourse of sexuality. Shifting the
novel into an interrogatory mode, these writers offer questions, not
answers, as they demystify the cultural production of the "good
woman." I began this chapter with an epigraph from *Daniel Deronda*.
The Princess Halm-Eberstein's bitter words need to be kept in mind as
we consider, in the next three chapters, novels that explore alternatives
to the Victorian opposition between motherhood and monstrousness,
novels that challenge more and more radically the ideological mono-
logue of nineteenth-century domestic realism.

4

Erotomania

I<small>N</small> "The Anti-Marriage League," Mrs. Oliphant objects vehemently to the "doctrine [Hardy] preache[s"] in *Tess*, whereby a woman "twice fallen from the woman's code of honor and purity" proves to be "specially and aggressively pure."[1] Extending her criticism to other New Woman novels, she attacks *Jude the Obscure* for its "grossness, indecency, and horror" (137). Referring to *Jude* as "the strangest illustration of what Art can come to when given over to the exposition of the unclean," she gathers vituperative energy for an assault on Grant Allen's *The Woman Who Did* (138). "The result of the struggle of the woman who did," she observes, "is to select, as the most important thing in existence, one small fact of life which natural instinct has agreed . . . to keep in the background, and which among all peoples who have ceased to be savage is veiled over by instinctive reticences and modesties of convention as well as by the everlasting truth of Love" (144). From Oliphant's perspective, *Tess* is less objectionable than *Jude the Obscure*, which is more "coarsely indecent" than any novel ever produced by the hand of a "Master" in English (138). And both of Hardy's novels are less objectionable than *The Woman Who Did*, which "puts life out of focus altogether, and distorts hopelessly its magnitudes and its littlenesses" (145). "Let us consider seriously what is the tendency of all this froth of literature," she advises her readers, reminding them that Allen's novel has been reprinted nineteen times in the year since its original publication. "[Let us consider] whether it is wise to give it the force of a popular movement, and to afford our sanction, the sanction of the modest and

the dutiful, to all the indecencies of a creed" that "displac{es] altogether" "[Love,] that faithful Union of Two upon which pure and
progressive society is built" (149, 144).

The phrases of note in the above are this last one about the displacement of Love and Oliphant's notion that the New Woman novelists
treat "one small fact of life" as if it were "the most important thing in
existence." While the novels discussed in Chapter Three "displace"
Love—hereby defined as the "faithful Union of Two upon which pure
and progressive society is built"—by rejecting both what Edmund
Gosse termed the "madonna heroine" and the "regulation finish" of the
marriage plot, the novels to be considered here put "life out of focus
altogether" as they make sexuality, not romantic love, their center of
attention. To put this another way, Oliphant is objecting to what those
critics discussed in Chapter Two referred to variously as the "sex mania," the "erotomania," and the "tommyrotics" of the New Woman
novel: the new thinking about the relation between sexuality and
human "character" that New Woman novelists introduced into the
literary marketplace once the circulating libraries lost their moral stranglehold on the novel and the structures of opportunity allowed for this
kind of "candour."

I discussed James Noble's essay, "The Fiction of Sexuality," in some
detail in Chapter Two, noting in particular his anger at the representation of sexuality as the "main-spring" of human action in the New
Woman novel. I will argue in this chapter that the "fiction of sexuality" is more diverse than Noble admits. On the one hand, in novels like
Sarah Grand's *The Heavenly Twins* (1893) and Dorothy Leighton's *As a
Man Is Able* (1893), for example, New Women criticize the sexual
corruption of men, invoking the Victorian ideal of female purity to
explain the moral superiority of the female sex.[2] On the other hand, in
novels like George Gissing's *The Odd Women* (1893), Percival Pickering's *A Pliable Marriage* (1895), and Arabella Kenealy's *A Semi-
Detached Marriage* (1899), New Women recognize their sexual desire
yet remain dominated erotically by a "New Man," a man who is more
aggressively and explicitly sexual in his approach to a woman than a
traditional Victorian hero could have been, given the conventions regarding "reticence in literature." In still other novels, such as Iota's *A

Yellow Aster (1894) and Victoria Cross's *The Woman Who Didn't* (1895), New Women "awaken" to the erotic dimension of maternal sexuality. And in yet others—such as Dorothy Leighton's *Disillusion: A Story with a Preface* (1894), Annie Holdsworth's *Joanna Trail, Spinster* (1894), and Edith Johnstone's *A Sunless Heart* (1894)—women act on their sexual desires only to have them denied by the men in their lives who see them as "spinsters," not as desiring women.

In "The Fiction of Sexuality" Noble assumes that all New Woman novelists build their narratives upon the same model of "human nature." But the diversity of ideas about sexuality promulgated in the novels discussed in this chapter invites a different interpretation. For in spite of what Noble says, these novelists are not mirroring and representing a sexuality that exists "in a domain of nature outside of and prior to representation."[3] Even if that is indeed what some of them claim to be doing, these writers are *producing* or constructing sexuality. In their narratives, the body of the New Woman serves as a proving ground for new conceptualizations of "human nature."

The New Woman and the Culture of Manliness

"One man in times of old, it is said, imparted vitality to the statue he had chiselled. Others may have the contrary gift of turning life to stone."

Moore paused on this observation before he replied to it. His look, at once struck and meditative, said, "A strange phrase: what may it mean?" He turned it over in his mind, with thought deep and slow, as some German pondering metaphysics.

"You mean," he said, at last, "that some men inspire repugnance, and so chill the kind heart."

"Ingenious!" responded Shirley. "If the interpretation pleases you, you are welcome to hold it valid. *I* don't care."[4]   (emphasis in original)

The passage from Charlotte Brontë's *Shirley* (1848) might serve to remind us that the project undertaken in the novels under consideration in this chapter is not entirely new in the 1890s. More so than perhaps any other mid-Victorian novelist, Brontë was concerned about the terrible price middle-class Victorian women had to pay for their recognition as moral beings, not creatures of reasonless passion. She addresses, particularly in *Shirley*, what Peter Cominos has identified as the central contradiction in the Victorian sexual ideology: the requirement that the middle-class lady deny her own body so as to body forth her culture's ideals, that she repress her sexual needs in order to emblematize the cultural ideal of innocence.[5]

Notably, New Woman novelists do not require their heroines to submit to this contradiction. What Brontë and other mid-Victorian writers perceived as a necessity, New Woman novelists view as "artificial," and therefore expendable.[6] As Brontë does in the above passage, they invoke the myth of Galatea and Pygmalion as they attempt to give the angel in the house her place " 'as flesh and blood.' "[7] Laura Marholm Hansson notes in *Six Modern Women*, for example, that "[women] feel themselves to be utterly different from what they were told they were, and which men believe them to be. . . . They are no longer a reflection which man moulds into an empty form[;] they are not like Galatea, who became a living woman through Pygmalion's kiss—they were women before they knew Pygmalion."[8] While Hansson rewrites the classical myth so as *not* to ascribe responsibility to Pygmalion for "awakening" Galatea to life, in the novels to be considered in this section the New Woman rejects the traditional Victorian conceptualization of female passionlessness only because a "New Man" takes it upon himself to initiate her sexually.

The following comment in the *Athenaeum*'s "Year in Review" essay for 1893 can serve to introduce this common dynamic, which I subsequently want to explore through a discussion of George Gissing's *The Odd Women*.

The year 1893, in its literary aspect, has been a year given over almost entirely to the younger writers, who have discovered one another throughout its course with unanimous and touching enthusiasm. The older men have been silent, while the juniors have enjoyed the distinction of limited editions and the luxury of large sales. . . . Along with the short story ("poisonous honey stol'n from France") has come a new license in dealing imaginatively with life, almost permitting the Englishman to contend with the writers of other nations on their own ground; permitting him, that is to say, to represent life as it really is. . . . Not so very many years ago Mr. George Moore was the only novelist in England who insisted on the novelist's right to be true to life, even when life is unpleasant and immoral; and he was attacked on all sides. Now every literary lady is "realistic," and everybody says, "How clever! how charming!"[9]

The only New Woman novelists the *Athenaeum* goes on to mention by name in this essay are Sarah Grand and George Egerton. In turning now to George Gissing's *The Odd Women* (also published in 1893), I want to emphasize the relevance to George Gissing's work of the *Athenaeum* reviewer's comment. Gissing knew Moore's work: knew that Moore had thrown down the gauntlet to English writers in encouraging them to "represent life as it really is." In addition, he knew both Hardy's work and the public's reaction to it. In *The Odd Women*, Gissing builds on the precedent set by these writers as he "constitut[es] sex as a problem of truth."[10] Perhaps because Hardy's fiction from first to last is "shaped by his desire to challenge *and keep within* the demands of the dominant [narrative] form, the three-decker novel," Hardy refrains from writing the body, to use the current phrasing.[11] As noted in Chapter Three, he lets Tess's confession fall into the white space between chapters. It might also be possible that the structures of opportunity in the publishing industry changed sufficiently between 1891 and 1893 to give Gissing more "license in dealing imaginatively" with "the unpleasant and immoral aspects" of life. Whatever the reason, Gissing colonizes the female body with unprecedented "candour" in *The Odd Women*. He documents Rhoda Nunn's transformation into a real "flesh and blood" woman with an explicitness not seen in *Story of an African Farm*, *The Wing of Azrael*, *Tess*, or *A Blameless Woman*. His protagonist, Everard Barfoot, pursues the "truth" about the New Woman's sexual desire with both an intellectual and a physical aggressiveness that remained unmatched in 1893.

As the narrator notes early in the novel, Rhoda Nunn initially seems like an "unfamiliar sexual type" to Everard Barfoot. Upon first meeting her, he wonders if she represents "the desire of a mature man, strengthened by modern culture and with his senses fairly subordinate to reason."[12] She is, he notes, "remote indeed from the voluptuous, but hinting at a possiblity of subtle forces that might be released by circumstances." And Barfoot sets about to do just that: to construct the "circumstances" that will "release" these subtle forces, thereby releasing Rhoda from the chastity figured by her last name.

It is worth noting the extent to which Gissing has borrowed from French naturalism in "designing" Barfoot's "experiment" with Rhoda. In "The Experimental Novel" (1880), Zola describes the naturalist's project in the following manner.

> The novelist starts out in search of a truth. . . . As soon as he has chosen his subject he starts from known facts; then he makes his experiment, and exposes [his character] to a series of trials, placing him amid certain surroundings in order to exhibit how the complicated machinery of his person works. . . . The problem is to know what such passion acting in such a surrounding and under such circumstances, would produce from the point of view of an individual and of society, and an experimental novel . . . is simply the report of the experiment that the novelist conducts before the eyes of the public. In fact, the whole operation consists in taking facts in nature, then in studying the mechanism of these facts, acting upon them, by the modification of circumstances and surroundings, without deviating from the laws of nature. Finally you possess knowledge of the man, scientific knowledge of him, in both his individual and his social relations.[13]

Substitution of the feminine for the masculine pronoun suggests that Barfoot borrowed from Zola the design of his "experiment" to reveal the "voluptuousness" hidden beneath Rhoda's Nunn-like exterior.

Where Gissing's characterization of the naturalist's project differs from Zola's is in his extreme self-consciousness about the confluence of erotic and "objective" scientific power in the relationship between the experimentalist and the female object of his study. Initially at least, Barfoot conceives of himself as a scientist in his dealings with Rhoda. He wants to expose Rhoda to a series of trials in order to "exhibit" her "complicated machinery," to use Zola's phrasing. The narrative account of these trials would thus be simply "the report of the experiment that [he] conducts before the eyes of the public." As Barfoot becomes more serious about his lovemaking, however, the character of his interactions with Rhoda changes. What was implicit in the scientific investigation becomes explicit in Barfoot's desire for sexual dominance over Rhoda. As sexual attraction complicates his "purely" scientific interest in her, his "investigation" into "her mechanism, her process of growth" becomes explicitly informed by a desire to control her, to have her acknowledge his power over her (101). As the narrator notes, Barfoot "delight[s] in [Rhoda's] independence of mind." But, significantly, his "last trial" of her is to prove her "complete subjugation to him" (261). If he can "inspire her with unreflecting passion," he will have "done his part," he thinks (261). The experiment will have been a complete success if Rhoda "foreg[oes] female privileges" and "obey[s] the constraint of love" (262).

Female privilege, as Barfoot uses the term, refers to Rhoda's status as an "odd woman" in late Victorian England. You will recall Grant Allen's argument in "Plain Words on the Woman Question" that the spinster, while she poses as "the cream of the universe," is really a "functional aberration."[14] "We ought not to erect into an ideal what is in reality a painful necessity of the present transitional age" (456), he advises his readers. Like Grant Allen, Barfoot refuses to endorse the "odd" woman's status as an independent agent. He would prefer that she obey the "constraint of love," by which he means that she should define herself solely in terms of her relationship with a male sexual partner. "Love," as he defines it, in other words, is not the idealized version of romantic love celebrated in the traditional marriage plot. It is erotic desire, desire, moreover, that is configured as domination.[15]

According to Barfoot, Rhoda should want to give up her existence as a "rational and responsible human being," to use his sister's phrasing, and give herself over to sensual experience (135).

In her important essay, "Making—and Remaking—History: Another Look at Patriarchy," Judith Newton describes the new culture of "manliness" that developed in the last third of the nineteenth century in England as a counterpoint to the powerful mid-century ideology of domesticity.[16] Middle-class Victorian women, she reminds us, were not merely victims of men's domination. Because women had a shaping and a defining hand in Victorian culture, and because men feared such female authority, the ideological power struggle between middle-class men and middle-class women took a new form in the 1860s and 1870s. Constituting itself in opposition to both the uneducated "masses" and female culture, a new male elite emphasized separation from women rather than appropriation of their virtues, while also valorizing "manliness," defined as "anti-effeminacy, stiff-upper-lippery, and physical hardness" (136). The interaction between the New Man and the New Woman in a novel like *The Odd Women* can best be understood, I think, in the context of this larger cultural formation. For the New Man in this narrative, the New Woman represents virgin territory: a territory to be colonized, a body to be known and mastered.

This attitude toward the New Woman perhaps also explains the plotting of novels like Arabella Kenealy's *A Semi-Detached Marriage* (1899), Frank Frankfurt Moore's *"I Forbid the Banns!" The Story of a Comedy Which Was Played Seriously* (1893), George Moore's novella, "Mildred Lawson" (*Celibates* [1895]), Percival Pickering's *A Pliable Marriage* (1895), and John Smith's *Platonic Affections* (1896).[17] In each of these novels, a sexually naive New Woman is pitted against an all-knowing male character or narrator. And in each novel the New Woman's discovery of her sexual desires—or rather, a male character or narrator's disclosure of her "real" self *for* her—is featured as the narrative climax. Halfway through *"I Forbid the Banns!"* for example, mocking Bertha Trevers' desire to establish a "free union" with her lover, Frank Moore's narrator announces in an aside to the reader that "the girl d{oes} not know herself" (2: 61). The last chapter of the novel finds her confirming this judgment of her. "I see all clearly. I did not know the world, Julian. I did not know myself. I thought that I was different from other women. I now know that I am not different," she confesses to her lover. "You did not cease to love me, Julian, did you?" she then asks in desperation (2: 245).

The situation is different in Percival Pickering's *A Pliable Marriage*, but the outcome is the same. Allen Drummond agrees initially to Dora Grant's conditions for their marriage: there are to be "no sentiments, nor pretense of sentiments. It is a practical commonsense agreement" only. They are "to remain friends only. The legal ceremony is an unavoidable concession to conventionality" (40). Allen confides to a friend, however, that he agrees to these terms only because he believes Dora "to be capable of a depth of feeling of which she was as yet unconscious" (244). And he waits patiently for her emotional and sexual awakening, which comes at the end of the novel under pressure of another woman's attempt to claim Allen's affection. "Give me a passion for God or man, but give me a passion. I cannot live without one," George Moore's protagonist cries at the end of "Mildred Lawson" (312). That is indeed what each of these writers does with the New Woman. Giving her a passion, they give the Victorian angel in the house a body. They "transform" the "pure woman" by inscribing her with a sexual "nature." But, notably, they also write the female body so as to maintain dominance over it in their narratives.

The Glory of Motherhood

What is the ideal that most of these modern women agitators set before them? Is it not clearly the ideal of an unsexed woman? Are they not always talking to us as though it were not the fact that most women must be wives and mothers? . . . Women ought . . . to glory in their femininity. A woman ought to be ashamed to say she has no desire to become a wife and mother. Many such women there are no doubt—it is to be feared, with our existing training, far too many: but instead of boasting of their sexlessness as a matter of pride, they ought to keep it in the dark. . . . They ought to feel

they have fallen short of the healthy instincts of their kind, instead
of posing as in some sense the cream of the universe, on the strength
of what is really a functional aberration.[18]

A determination to write the female body so as to master it also
informs a novel like Grant Allen's *The Woman Who Did*, but with a
difference. As the above quotation from Allen's "Plain Words on the
Woman Question" might suggest, he is less interested in simply exca-
vating or uncovering the New Woman's repressed sexuality than he is
in reclaiming her biological obligations to the human race. The
former, however, is a prerequisite for the latter. And Allen sets out to
teach both his protagonist, Herminia Barton, and his female readers
that their duty lies in obeying not the conventional social code governing sexual relations but "the laws of nature."
    With this goal in mind, Allen's narrator indulges himself in the
following intrusive commentary after Herminia Barton gives birth to
her illegitimate daughter, the product of her "free union."

Every good woman is by nature a mother, and finds best in maternity
her social and moral salvation. She shall be saved in child-bearing.
Herminia was far removed indeed from that blatant and decadent set
of "advanced women" who talk as though motherhood were a disgrace
and a burden, instead of being, as it is, the full realization of woman's
faculties, the natural outlet for woman's wealth of emotion. She knew
that to be a mother is the best privilege of her sex, a privilege of
which unholy manmade institutions now conspire to deprive half the
finest and noblest women in our civilized communities. Widowed as
[Herminia Barton] was, she still pitied the unhappy beings doomed to
the cramped life and dwarfed heart of the old maid; pitied them as
sincerely as she despised those unhealthy souls who would make of
celibacy, wedded or unwedded, a sort of anti-natural religion for
women.[19]

What interests me in this passage is Allen's invocation of the Victorian
iconography of womanhood. Good woman, spinster, advanced woman:
all are mentioned by way of indicating what Herminia is not, how she

falls through the cracks of that classification system. Because Herminia has sex with a man who is not her legal husband, she is not a "good woman" by Victorian standards. Because she neither practices celibacy nor views motherhood as "a disgrace and a burden," she is not what Allen terms a "spinster" or an "advanced woman" either. Her behavior, in other words, cannot be codified within the marital system of the bourgeois social order. Instead of living in accordance with the laws of "unholy manmade institutions," she obeys what Allen refers to as natural law. Notwithstanding the fact that it will bring her, personally, nothing but misery, she is a "good woman," not because she is chaste but because she knows that mothering is "the best privilege of her sex."

It has been argued that all New Woman novels recuperate mid-Victorian sexual ideology. The "ideology of womanhood" espoused in novels like *The Woman Who Did* is said to be indistinguishable from "the womanly ideal against which it had defined itself."[20] I would stress instead the more aggressive naturalization of cultural phenomenon that distinguishes the former from the latter. Mid-Victorians argued that their rigidly binary modeling of gender roles was "natural." But Darwinian science, specifically the conceptualization of "instinct," made it possible at the end of the century to naturalize behavior that mid-Victorians would not have sanctioned. This is still clearer in the novels I turn to next than it is in Allen's novel. As in *The Woman Who Did*, the New Women in Iota's *A Yellow Aster* (1894), Lucas Cleeve's *The Woman Who Wouldn't* (1895), and Linton's *The New Woman in Haste and Leisure* (1895) discover their "true nature" as mothers. But unlike Allen, these novelists eroticize maternity in a way that would have been completely incompatible with the Victorian code of womanliness.

As an adolescent, Iota's protagonist had wanted to achieve what she termed "her glory" through "other channels" than her heart.[21] When Gwen Waring reluctantly accepts a proposal of marriage, she tells her prospective mate in no uncertain terms that she does not love him. "Whether or not it is fair to try experiments in lives," she agrees to marry him rather than continue to play the social butterfly as a debutante (52). As the narrator notes, their subsequent life together is a model of "lovelessness and fair living," even if it leaves them both unsatisfied (155). Thinking herself "sexless," characterizing herself as a "sort of Dead Sea apple"—looking on the outside "so very sound and complete, but "rotten at the core"—Gwen refuses to feel anything for her husband (64). Even motherhood leaves her indifferent, at least until her son's illness brings out what the narrator terms the "latent truth in her own nature" (167).

Then and only then are "the splendid reserves of her tenderness" expressed in "her lovely frank abandonment to her new-found mother-hood" (172). Then and only then does Gwen become, again quoting the narrator, a "beautiful sexual mother-woman." And she exclaims:

> "I am a woman at last, a full, complete, proper woman, and it is magnificent. No other living woman can feel as I do; other women absorb these feelings as they do their daily bread and butter, and they have to them the same placid, every-day taste. They slip into their womanhood; mine has rushed into me with a great torrent. I love my husband, I worship him, I adore him." (172)

A "full, complete, proper woman:" a woman who "abandons herself" to motherhood; a woman who "lavishes" her son with "the splendid reserves of . . . tenderness" she previously had withheld from her husband. Notably, at this point in Iota's narrative, a new, and newly potent sexual ideology centered on motherhood supplants the Victorian ideology of female passionlessness. Prior to this scene in the novel, Gwen was unrelentingly cold and distant with her husband. She was, in effect, disembodied, for she lived at one remove from her physical being. Here, however, Iota describes her sudden sense of embod-iedness. Gwen is quite literally fleshed out and filled up by her new sense of sexuality: other women "slip into their womanhood; mine has rushed into me with a great torrent." Like mid-century novelists, Iota endorses motherhood only within conventional marriage as an end to the New Woman's quest for identity. She defines female sexuality *only* as a function of maternal instinct, declining to make a distinction between the two. At the same time, she reinforces the conventional Victorian conceptualization of a woman's necessary choice between biological and cultural labor, procreativity and creativity. Interestingly enough, however, she will still be condemned by her contemporaries for "domesticat[ing] the refinements of lust" and "permeat[ing] marriage with the ardours of promiscuous intercourse."[22] In other words, her sexualization of motherhood will be perceived as very threatening to the traditional social values she wants to uphold.

I mentioned earlier Iota's endorsement of the idea that women should be biological, not cultural, laborers. I want to go back to that point by way of introducing a discussion of two other New Woman novels that celebrate "the glory of motherhood" by predicating the New Woman's "exquisite, incomparable joy [in] maternity" upon her renunciation of all labor in the cultural sphere.[23] While her husband is away in Africa, Gwen Waring manages his farm quite successfully. After the birth of her child, however, she relinquishes all of those responsibilities to her husband. Readers are invited to believe at the end of Iota's novel that Gwen is completely absorbed by the responsibilities of childcare. In "A Defense of the So-Called Wild Women," you will recall Mona Caird arguing that women have "a thousand emotional and intellectual attributes that are wholly superfluous to . . . maternal activities."[24] Caird claims that women should be allowed to develop these "superfluous" attributes and realize their ambitions as well as their erotic fantasies. In *A Yellow Aster* Iota tries to squelch this particular controversy in the debate on the New Woman by naturalizing motherhood. She endorses the view that women should be involved in the reproduction but not the production of culture.

While Iota makes this issue a minor part of her presentation, both Lucas Cleeve and Mrs. Linton make this their central claim in, respectively, *The Woman Who Wouldn't* (1895) and *The New Woman in Haste and Leisure* (1895). Cleeve's Opalia Woodgate, for example, maintains her New Womanly independence of her husband by refusing to sleep with him and devoting herself to charity work in the East End of London. Anything else, she claims, would be politically and morally objectionable, a selfish preoccupation with private life in a world that allows very few people to enjoy that luxury. Her rejection of romantic idealism even informs her work in the East End, where she finds herself dealing with situations and people quite different from those the Victorian lady might expect if she projects her own bourgeois values onto the working class. "In books," she notes,

> the poorest cottage always has a spotless floor and a flower in the window, and the heroine, probably the mother of five or six children, after cooking and washing all day, and doing in a few hours work that would occupy several days in reality, clean and tidy, and, with a smile on her beautiful countenance, appears cheerfully at her tea-table to welcome her husband. In real life the floor is invariably dirty, and a beer jug stands on the window-sill, a ragged, unkempt, slatternly woman dispenses oaths to her numerous offspring, or sends them out to get a "pint" for which she cannot afford to pay.[25]

Although she is frustrated with the bureaucracy of the charity organizations and at times all but overwhelmed by a sense of personal disempowerment—for what can she do in the face of so much poverty and disease in the East End—Opalia perseveres. That is, until she returns to her West End home one night to find her husband kissing the woman whose portrait he has been commissioned to paint. Reluctantly, she relinquishes her virginity to him at this point, even though she is not physically attracted to him. As the narrator suggests, only the "compensating joy" Opalia experiences in waking to see her first-born son will make up for "all the degradation, all the expiation, all the suffering" associated with fulfilling her sexual "duty" to her husband (225). As the narrator also stresses, it is this "exquisite, incomparable joy of maternity" that finally makes Opalia realize how misplaced all her efforts have been to help families in the East End rather than cherishing her own.

Perhaps because the heroine of Linton's *The New Woman in Haste and Leisure* rebels more violently against the Victorian cult of womanhood than Opalia Woodgate, her return to the fold is even more spectacular. Having eloped with her childhood sweetheart, Phoebe Westgate, a bride of one month, returns home to her mother pregnant—and too emotionally immature to be either a wife or a mother. Prior to her marriage, Phoebe had been even more willful than Eliot's Gwendolyn

Harleth, still more difficult for her widowed mother to handle; she is even more self-centered now, and it is not long before she abandons her child to its grandmother's care and joins the Excelsior Club, a club where "women of independent character" meet to discuss

> the diabolical nature of husbands, the degrading institution of marriage, the shameful burden of maternity, woman's claims to be a County Councillor, a voter, a lawyer, a judge, an M.P., as well as to usurp all the offices at present filled by men only—the initiation of unmarried girls into all the secrets of life and vice, and the right of the sex in general, married or single, to live like men in every particular, if they chose to do so.[26]

While three quarters of the novel concerns the escapades of this group, which runs a newspaper, organizes a political campaign to overthrow the patriarchy, and finally splits over the issue of universal suffrage, Linton provides her narrative with what W. T. Stead terms a "boomerang" ending.[27] Betrayed sexually by a man whose political support she has been courting, Phoebe breaks rank with her New Womanly cohorts at the end of the novel and attempts to reestablish a relationship with her husband, whom she has sought out over the years only when she was short of funds. Now a fine, upstanding, and extremely conservative country gentleman, her husband refuses to be reconciled with her, telling her point blank that he is in love with a missionary in Africa—a woman who is sexually unavailable to him but who nonetheless embodies his ideal of "womanliness." Phoebe has ruined her chances to be a good Victorian wife; Linton nonetheless allows her the opportunity to redeem herself as a mother. The last chapter of the novel does not find her once again secure in her husband's arms, but at least she kisses her much-neglected daughter for the first time with "a mother's profusion of tenderness and love" (461).

Interestingly enough, in her first New Woman novel, *The Rebel of the Family* (1880), Linton had rejected "materialism," the idea that the individual's behavior is governed by instinct, not free will. "It is sinful and atheistic to speak of an immortal soul as if it were nothing but a bit of matter, as if the spirit were subject to the condition of the nerves and the blood!" the character in the novel most closely aligned with Linton's own views had exclaimed.[28] Fifteen years later, she seems to have recognized the political efficacy of "the laws of nature," for she is as willing as Grant Allen to "go to nature," to make reference to maternal instinct, as she attempts to educate Phoebe Westgate out of her allegiances to the Excelsior Club. Significantly, however, she does not reproduce Allen's dysphoric resolution to the New Woman's life. Rather than dying, repentant, Phoebe is to live on as a "womanly" woman. As is also the case in *The Woman Who Wouldn't*, readers are led to believe in the novel's closing pages that the New Mother is the phoenix who rises out of the ashes of the "old" New Woman's radical ideals.

Antinaturalism in the New Woman Novel

"By what form of bribery, by what appeal to the magic of hereditary instinct, [can we] charm the New Woman—sexless, homeless, unmaternal as she increasingly is—back to the store-closet and the nursery?" asks Lucas Malet in an essay for *Fortnightly Review* in 1905.[29] Malet helps us see what Iota, Cleeve, and Linton accomplish in their narratives. By eroticizing maternity, they do indeed "transform" the "pure woman." But by focusing on maternal rather than nonmaternal sexuality, they also catapult the New Woman back into domesticity. If this is one trajectory in the debate over the New Woman, if this is one line of development in the discourse about the New Woman, there are others to be traced below. I begin this section by discussing a text that was mentioned earlier but only in passing. The editors of the *Athenaeum* described George Egerton's *Keynotes*, her first collection of short stories, as "remarkable chiefly on account of the hysterical frankness of its amatory abandonment."[30] Invoking once again the metaphor of the Fall, other critics vilified Egerton for bringing women's literature into disrepute by "cast[ing] aside all reticence in the mad desire to make others eat as freely as themselves of the forbidden fruit of the tree of knowledge."[31] While such charges of "sex mania" were brought against many New Woman fictions, Egerton's characterization of the New Woman's sexuality in *Keynotes* differs significantly from its treatment in the novels discussed above.

In one respect, Egerton's celebration of female eroticism seems to be of a piece with George Gissing's "experimentation" with Rhoda Nunn. Like Gissing, Egerton displays—and thereby "proves"—her female characters' sexuality, the most notorious instance of this being the unnamed protagonist's fantasy at the end of "A Cross Line."

> Her thoughts shape themselves into a wild song . . . an uncouth rhythmical jingle with a feverish beat . . . to the untamed spirit which dwells in her. Then she fancies she is on the stage of an ancient theatre out in the open air, with hundreds of faces upturned towards her. Her arms are clasped by jewelled snakes and one with quivering diamond fangs coils round her hips. . . . She bounds forward and dances, bends her lissom waist, and curves her slender arms, and gives to the soul of each man what he craves, be it good or evil. And she can feel now, lying here in the shade of Irish hills . . . the grand intoxicating power of swaying all these human souls to wonder and applause. She can see herself . . . sway voluptuously to the wild music that rises, now slow, now fast, now deliriously wild, seductive, intoxicating. . . . She can feel the answering shiver of feeling that quivers up to her from the dense audience, spellbound by the motion of her glancing feet, and she flies swifter and swifter, and lighter and lighter. . . . One quivering, gleaming, daring bound and she stands with outstretched arms and passion-filled eyes, poised on one slender foot, asking a supreme note to finish her dream of motion. And the men rise to a man and answer her.[32]

In this passage, Egerton seems to historicize George Moore's model of the artist's exploration of "nature." She presents Victorian social conventions as a façade to be punctured, below which are to be found archaic truths about woman's "complex nature." Victorian man's "denseness," his Ruskinian "chivalrous conservative devotion to the female ideal he has created[,] blinds him" to this nature, Egerton's unnamed protagonist notes. "Stray words, half confidences, glimpses through soul-chinks of suppressed fires, actual outbreaks, domestic catastrophes": all hint at the "untamed spirit" this neatly dressed and well-manicured Victorian lady usually represses. In her dream-vision these "memor[ies] of hidden things," things "born with her, not of this time" (20), stand revealed as she dances "voluptuously" on an ancient stage—wishing that the men of her own time would offer her a "supreme note to finish her dream of motion."

But this passage in "A Cross Line" does not simply reinscribe an essentialistic definition of female sexual nature. Instead, Egerton's endorsement of both female eroticism and ambition in this fantasy works with and *against* the naturalistic imperative regarding the discovery of "female nature" we have seen other New Woman novelists invoke.[33] Significantly, Egerton's protagonist fantasizes about her life in a different cultural context. In the "ancient" culture she dreams about, she would be able to take pleasure in both her erotic fantasy and her fantasy of success as an artist in a public forum. Thus, in her dream-vision, Egerton's protagonist crosses not one but two lines. She moves from culture into nature—and exposes the latter as culture's vision of what lies below or behind itself in a primitive or archaic cultural formation. And she moves outside the circle Victorian middle-class culture draws around "correct" female behavior: erotic and ambitious fantasies are commingled in this dream in a way that the ideology of passionlessness would not have allowed. I will pursue discussion of this second crossing, the commingling of erotic and ambitious fantasies, in Chapter Five. What I want to discuss here, however, is the precedent Egerton sets for other New Woman novelists through the first crossing identified above: the acknowledgment that "nature" is something defined by culture as the place where culture's most cherished ideas and ideals can be kept safe from history. The intertextual dynamic to be explored can best be described by recalling the characterization of the New Woman novel's initial relationship to French naturalism. Writers contributing to the *New Review*'s symposium on "Candour in English Fiction" in 1890 took up George Moore's challenge to "correct" English realism by representing the "real" New Woman, the woman whom even French naturalists had not yet represented "scientifically." In turn, the novelists to be discussed in this section can be said to have set themselves the task of correcting these corrections of realism. In other words, the precedent set by writers such as Iota, Linton, and Grant Allen becomes another precedent to be uprooted and tilled under as New Woman novelists reseed what Edmund Gosse, in *Questions at Issue*, referred to as the hundred acre "estate called life."[34]

Even though it captures the sense of historical movement to be emphasized in the last section of this chapter, Gosse's metaphor is misleading, however. For the novelists to be considered here define their literary project differently than did the New Woman novelists most directly influenced by French naturalism. Like George Egerton, they expose "nature" as culture's label for the cultural formations it wants to make inaccessible to social change. Unlike the writers discussed previously, novelists such as Emma Frances Brooke, Ella Hepworth Dixon, Annie Holdsworth, George Paston [Emily Morse Symonds], and Netta Syrett make history, not nature, the site of their representations. In this regard, their work represents a rejection of both the themes and the narrative strategies of other New Woman novelists.

Consider, for example, Annie Holdsworth's *Joanna Trail, Spinster* (1894), a novel about a working-class prostitute who challenges middle-class prejudice as this is reinforced "scientifically" through a theory of genetic determinism. Originally "saved" from prostitution to be trained as a housemaid, Christine, the young protagonist in Holdsworth's novel, soon becomes a surrogate daughter for the aging Miss Trail, a woman who has dutifully played the role of spinster aunt all her life and now defies her very proper family for the first time by agreeing to take this London waif into her home. Although Christine initially wants to leave the "deadly dulness" of her new drawing-room existence for "the old vivid life" on the streets of London, she begins to think of herself as a member of the middle classes once her friendship with Miss Trail begins to blossom.[35] Proof of her successful gentrification comes when she receives a marriage proposal from a young journalist. Much to her horror, however, this man reveals himself to be one of those men whose " 'voluptuous egoism' . . . clamours for infinite purity in woman" when she tells him about her past (140–141). As the narrator notes, Bevan has a " 'voracious aesthetic gluttony for feminine

spotlessness.' " Thus, not unlike Hardy's Angel Clare, he rejects the
woman he supposedly loves when her past proves less than "aesthetically" pleasing. Humiliated by his contempt for her, Christine decides
to return to London. "Girls like me can't be saved" (153), she tells
Joanna in a brief note advising her not to try to find her.

Up to this point in *Joanna Trail, Spinster*, there are at least two
obvious parallels between Holdsworth's novel and a novel like *Tess of the
D'Urbervilles*. Both focus on a lower-class woman's rise into the middle
classes; both feature her rejection by a man more in love with his image
of her than with her impure reality. But here all parallels with *Tess* end,
for Holdsworth's protagonist finds it impossible to take up again her
"old vivid life" as a prostitute. As she tells Joanna upon her return to
Joanna's village, she arrived in London only to find she could not shed
her new bourgeois sensibility, specifically her new middle-class attitudes toward sexuality, as easily as she could her middle-class clothes.
Tess Darbeyville lets Alec talk her into becoming his mistress after he
finds her working in the fields as a common day laborer. In contrast,
Christine tries to act upon her conviction that she cannot be "saved,"
that she cannot escape the fate determined for her by her early promiscu-
ousness. When she finds, instead, that she now has nothing in common with her youthful "pals," she returns to the village to lead a very
retired life with her friend Joanna. Hers will be a life governed not by
grand passion, grand corruption, or grand tragedy. It escapes such
categorization, it resists such tidiness.

Certain aspects of a novel like *Joanna Trail* suggest its derivation as
well as its deviation from a model like *Tess*. Similarly, Mona Caird's
second New Woman novel, *The Daughters of Danaus* (1894), invites
comparison with Iota's *A Yellow Aster*. We saw earlier how the discovery
of Gwen Waring's maternal instinct figured into the plot of Iota's novel.
Caird counters such celebrations of motherhood as woman's natural
vocation in her second New Woman novel, a novel about a New Woman
who feels completely hemmed in by her maternal responsibilities.

Like Gwen Waring in *A Yellow Aster*, Caird's protagonist does not
initially love the children born of her loveless marriage, a marriage
made to satisfy her parents. But unlike Gwen, Hadria Temperley never
discovers what Iota had referred to as the "latent truth in [Gwen's]

nature." Indeed, Hadria goes so far as to call her children "the insult of society," "the tribute exacted of my womanhood. It is through them that I am to be subdued and humbled," she complains, revealing that she understands all too well how the ideology of mother love can be used to curtail women's pursuit of nondomestic activities.[36] Because of her responsibilities as a wife and mother, the narrator suggests, Hadria never had the chance to develop her talents as a musician and composer. As other characters will note as well, "her genius is necessarily stifled by a [life that] is conventional through and through" (268). And the "tyranny of affection"—the tyranny of husbands and mothers who insist that she occupy herself solely with the care of her children—leaves her feeling both "starved and aimless in the midst of what might have been plenty" (268, 467). Thus, like the fifty daughters of Danaus alluded to in the novel's title, Hadria is condemned to the "idiot's labour of eternally drawing water in sieves from fathomless wells" (467).

We have already seen how Grant Allen counters this critique of a patriarchal ideology of motherhood in *The Woman Who Did*. Allen's Herminia Barton is a New Woman, of course, but Allen underscores the fact that she is "far removed indeed from that blatant and decadent set of 'advanced women' who talk as though motherhood were a disgrace and a burden, instead of being, as it is, the full realization of woman's faculties, the natural outlet for woman's wealth of emotion" (138). If Allen counters Caird, his representation of the New Woman is countered in turn not only by Lucas Cleeve and Victoria Cross in *The Woman Who Wouldn't* and *The Woman Who Didn't* but also by Netta Syrett and George Paston in, respectively, *Roseanne* (1902) and *A Study in Prejudices* (1895).

Interestingly enough, in spite of the fact that Allen was instrumental in getting Syrett's first novel, *Nobody's Fault* (1896), published, her second novel calls into question the representation of cultural mandates as "natural law."[37] The child of an alcoholic artist and a Parisian dancer, Syrett's protagonist in *Roseanne* is haunted by the memory of her father's words in showing her his portrait of her mother and threatening that it prophesied her future. Roseanne never forgets the painted figure, which both fascinated and horrified her when she first saw it as a ten-year-old: "the frankly revealed shapely limbs . . . the muslin frill which did duty for a skirt . . . the strip of satin which formed the bodice . . . and the beautiful insolent face, with its suggestion of cruelty, of coarseness, and of something else which the girl only dimly understood" (68–69). Until she saw this portrait, Roseanne had never thought it was "wicked to feel the joy she experienced in the rhythmic movement of her body to . . . dance music." Looking at the painting, however, "all the barriers" to her understanding of adult sexuality and sexual corruption "which, in the case of most girls, yield so gradually, so slowly—went down with a jarring, soul-shaking crash," the narrator notes (70–71).

Not until she is an adult does Roseanne understand the point Syrett makes in this scene: the concept of genetic determinism is itself based in culture rather than in nature. That is, it has its source in a painting, a representation, not in nature. Showing his daughter his portrait of her mother is a particularly manipulative gesture on the part of Roseanne's father. But of course it has the desired effect on his impressionable daughter. Thereafter Roseanne forswears both drinking and dancing in order to avoid repeating the pattern of her family's history. Years later, the trauma of her attraction to a married man will bring this family legacy back into mind as her inevitable destiny. Unable to marry the man she loves, Roseanne flirts with the idea of becoming the mistress of one of her father's friends, a man who had said of her when still a child, "if temperament, physique, heredity, and what do you call it—environment, I mean—count for anything, she is damned already" (17). The night she is to elope with him, however, Roseanne finally overthrows the naturalistic teleology of character that has been dogging her all of her life. Instead of becoming this man's mistress, she travels alone to San Francisco to find work. Of what sort readers are never to know, yet we are meant to be reassured by a friend's observation that Roseanne's escape has "taken away the horrible sense of a meaningless existence" (332).

The narrative climax in *A Yellow Aster* finds Gwen Waring claiming for herself what the narrator had already proclaimed on her behalf, her new-found identity as a "sexual mother-woman." It also finds her living the life prefigured for her in a painting done of her as a young bride (a painting she detested at the time). Similarly, at the end of *Tess*, Tess accepts the role Hardy assigned to her in his tragedy. In *Roseanne* Syrett rejects both the thematization of biological determinism and the narrative architectonics Iota and Hardy practice in their New Woman novels. Syrett establishes the fatedness of Roseanne's sexual corruption—and then lets her protagonist reject this destiny. She lets her readers believe in the "scientific" "progress" of her narrative, then disrupts the chain reaction. She refuses to valorize either genetic law or the generic conventions of naturalistic tragedy.

With equal insight, George Paston [Emily Morse Symonds] points up the subjective interests fueling such "objective" representations of natural law in *A Study in Prejudices*, her novel about a New Woman who marries a conventional man because she is "tired of doing as [she] like[s]" and is ready to give up her Bohemian life style for a more settled domestic routine.[38] Cecily Tregarthen soon chafes under her writer husband's rigid rules: she is not to pose for an artist friend; she is not to go out alone; she is to be his "domestic treasure" (204). When her husband discovers that Cecily is not an angel in the house but instead "a mere every-day young woman who had romped and flirted, and said and done foolish things without any prophetic consciousness of the high honour that fate held in store for her" as his wife, he leaves her (205). Not until he receives a telegram announcing the death of their baby does he begin to regret the effort he made to make Cecily "the most desirable mother of a race" by restricting her freedom (308). But it is too late: he knows now that his attitude toward her has been not a "high and holy principle but rather a stupid and ignorant prejudice, the outcome of the short-sighted selfishness and petty jealousy of the average man" (310). Yet this knowledge cannot bring Cecily out of her postpartem delirium. The birth of their child does not save their relationship; it does not instill Cecily with "womanly" instincts. Instead, the death of both mother and child represents an indictment of the social customs Cecily's sister characterized in the following way upon first learning of Cecily's engagement: "monogamous marriage happens to be the custom of the country; but custom is not nature, though thanks to a woman's fatal adaptability it is apt to become second nature" (86).

Joanna Trail, Roseanne, The Daughters of Danaus, and *A Study in Prejudices* challenge essentialistic thinking about class, genetics, and maternal instinct, respectively. The novels I turn to now challenge a fourth kind of essentialism practiced by other New Woman novelists. Sexual determinism can be defined as the characterization of sexual instinct as *the* factor, *the* force, that determines the course of events in a woman's life. Instead of positing a biologically based model of personality—sexuality being the central core of identity, which pushes up through the layers of civilization and blossoms into the "rose" of Iota's "sexual mother-woman," for example—these writers take a socio-logical approach to both sexuality and character. Rejecting what Janet Hogarth terms "the divine right of instinct," they refuse to ground or center the New Woman's life upon her sexuality.[39]

Midway through Emma Frances Brooke's *A Superfluous Woman*, for example, the protagonist withdraws from a relationship with a lower-class man to whom she finds herself sexually attracted. What keeps Jessamine Halliday from giving herself to this "noble peasant" is the difference between their understanding of the terms in which a sexual relationship will be played out between them.[40] Colin wants to love Jessamine, passionately, as his wife. Still conscious of class distinctions and reluctant to be assimilated into his class, Jessamine wants to love him as a "lover;" that is, with the romantic abandonment and the "air of the grande dame" (127). On the very verge of accepting her passion for Colin as her fate, she rejects both him and it. Later she will realize she has made the wrong decision; but she also acknowledges the inevita-bility of that choice, given what she calls the "Aunt Arabella in me," that part of herself symbolized by the maiden aunt who raised her which cannot see beyond or around class divisions (36).

In Ella Hepworth Dixon's *The Story of a Modern Woman*, Mary Erle dismisses "the only man she [has ever] loved," the only man who "desires her as a woman," when he offers to rescue her from her strug-gle to support herself as a writer.[41] When Vincent Hemming tells her he is miserable in his marriage; when he asks her to run off to Europe with him; when he challenges her—"Dare to be yourself. Come to me. Let us begin a new life, a real life, dear. You are above the prejudices of our false civilization, you are capable of being a true woman, of giving up something for the man you love" (302–303)—Mary refuses. "I can't, I won't deliberately injure another woman" (i.e., his wife), she tells him. Instead, as she notes to herself in private once he leaves, she injures herself by denying herself "the best that life had to offer" (312).

In a very similar situation, Brigit, the protagonist of Netta Syrett's *Nobody's Fault* (1896), complains: "Often I wish . . . that I might *take* my own way, lead my own life,—be myself. But one can't—one can't. It wouldn't be *you*, after all, if you trampled other people underfoot, and yet how they hinder you" (emphasis in original).[42] Other people hinder her to the extent that she will decide not to live with her lover. Her reasoning is thus: when she left her husband, she purchased her own self-respect at the price of her mother's pride in her daughter's having made a society marriage. Brigit would live with her new lover now, she would have a family out of wedlock, except that it would be "treading down part of my nature in hurting mother" (229).

The phrase to note is the last. It would be "treading down part of my nature in hurting mother." "Nature," as Brigit uses the term, does not refer to a sexual nature that is more primary than her identity as a member of a human community. Her nature is something that, in fact, deters her from satisfying her own sexual and emotional needs because these would conflict with her mother's selfish desire for the social status she derives from her daughter's first marriage. In other words, in *Nobody's Fault*, as in *The Story of a Modern Woman* and *A Superfluous Woman*, sexuality is not the "keynote" of a woman's identity, to use George Egerton's phrase. Human sexual "nature" is not an "untameable quantity that may be concealed but . . . never eradicated by culture."[43] Moreover, sexual desire is not something that will enable the New Woman to achieve any kind of psychic integrity—even though these women's lovers promise them they will achieve such integrity through sex.

Instead, what is emphasized in these narratives is that a woman's expression of sexual desire entails either infantalization or a renunciation of all other interests. Had Netta Syrett's Roseanne gone off with Wyngate to be his mistress, she would have succumbed to a "child's impatience for escape from herself," a child's longing to "forget her misery, if only for a while, to drown thought in [the] excitement" of an adventure on a "real Greek island" (316). For Jessamine Halliday, desire brings not a child's sense of powerlessness but a prisoner's fear of entrapment. The first time she responds physically to Colin, Jessamine feels "her heart [run] down to some remote place of weakness in her being." Having been taught by her aunt that "[passion] was an offensive word and an unladylike allusion," she now feels a "helpless sliding, strange, delicious, fatal—and full of th[e] peace [of complete passivity]" (91, 218). As she "slip[s] darkly and helplessly toward some moral abyss," it also seems to her that she has been "set upon some dim-washed islet of earth, where a tremendous and inexplicable chain grasped and held her" (218, 100).

Similarly, Ella Hepworth Dixon emphasizes the loss of individuality Mary Erle will sustain if she becomes Vincent Hemming's lover. Long before the incident described above, Hemming had offered to marry her. Shortly after her father's death, he had visited Mary to pay his respects. Moved by her expressions of frustration at her lack of education and thus her lack of any means to support herself, he proposed to her. She accepted, then immediately found herself thinking,

> Only a minute [ago] . . . she had been ready to face the world alone, to be herself, to express herself, to work out her own destiny. And now it was all changed. Something held her against her will. The demands of the flesh clamoured louder than those of the spirit. This man—a minute ago her friend, and now . . . her lover, [held her by the wrists and his hands] felt like links of iron.
>
> In that one supreme moment Mary Erle tasted for the first time, in all its intensity, the helplessness of woman, the inborn feeling of subjection to a stronger will, inherited through generations of submissive female intelligence. (79)

As is noted explicitly in *The Wing of Azrael*, though not *The Story of a Modern Woman* or *A Superfluous Woman*, the mythic analogue for the situation in which the New Woman now finds herself is the story of Andromeda.[44] In the classical myth, Andromeda is a king's daughter who is punished for her mother's hubristic vanity. Like Iphigenia, she is a virgin martyr, an innocent woman whose life is sacrificed to appease the offended gods. When New Woman novelists retell this myth of female sacrifice, one of three things happens. Andromeda remains chained to her mother's tea service, fulfilling the duties of an unmarried daughter in her parents' household. Or, like Hadria Temperley in Caird's *The Daughters of Danaus*, she marries against her will, saving her parents' estate—and ruining her own chances for happiness. Or, like Jessamine Halliday and Mary Erle, the New Woman escapes the entrapment of family obligations, only to be imprisoned by sexual desire. As noted in the passage from *The Story of a Modern Woman*, sexual desire dooms Mary to "helplessness," to "subjection," to "submissive female intelligence." It makes Perseus her captor, not her liberator. In these novels, sex represents that which precludes the individual from working out "her own destiny" or "express[ing] herself."

It might help here to recall the work of other New Woman novelists. Grant Allen and Iota defy the Victorian ideology of sexual passionlessness by describing sexuality as the core, the center, of human personality. Sex is character, and thus sex is fate in *The Woman Who Did* and *A Yellow Aster*. But even if Allen and Iota discredit the Victorian notion of female purity, they continue to accept the traditional mind-body dualism upon which the Victorian ideology of passionlessness depends. Their references to sexual instinct simply increase the traditional polarization of mind and body (reason and passion) even as they establish body (sexuality) as the determinant of mind (subjectivity). When New Woman novelists like Dixon, Syrett, and Brooke reject sexual determinism, however, they also reject this reinforcement of mind-body dualism. And as they rethink dualism, they begin to model subjectivity in a new way.

Before developing this idea, let me suggest how my reading of this material differs from other recent interpretations of these novels. Scenes like those discussed earlier in *The Story of a Modern Woman*, *Nobody's Fault*, and *A Superfluous Woman* have prompted critics to characterize turn-of-the-century women writers as women "disgusted by sex and terrified by childbirth," women anxious to "break away from the yoke of biological femininity."[45] What such interpretations ignore, I think, is the New Woman novelists' sensitivity to the *social* construction of that "yoke of biological femininity," their awareness of how an essentialist sexual ideology can be wielded to keep the New Woman from "swarming out at all doors," as Elizabeth Linton has it.[46]

Consider again the scene in *The Story of a Modern Woman* in which Vincent Hemming offers Mary the chance to begin a new life, "a real life," as his mistress. "You are capable of being a true woman," Hemming says, by way of flattering her into capitulating to him. "You are capable of being a true woman, *of giving up something for the man you love*" (302, 303, emphasis added). For Dixon's protagonist, the alternatives are clear. Either she can go with Hemming to lead a "new life, a real life" (i.e., a sexually active life) as his "little girl," or she can remain in London to "face the world alone, to be herself, to express herself, to work out her own destiny" (79). With such choices there is no choice. As is true for so many other New Women, Mary chooses celibacy because celibacy is the only way she can possess her "self" in a culture that conceives of a sexual relationship as a man's "possession" of a woman. Mary is neither "frigid" nor "hysterical"; she is neither "disgusted by sex" nor "terrified by childbirth." Rather, her celibacy seems to be a necessary means of self-protection when confronted with the aggressive demands of the New Man, the man who wooes her with Darwinian law.

It is worth looking again at Gissing's *The Odd Women* because the title of Chapter Thirty-One, "Retreat with Honour," gives us a label for Mary Erle's—and so many other New Women's—experience. I considered Everard Barfoot's "experiment" with Rhoda, his "trials" designed to reveal the sexuality repressed by the nun-like "woman-worker," earlier in this chapter. What deserves mention in this context is Rhoda's reaction to this trial. Barfoot succeeds in eliciting a physical response from her, but he does not convince her to "forgo female privileges [and] obey the constraint of love."[47] In the aptly named Chapter Thirty-One of *The Odd Women*, Rhoda "retreats with honour" not only from her last conversation with Barfoot but also from their relationship when she realizes that he was "never quite serious about anything [he] said" during their "perfect day" in Wales the previous summer (326). Rhoda retreats, in other words, from the "voluptuous-[ness"] Barfoot intends her to body forth. She resumes her nun-like chastity; she refuses to endorse "the determining typicality of sex."

Because the New Man tries to "retur[n the New Woman] to her sex," to "identif[y], analys[e], and . . . explain he[r"] on the basis of her sexual nature, she herself seeks to escape such determinism—even if it means denying herself expression of her sexual desire.[48]

The *honorable* nature of the New Woman's retreat into celibacy is also underscored in *The Story of a Modern Woman* in the scene that follows the one in which Hemming invites Mary Erle to travel to France with him as his mistress. The night after Hemming proposes to her, Mary sits in front of her mirror combing her hair and mulling over her decision. She knows she will not go to France with him, but nonetheless she resents having to make that decision. "What had she done that she was always to be sacrificed? Why was she to miss the best that life had to offer?" she wonders, staring at her reflection in the looking glass. At this point, the scene itself becomes emblematic of what Mary describes as her "strange sense of dual individualty" (312). The woman in the mirror demands the "present moment of happiness." She demands, in other words, the satisfaction of a sexually active life; however, Mary, the flesh-and-blood woman who sits in front of the mirror, prefers to remain *dis*embodied, sexually inactive, because of what she stands to lose if she identifies her "self" with (as) the woman reflected in the mirror.

Notably, the sexuality imaged in Mary Erle's mirror parallels what Luce Irigaray describes as "female sexuality as it has been defined with respect to the masculine": female sexuality as it occurs "only within models and laws devised by the male subject."[49] When Mary Erle rejects the mirror image of herself, she rejects not only Hemming's *image of her* but also heterosexuality as it could be practiced at the end of the nineteenth century in England. In other words, Mary rejects not sexuality per se but patriarchal culture's construction of sexuality, its normalization of erotic domination.[50]

The fact that Mary experiences sexual desire schizophrenically suggests how difficult it was for New Women to claim their sexuality without being claimed by it. In this key scene in *The Story of a Modern Woman*, Mary stops trying to integrate her sexuality into her "character"; she stops trying to acknowledge her sexuality as part of herself. Because Hemming is not offering her the opportunity to "be herself" in a sexual relationship with him—she will be his "little girl" if she goes with him to the continent—Mary responds to the trauma of a split perception of herself by rejecting one self and claiming the other.

Although Dixon takes this no further in *The Story of a Modern Woman*, in other New Woman novels similar perceptions of "dual individuality" become a preliminary to still more extreme experiences of psychic fragmentation, which in turn lead to a new modeling of "character." This process is most clearly described in Emma Frances Brooke's *A Superfluous Woman*.

When she is forced to decide between marrying the Scottish farmer she is attracted to sexually and making a society marriage, Jessamine Halliday complains: "There are two me's—the Jessamine who [wants] to throw herself at the feet of a peasant" and the "Jessamine that [is] ready to sell herself to [Lord Herriot]," the "greatest catch in Europe" (138, 121). In fact, she has already identifed at least three "me's," three selves in the novel: the Jessamine who is attracted to Colin, the Jessamine who eventually will marry Lord Herriot, and the "Aunt Arabella in me," the internalized voice of her class-conscious maiden aunt, who believes that a loveless marriage to a propertied gentleman is preferable to de-classing oneself by marrying a farmer. Early in the novel Jessamine had expressed her contempt for this last part of herself. Generalizing from her own experience, she observed, "hate, hate, hate her as you may, your Aunt Arabella has become part of you" (36). Venting her anger in an extravagant biblical metaphor, she proclaimed she would like nothing better than to "dip in the pool of Siloam" to rid herself of the "Aunt Arabella in me" (36).[51] She then observed, on a much more subdued note, that she is "so mixed and fictitious a creature" that even this would not cleanse her, purge her, of that hated part of herself.

Jessamine is "so mixed and fictitious a creature" that she does not know what part of her is the real Jessamine. As her rejection of the Siloam metaphor indicates, the Judeo-Christian paradigm of "character" cannot contain her, cannot provide her with a sense of psychic integrity. As she experiences it, sexual desire is anything but "natural." It is socially conditioned, but not determined, for it is tied up with class consciousness and economic concerns. Moreover, Jessamine's "self" is both "mixed and fictitious:" mixed because of her sense of multiple selves desiring more than one thing and lacking continuity over time; fictitious because none of these selves is more real than the others. They are all parts of her, they are all parts she plays.

Jessamine's recognition of her "fictitiousness" is, I think, an important moment in the history of the New Woman novel. For this scene describes a shift from one conceptualization of identity to another. The "self," as Jessamine experiences it, is not total and present-to-itself. Instead, identity is relational. The "I" is constructed through and by relationships with other people. Even if other people would still impose upon Jessamine a model of single and integrated identity, she experiences her self as a plurality.

Juxtaposition of this scene in *A Superfluous Woman* with James Noble's comments in "The Fiction of Sexuality" and Mrs. Oliphant's complaint in "The Anti-Marriage League" might help us understand how the antinaturalistic novels considered in this chapter have altered the discourse on the New Woman. Oliphant objected to the "displacement" of Love, "that faithful Union of Two upon which pure and progressive society is built." Both she and Noble argue that the New Woman novel "puts life out of focus altogether" by treating sexuality as if it were "the most important thing in existence" or "the main-spring" of human action. Neither can acknowledge what is highlighted in novels like *A Superfluous Woman*, *The Story of a Modern Woman*, or *Roseanne*: the "fiction of sexuality" exposes the *fiction* of sexuality; that is, the fiction written about the New Woman's sexuality reveals the fictitiousness of all definitions of female "nature."

This suggests, I think, that efforts to write—and rewrite—the body of the New Woman did not culminate in complete agreement about the "nature" of woman, New or otherwise. Instead, two important concepts were invalidated as novelists continued to write on this subject in the 1890s: first, the idea that there is such a thing as "female nature" that can be discovered—brought to the surface, brought to the public's attention through the authoritative gaze of the novelist; and second, that identity is single, seamless, and coherent. In other words, Oliphant's argument notwithstanding, Love is not the only thing displaced in these narratives. Gone as well is the humanistic model of

integrated selfhood or "character."[52] A monolithic model of New Womanliness will not be substituted for the old model of the "pure woman."
Plurality succeeds singleness, and, as we shall see in Chapters Five and
Six, the heterogeneity introduced in the fiction discussed here will only
give way to more heterogeneity, more deviation from traditional Victorian values and literary forms, before the controversy over the New
Woman is subsumed in the rise of high modernism.

5

Crossing the Line:
Figuring Revolutions

I ARGUED IN Chapter Four that George Egerton's celebration of female eroticism in the infamous dream sequence in "A Cross Line" both is and is not like other naturalistic "experiments" with the New Woman's sexuality. The dream of dancing on an ancient stage before a crowd of men does not simply reinscribe an essentialistic definition of female sexual nature. Egerton's protagonist moves from culture into nature—and exposes the latter as culture's fantasy of what lies "below" or "behind" itself in a primitive or archaic cultural formation.[1] She also crosses the line Victorian culture draws around "correct" feminine behavior: she not only dreams about active female sexual desire, she also figures this in conjunction with a woman's artistic ambition. What I did not note in Chapter Four is that Egerton's protagonist crosses back over these lines once she wakes up from her dream. Realizing she is pregnant by either her husband or her lover, she ends her affair with the "man in gray" she met at the opening of the story. Abandoning both her fantasy of artistic success and her erotically charged relationship with this man who is not her husband, she commits herself to motherhood. The story ends when she asks her maid how fine lingerie from her trousseau can best be remade into infant clothing.

I mention "A Cross Line" again here because New Women in the novels to be discussed in this chapter cross the same lines highlighted in Egerton's story. Unlike Egerton's protagonist, however, these women will not return to convention. These narratives figure ambitions that cannot be recuperated into the Victorian ideology of domesticity. In this respect, these fictions remain outside the tradition of domestic realism to which the novels discussed in Chapters Three and Four still belong, even if they subvert its conventions.

Both of these points deserve clarification. Let me begin by recalling, by way of contrast, the original agenda of the New Woman novel. Novelists who contributed to the 1890 *New Review* symposium on "Candour in English Fiction" criticized the conventions of nineteenth-century literary realism. They complained about the "censorship of prudery," the "schoolgirl standard" of "accessive scrupulosity" in fiction that produces "fairy tales, not facts," about contemporary life.[2] As we have already seen, in the fiction they wrote subsequently, these writers replaced "the false colouring best expressed through the regulation finish that 'they married and were happy ever after' " with more "realistic" representations of "sexual relationship as it is."[3] Unlike the above, the novelists to be considered in this chapter do not use the conventions of realism as their point of departure. They imagine lives for New Women that are in no way constrained by the conventions of domestic realism. Rather than working within the conventions of realism, rather than attempting to modify those conventions, these novelists simply conceived their task differently.

Lady Florence Dixie, for example, makes no mention of the English literary tradition in her preface to *Gloriana; Or, The Revolution of 1900*, which was published the same year the *New Review* ran its symposium on "Candour in English Fiction." Dixie's brief preface explains that *Gloriana* is "to speak of evils which *do* exist [in society today]." It will "study facts which it is a crime to neglect . . . [and] sketch an artificial position [i.e., the class and gender system]— the creation of laws false to Nature—unparalleled for injustice and hardship."[4] But Dixie then warns her readers that "the stern reality" depicted will be "mingled with visions of a future day" when her heroine, a middle-class woman born out of wedlock, will run for Parliament and lead the socialist Revolution of 1900. Dixie notes that her story "will not have been written in vain" if it "awaken[s] the sluggards among women to a sense of their Position, and should thus lead to a rapid Revolution"—in real life, not just in the fictional world of her heroine (ix–x).

We have seen this kind of preface before. In very similar terms Lucas Cleeve justified entering the public fray in countering Grant Allen's *The Woman Who Did*: "if one young girl is kept from a loveless, mistaken marriage, if one frivolous nature is checked in her career of flirtation by the remembrance of Lady Morris, I shall perhaps be forgiven by the public for raising my feeble voice in answer to 'The Woman Who Did.' "[5] The irony here is that while the 1890 "Candour in English Fiction" symposium contributors are sparring over literary convention, Dixie simply asserts in all confidence that her novel will spark a social revolution. She could care less whether the novel maintains its "hegemony" vis à vis poetry and drama, to recall Edmund Gosse's phrasing.[6] The literary conventions of representation are superfluous to her concerns. She is interested solely in effecting social change through her fiction.

If the original agenda of the New Woman novel was to "correct" nineteenth-century realism; if antinaturalists like Netta Syrett, Ella Hepworth Dixon, and Emma Frances Brooke "corrected" the corrections of other New Woman novelists, the work of writers such as Florence Dixie represents a third line of development in the New Woman novel, which I can best introduce by invoking the distinction Roland Barthes makes in *The Pleasure of the Text* between representation and figuration.

As Barthes notes in a discussion of what he terms "classic" nineteenth-century realism, to represent something means presenting it both as if it had already happened (thus the term "re-presentation") and as if the subjective values of the observer do not inform the account. In a text of representation, desire "never leaves the frame, the picture."[7] In this kind of writing, desire "circulates among the characters," but "nothing emerges, nothing leaps out of the frame" (57). In contrast, figuration assumes a different relationship between author and text, text and reader. To figure something is to give up the pose of objectivity, to acknowledge that you are not simply reproducing something that exists in the "real" world. Figuration means acknowledging the subjective desires that inform your textual constructions of the world. To use

Barthes's distinction, then, writers like Dixie, Jane Hume Clapperton, and Edith Johnstone are not interested in re-presenting reality. They figure it: create it, imagine it. And such imaginings, it is worth emphasizing, are in no way constrained by their knowledge of what has been done within the tradition of domestic realism. Rather than establishing a transgressive relationship to literary convention, these writers simply desire something else. Their figurations are unmediated by the domestic ideology informing nineteenth-century realism.

A Happy Marriage
of Socialism and Feminism

In Chapter Two I distinguished the New Woman from three other groups of women who were "revolting" against the bourgeois social order at the turn of the century: single-issue social reformers, "Independent Women," and socialists. I also noted in that chapter the common association of New Women with socialists by critics for whom unconventional sexual behavior served as a trope for radical politics. The New Woman is "intimately connected" with "the spread of Socialism and Nihilism," according to the author of "The Apple and the Ego of Woman." She is the nineteenth century's version of the Parisian anarchists, both Elizabeth Linton and the author of "The Strike of a Sex" claim.[8] Even as these critics try to malign the New Woman by associating her with socialism, the novels to be considered here cast this association in a very different light.

Consider, for example, Jane Hume Clapperton's *Margaret Dunmore; or, A Socialist Home* (1888).[9] As the title of Clapperton's novel indicates, Margaret Dunmore does not just join a socialist organization; she is one. Spending her inheritance to set up a "home" for her "family"— two couples and their children, an ex-prostitute, and a widowed socialist now working as a free-lance artist—Margaret initially earns nothing but the opprobrium of her middle-class family and friends. In the face of such resistance, however, she perseveres. Ultimately, the middle-class neighbors of her socialist collective begin sending their children to the school Margaret runs as one of her home's business ventures. As the narrator emphasizes, the success of the school symbolizes the peaceful coexistence of the bourgeois community at large and the socialist "home" in its midst. More particularly, it symbolizes Margaret's personal success in creating a life for herself other than that assigned to her in the traditional Victorian scheme of things. Margaret Dunmore has, quite literally, done more than she would ever have been expected to accomplish as a "spinster." She has sustained her vision and realized her fantasy of a "new life" in a socialist community. She has created, moreover, a "happy marriage" between socialism and feminism.[10] For in this collective, women like Margaret can ignore the class *and* the gender ideology of their middle-class families.

Similar advantages accrue to Hector/Gloriana D'Estrange, the transvestite protagonist of Florence Dixie's *Gloriana; Or, The Revolution of 1900* (1890). Gloriana is the illegitimate child of a woman who left an arranged marriage to live in Italy with her lover. That lover, Gloriana's father, is murdered by her mother's husband's family, forcing Gloriana and her mother to return to England, where Gloriana grows up determined to tell little girls about "all the wrongs that girls and women have to suffer, and . . . bid them rise as one to right these wrongs" (xxx). To realize this ambition, she assumes a male identity and pursues a gentleman's education at Eton and Cambridge before winning a seat in Parliament.

In her preface to the novel, Dixie wrote of her interest in "speak[ing] of evils which *do* exist [in contemporary society]" before "mingl[ing]" "stern reality" "with visions of a future day" (vii, x). Obviously, by this point in the novel "stern reality" has already given way to "visions of a future day." As "Hector D'Estrange," Gloriana wins considerable support from the population at large for her radical views on women's rights. She introduces a bill into Parliament advocating the "absolute and entire enfranchisement of women," the mixed education of the sexes, the extension of the right of primogeniture to women, and the eligibility of women to Parliament (119). Her most significant early triumph, however, is not the passage of this bill by general referendum but the general public's endorsement of her, once she reveals her real

identity. Banished from Parliament for her unpopular feminist popu-
lism, hunted down by a battalion of troops commissioned by Parliament to bring her into custody, "Hector" quite literally disrobes before
a crowd of working-class men and women. This crowd not only accepts
Gloriana gratefully as their leader, they also stand their ground before
the armed soldiers, allowing her to slip away unnoticed.

This scene is of particular interest because it highlights the difference in class-based attitudes about what constitutes appropriate "womanly" behavior. Unlike the men of her own class, Gloriana notes, "it
never enters the minds" of these rough working-class men "to depreci-
ate [*sic*] her deeds, to belittle her acts, because she is a woman" (182).
In other words, these men do not promulgate the doctrine of separate
spheres; they do not see her political activism as an "unwomanly"
usurpation of male prerogative. Instead, these men rally to protect her
against the men of her own class, who would imprison her now for so
successfully flaunting their sexual code. Gloriana is both grateful for
and surprised by their enthusiastic support.

> Their reason tells them that she understands their wants, that her
> great heart is in sympathy with their needs, that she has sought to
> help them when in power, and that now her enemies have got the
> upper hand, all their loyalty and devotion is needed to support the
> cause, which she has told them lies at the root of all future social
> reform, which means progress, comfort, and happiness for the
> toiling millions.   (182)

Clearly, Gloriana's working-class audience does not view universal
women's suffrage as something antagonistic to the more general cause
of "progress, comfort, and happiness for the toiling millions." Where
other socialists might subordinate gender to class issues, these men are
willing to follow Gloriana in seeing women's suffrage as the first step
toward universal social reform. Women's oppression in the bourgeois
system is analogous to their own—and they voice their willingness
here to overlook other differences in the interest of achieving a common
goal.

It is worth noting as well that Gloriana does not assume that her appearance in public in a political capacity is "unseemly" or "unwomanly." If the working-class men in this scene identify with Gloriana, thereby violating the social code regarding cross-class (and cross-gender) identifications, Gloriana herself refutes two of the central tenets in the Victorian ideology of domesticity: the general separation of public and private spheres (and the relegation of women to the latter); and the related assumption that work in the public sector "unsexes" a woman, exhausts her biological capital. Victorian "daughters of educated men" had two choices: they could grow up to be wives and mothers; or they could, like George Gissing's character, Rhoda Nunn, remain celibate and dedicate themselves to work for "unknown humanity" in all manner of philanthropic (volunteer) social organizations.[11] While Gloriana's appearance before the crowd is not exactly analogous to George Egerton's erotic dream-vision in "A Cross Line," she obviously enjoys the attention she receives from the crowd. If the situation is not erotically charged in the explicit manner that Egerton's is, neither does Gloriana "unsex" herself by appearing in public. She disrobes, removes her masculine costume—and thereby gains the crowd's political support. Having gained their support, she then goes on to instigate the changes that will culminate in "the Revolution of 1900." Thus, after much ado and many adventures, she becomes Prime Minister, and the novel ends in 1999 with a balloon-view vision of a London rid of poverty and full of green spaces.

Lest the thread of argument be lost in the fantastic details of this plot, I would stress the challenge to the traditional Victorian conceptualization of the relation between (private) female sexuality and public labor. Unlike George Eliot's Dinah in *Adam Bede*, for example, Gloriana is not claiming to forget her body when she speaks before a "promiscuous" audience.[12] Instead, she stands *as a woman*, as a female body, in front of that crowd. And she brings "a woman's passion" to her political campaign. The rhetoric in the passage cited earlier about her "great heart" invokes the traditional iconography of femininity; yet this iconography, paraded in a public space, refutes the doctrine of separate spheres. In other words, Dixie rejects out of hand the conventional Victorian notion that women's erotic and ambitious desires cancel each other out. She refuses to honor the overdetermined opposition between love and labor when she figures Gloriana as a middle-class female body on a public stage.

As I will show in the next section, this reconceptualization of the relation between public and private spaces, erotic and political ambitions, is also taken up by New Woman writers who are not interested in socialism and the "new life" it offers middle-class women. Turning first to Rhoda Broughton's *Dear Faustina* (1897), I want to consider a challenge specific to the novels that figure the New Woman as a socialist: the challenge of collectivism.

As Rhoda Nunn notes in *The Odd Women*, Victorian middle- and upper-middle-class society would prefer that its women had "no life . . . but in the affections."[13] Such a precept not only bases the achievement of emotional satisfaction on a denial of public ambition, it also presumes a belief that women's reward for such behavior comes in her exclusive ownership, so to speak, of the people she loves. *Her* family, *her* husband, *her* children: these are a woman's private property; these are the people who confirm her value as an individual through their affection for her. Rhoda Broughton flaunts her protagonist's relinquishment of this value system in *Dear Faustina*, a novel that pits a radical mother against her naive daughter and then shows the daughter choosing a more radical life than either her mother or the friend who has set out to radicalize her.

The novel opens with a Vane family confrontation. Now that her husband has died, Mrs. Vane announces that she is going to join "a band of women thinkers and workers . . . whose object and aim is 'the redressing of the balance: the balance as between man and woman, as between rich and poor, as between the treader-down and the trodden.' "[14] She has been telling her children for years that she "ought never to have married . . . that was the root-mistake of her life, as it has been for so many millions of other women" (11). "Now that she has regained the use of her wings," she is going to become president of this organization, which demands "the whole being, the entire life, with no reservations—the soul, body, heart and energies of each of its members" (11, 16). Renouncing "the desire for selfish, individual happiness," she dedicates herself to "higher and broader uses"—and advises her children not to expect anything more from her in the future (23, 18).

Rather than live with her married sister and brother-in-law, Mrs. Vane's daughter Althea moves into a flat in Chelsea with Faustina Bateson, a friend who supports herself as a journalist. Faustina had been living in the Notting Hill slums in order to "[get up] the subject of the Housing of the Working Classes" (46). Having parted ways with her previous flatmate over their differing views on "the employment of Infant Labour," she suggests the move to Chelsea—as Althea finds out after the fact—because she wants Althea to use her society connections to acquire inside information for her. Even though Althea no longer lives in her parents' home, she can still attend society functions; in other words, she can be paired for dinner with secretaries and under-secretaries. As someone who "gets up" articles on working-class housing, Faustina is too well known and too déclassé to be offered society invitations. The halcyon days of this friendship are soon over, however, as Althea finds herself replaced in Faustina's affections by someone who proves to be better than Althea at using her womanly charms to woo information out of politicians. Althea is also offended by Faustina's unwillingness to do an article on "Dangerous Trades" because it would mean implicating the newspaper for whom she does her "bread and butter" articles. In a violent argument, Althea accuses Faustina of abandoning her principles and protecting her own private interests; in turn, Faustina defends herself by suggesting that such self-interest is entailed by her professionalism. Only amateurs with other means of financial support can afford to take on every liberal cause, she claims, mocking Althea's continued dependence on her family.

At this point in the novel, Althea chooses for herself a life more defiant of bourgeois ideology than either her mother's or Faustina's. Mrs. Vane's commitment to radical feminist politics never took her outside the middle-class world. Faustina's journalism takes her into the East End, but only long enough to gather copy for her stories—stories, at that, whose politics keep her gainfully employed. In contrast to both, Althea first visits, then permanently joins, a settlement house for working-class women in south London. And the plot of Broughton's novel highlights the difference between Althea's first experience of "the masses" and her later ones. Asked to help organize a social event for the Canning Town settlement workers, Althea initially looked forward to "the glory" of "humanizing them" (258). She anticipates the self-satisfaction involved in introducing them to "civilized" middle-class social rituals. When "the girls" get unruly, however—raiding the food tables when the drawing-room charades prove too staid an entertainment for them—Althea finds herself caught in a crowd over which she has no control. Panicking at the idea of being crushed to death, she becomes frightened at her own powerlessness. At this moment her sense of self-obliteration in the presence of this collective is anything but pleasant. She regains her poise only when the middle-class gentleman who is the chief financial backer for the settlement enters the room and, in a booming voice, restores order. At the end of the evening, she tells him that if it were not for her living arrangement with Faustina, she'd "come among you" for good. Clearly, though, she can make this statement only after the fact, after her initial terror is forgotten.

Shortly thereafter, the argument about Faustina's unwillingness to implicate her employer resurfaces, and Faustina sends Althea packing to her sister and brother-in-law's home. But Althea's physical return to the middle-class world does not return her to political quietism. Much to her sister's chagrin, she disrupts the household by, for example, informing her nieces and nephews that the carbon bisulphide emitted in the factories where their new mechanical toys are produced makes workers go mad if they are exposed to it over long periods of time. Such incidents suggest that Althea has become more Faustian than Faustina Bateson. While supporting herself outside the traditional family structure, the latter still retains the values of bourgeois individualism; she does not let her concern for the working classes interfere with her ability to make a living. Althea is the one who proves herself true—as her name suggests—to the workers' cause. At the end of the novel, she agrees to organize a cooperative sewing workroom in the Canning Town settlement, leaving her bourgeois family for good.

When the protagonist of Gertrude Dix's *The Image-Breakers* (1900) has a similar experience with a crowd, her commitment to socialism is reconfirmed.[15] Married to a wealthy landowner who had socialist sympathies before his brother died and he inherited the family estate, Rosalind Dangerfield has been publishing essays attacking the capitalist system under the name "R. Dangerfield." Shortly after the novel begins, however, she decides that she can no longer sustain her schizophrenic existence as a lady of the manor and a socialist writer. As Leslie Ardant, a young working-class girl Rosalind has befriended, notes, "the [middle-class] philanthropists don't like her because she goes too far for them, and the Socialists dislike her because of her position" (16). Given such internal and external tensions, Rosalind decides to leave her husband and join a socialist collective household in the local village.

Having previously felt like "an alien and a stranger" in her own community (22), Rosalind gains an altogether different sense of life in the village when she attends a rally organized by a national socialist organization on behalf of the women workers in the local factory. "There had been something very wonderful in the great mass of humanity which shifted, swayed, [and] converged, like water finding its level, subsiding into silence as the speaking began," she notes afterwards (22). She is uncomfortable when the first speakers, agitators down from the north of England, work the crowd up "like water for the wind to play with" (22). Yet, the editor of the socialist journal for whom she has been writing has a very different effect on herself, as well as the rest of the crowd. "As he spoke of wisdom and of courage, she could almost have believed that a miracle took place under her eyes, as the members of the crowd, so lately whipped to rabid anger, seemed, as it were, invested with the armour of steadfast soldiers, ready to defend their own and children's rights" (23). The crowd then disperses in "disorderly array"—but she and they have been changed fundamentally by this experience.

From this point forward, Rosalind's life will be dedicated to "destroy-[ing] systems," to "strik[ing] a blow at the foundations of poverty and sordid life" (155). Even when she becomes sexually involved with Justin Ferrar, her editor and the leader of the local socialist cell, she refuses to conceive of this relationship as in any way separate from her political commitment. As she explains to Leslie, "the work is first. Our desire to help humanity makes us feel that much should be sacrificed for the sake of that work" (74). To Leslie's suggestion that "if you love him, you care for nothing, except for him," Rosalind responds by chiding her: "you make too much of mere personal feeling. . . . I am not in love with [Justin]. I hope our comradeship will never be touched with a breath of the hateful selfishness *à deux* people mistake for love" (76). Notably, Rosalind—unlike either Gissing's Rhoda Nunn or Lucas Cleeve's Opalia Woodgate—does not renounce her sexual relationship with Justin in order to pursue her ambitions as a "woman-worker." Nor does she subordinate the latter to the former; that is, she does not make her political work contingent upon her sexual relationship with Justin. What Dix figures here, and what Rosalind Dangerfield enjoys, is the complete commingling of her erotic and ambitious fantasies. As noted in Chapter Four, Mrs. Oliphant condemned "The Anti-Marriage League" of New Woman novelists for "displac[ing] . . . Love, that faithful Union of Two upon which pure and progressive society is built." Rosalind does indeed displace Love in this conversation with her friend Leslie. More importantly, however, her rejection of "the hateful selfishness *à deux* people mistake for love" represents only the beginning of what she and Justin would like to achieve: namely, the destruction of the entire bourgeois social order.

Reconceiving Maternity

What follows next in *The Image-Breakers* brings us back to an issue broached earlier, the reconceptualization of the relationship between public and private cultural spheres and between women's erotic and nonerotic ambitions.

In *The Flesh Made Word* Helena Michie argues that mid-Victorian women writers used the conventional Victorian rhetoric of motherhood to place their writing on "a natural continuum" with their responsibilities as wives and mothers.[16] "In a culture where housework was one of the few sanctioned physical activities even marginally available to women of the upper classes, domestic and maternal metaphors are coded expressions of various forms of female energy," she notes (64). "Writers like Dinah Mulock Craik, Catherine Maria Sedgewick, Mrs. Humphrey Ward [*sic*], and Elizabeth Gaskell went out of their way to domesticate their art," because they could thus "escape the constrictions of the female role without leaving the safety of home and domesticity" (64, 63). The traditional Victorian characterization of female vocation, in other words, was not always or necessarily put to conservative uses; it could also be used to subvert conventional expectations.

As Martha Vicinus notes, the "Independent Women" of the 1870s and 1880s manipulated this same rhetoric of domesticity as they sought to legitimize their work in the public sector. The professionalization of nursing and social work; the establishment of women's religious communities, schools, and universities; the development of philanthropical organizations: all were defended through reference to the "superfluous" woman's "duty" to "mother the public" if she had no family of her own. By arguing that their single-sex organizations represented extensions of the Victorian lady's volunteer social ministry, Vicinus suggests, "Independent Women" created domestic or "female" spaces for themselves in the public domain. In other words, they violated the doctrine of separate spheres—but without challenging the gendered division of human labors.

If New Woman novelists such as Gertrude Dix also wield the Victorian rhetoric of motherhood, their use of this rhetoric differs from that of either the mid-century novelists or the "Independent Women" in one important respect. As the title of Dix's *The Image-Breakers* suggests, the cultural icon of "the good woman," the domestic angel who channels all of her desire into marriage and motherhood, is invoked in this novel only to be shattered. Dix accomplishes this, first, by asking her readers to identify with a protagonist who leaves her husband to join a socialist collective and later establishes herself in a common-law marriage with one of her "comrades." But, equally importantly, she attacks the cultural myth of femininity by rethinking maternity in nonbiological terms. This last point is the one I want to pursue at present through a discussion of revelant scenes in both *The Image-Breakers* and Mary Cholmondeley's *Red Pottage* (1899).

Shortly after Rosalind's conversation with Leslie about her relationship with Justin, Rosalind begins work with him on a book-length critique of the capitalist system. In all subsequent conversations with Leslie, she refers to this manuscript as her child. It is the product of her intellectual and emotional intimacy with Justin. She labors over it, she loves it, she gives it everything she would give a "real" child. In other words, Rosalind does not figure creativity and procreativity as antithetical terms. Rather, the latter serves as a trope for the former. Paradoxically, literal or biological mothering becomes a metaphor for figurative or cultural mothering.[17]

Mary Cholmondeley makes this same idea a source of conflict in *Red Pottage* (1899). When Hester Gresley discovers that her brother has burned the manuscript of her second novel, she tries to make him understand the wrong he has done her by offering him the following analogy: "When Regie [her nephew] was ill, . . . I did what I could. I did not let your child die," she reminds him. "Why have you killed mine?"[18] Child, book: both are—were, in the latter's case—things Hester loves.

This bold analogy is quietly reinforced throughout *Red Pottage*. As the narrator notes quite early in the novel, for example, Hester talks with her best friend, Rachel West, about her book the way "a young girl talks of her lover" (80). Absorbed in her project, she "live[s] constantly in the world which the greater number of us only enter when human passion [i.e., sexual intimacy between man and woman] lends us the key" (80). Her clergyman brother and all of his parishioners think of her as a spinster; indeed, they remind her constantly of her unfortunate unmarried state. But Hester herself feels deprived of nothing but time to write. She abides by the rules of her brother's household, devoting what little spare time she has to his children. And she "spends herself," as she puts it—"spends" in the Elizabethan sense of the term—on her writing. She tells a friend the following story in explaining the severity of her grief over the manuscript's destruction.

> "If I had a child . . . and it died, I might have ten more, beautiful and clever and affectionate, but they would not replace the one I had lost. . . . If [my book] were a child . . . I should meet it again in heaven. There is the resurrection of the body for the children of the body, but there is no resurrection that I ever heard of for the children of the brain. . . .
>
> "A great writer who had married and had children whom she worshipped, once told me that the pang of motherhood is that

even your children don't seem your very own. They are often more like some one else than their parents, perhaps the spinster sister-in-law, whom every one dislikes, or some entire alien. Look at Regie. He is just like me, which must be a great trial to Minna [her sister-in-law]. And they grow up bewildering their parents at every turn by characteristics they don't understand. But she said the spiritual children, the books, are really ours.

. . . "I suppose love is worship. I loved [my book] for itself, not for anything it was to bring me. That is what people like Dr. Brown don't understand. It was part of myself. But it was the better part. The side of me which loves success, and which he is always appealing to, had no hand in it. My one prayer was that I might be worthy to write it, that it might not suffer by contact with me. I spent myself upon it. . . . I knew what I was doing. I joyfully spent my health, my eyesight, my very life upon it." (334–335)

Unlike either the mid-Victorian writers about whom Michie writes or the "Independent Women" who would have been her contemporaries, Hester is not simply enlarging the domestic or female sphere to include (and thereby legitimize) activities once coded "unwomanly." In the above passage, she is conflating the public and private spheres, imagining them as one and the same cultural space so as to discredit entirely the gender-based division of human labor. Significantly, production and reproduction become one here: they are not presented either as different kinds of activities or as activities that take place in different cultural spheres.

Before saying anything further about Hester's reaction to the loss of her manuscript, I want to consider in some detail an early scene in the novel. A brief explanation of Hester's relationship with her childhood friend, Rachel West, is necessary to understand how this scene in Chapter Six initiates the chain of events that will culminate in a confrontation between Hester and her brother.

As the narrator emphasizes in the opening paragraph of Chapter Six, Hester and Rachel have the kind of friendship men often assume women cannot sustain.

The passing judgment of the majority of men on [women's friendships] might be summed up in the words, "Occupy till I come." It does occupy till they do come. And if they don't come the hastily improvised friendship may hold together for years. . . . But nevertheless here and there among its numberless counterfeits a friendship rises up between two women which sustains the life of both, which is still young when life is waning, which man's love and motherhood cannot displace nor death annihilate; a friendship which is not the solitary affection of an empty heart nor the deepest affection of a full one, but which nevertheless lightens the burdens of this world and lays its pure hand upon the next.

Such a friendship, very deep, very tender, existed between Rachel West and Hester Gresley.   (29)

Friends since childhood, Rachel and Hester have not traveled in the same social circle as adults since Rachel's father died and left his income to his business partner, not his daughter. While Rachel struggles to earn her living in the East End of London as a "typewriter," Hester, a dependent of a wealthy aunt, continues to make the rounds in society. Yet the two remain close, and in this scene in Chapter Six, Rachel's reluctance to let Hester make a private gesture of charity startles Hester into recognition of her public vocation as an artist.

Refusing to accept the rabbit coat Hester has bought her out of her small allowance, Rachel insists that Hester's love and sympathy have meant more to her than any amount of money Hester has given her. This confession of love on Rachel's part sparks a sudden insight for Hester. As the two women sit closely together, Hester's sense of her economic powerlessness gives way to an exhilarating sense of her ability, as an artist, to transform the world. I quote at length because the following passage epitomizes Cholmondeley's effort to reconceptualize the public/private split and the overdetermined opposition between women's erotic and ambitious fantasies.

Rachel remembered that conversation often in after years with a sense of thankfulness that for once she who was so reticent had let Hester see how dear she was to her.

The two girls stood long together cheek against cheek.

And as Hester leaned against Rachel the yearning of her soul towards her suddenly lit up something which had long lain colossal but inapprehended [*sic*] in the depths of her mind. Her paroxysm of despair at her own powerlessness was followed by a lightning flash of self-revelation. She saw, as in a dream, terrible, beautiful, inaccessible, but distinct, where her power lay, of which restless bewildering hints had so often mocked her. She had but to touch the houses and they would fall down. She held her hands tightly together lest she should do it. The strength as of an infinite ocean swept in beneath her weakness, and bore it upon its surface like a leaf.

"You must go home," said Rachel gently, remembering Lady Susan's punctual habits.

Hester kissed her absently and went out into the new world which had been pressing upon her all her life, the gate of which Love had opened for her. For Love has many keys besides that of her own dwelling. Some who know her slightly affirm that she can only open her own cheap patent padlock with a secret word on it that everybody knows. But some who know her better hold that hers is the master-key which will one day turn all the locks in all the world.   (37–38)

The last paragraph of this passage requires some unpacking. As in the passage from a later chapter cited above, Cholmondeley's narrator is invoking conventional Victorian patterns of domestic life in the allegorical figure of "Love." Love's "own dwelling" is, of course, the Victorian home. The "secret word . . . that everybody knows" is the marital bond, the commitment to monogamy and emotional exclusivity a heterosexual couple makes when it establishes a nuclear family in Love's "own dwelling." But Love, as the narrator insists, has keys to other dwellings as well. What is being modeled for us in this scene—visually, in Hester's and Rachel's physical closeness, and more abstractly in the allegory of Love—is both a relationship and an understanding of cultural labor that cannot be accommodated by Victorian convention.

Consider, by way of contrast, Freud's understanding of the relationship between "lower" and "higher" forms of human activity. As Freud would have it, we sublimate our primary sexual desires in order to participate in culture; inadequate as they sometimes are, cultural activities are substitutes for physical gratification. Something is inevitably lost, yet something else is gained—the satisfaction of attaining a "higher" form of expression.[19] Significantly, the movement Cholmondeley describes here through the metaphor of Love's houses is not a movement from "lower" to "higher" forms of cultural activity, from direct to sublimated expressions of sexuality in art. In fact, the situation Cholmondeley describes does not fit the classic Freudian model for two reasons, not one. First, the love fueling Hester's discovery of her cultural ambitions is for another woman. It is not a bonding that Love claims as her "own dwelling"; it is not a heterosexual partnership that will provide the basis of a nuclear family. And second, the movement Cholmondeley charts is horizontal rather than vertical. Hester moves not "up" toward higher forms of expression but across—toward "other houses," toward her friend Rachel. Thus, when she writes her first New Woman novel, she writes about a woman she knows and loves in her "real" life. She never accommodates herself to the traditional model of the artist's "objectivity" with regard to his material.[20] She loves her characters, even as she loves the people upon whose lives she has modeled them.

In other words, life and art exist on a continuum for Hester. They are no more separate than the so-called "public" and "private" spheres. By figuring life and art as contiguous planes of existence, Cholmondeley imagines her release from the domestic ideology that would isolate her in the latter, the private world. Moreover, she imagines this not as an isolated individual's experience but as an understanding that will change the world order as well: "Some who know her [Love] better hold that hers is the master-key which will one day turn all the locks in all the world" (38). "[Hester] had but to touch the houses and they would fall down" (37). As is also the case in *The Image-Breakers*, the individual's experience becomes an emblem of what is also desired for the collective. On the one hand, giving Rachel a rabbit coat is a private act of charity. On the other hand, writing a novel about her—a novel that displaces the idealization of heterosexual love, a novel that figures life in a world where people are not constrained by what Rosalind Dangerfield terms "selfishness *a deux*"—is a revolutionary act. To use Egerton's phrasing again, Hester Gresley "crosses the line" in this scene in *Red Pottage:* she images a life for herself different from the one she led as a Victorian Andromeda, chained to the rock of her aunt's tea set. "She had but to touch the houses and they would fall down. She held her hands tightly together lest she should do it. The strength as of an infinite ocean swept in beneath her weakness, and bore it upon its surface like a leaf" (37).

The Lesbian Continuum

I discussed antinaturalistic New Woman novels such as Netta Syrett's *Nobody's Fault* (1896), Ella Hepworth Dixon's *The Story of a Modern Woman* (1894), and Emma Frances Brooke's *A Superfluous Woman* (1894) in Chapter Four, where I argued that these writers refuse to endorse the modeling of women's sexual "essence." I want to call attention now to a common patterning of events in these novels, whereby the balance of power in triangulated relationships between a man and two women shifts significantly as the heroine rejects the man's invitation to define herself solely in a sexual relationship with him. Thus, for example, in *Nobody's Fault*, Brigit decides that she cannot live with her lover out of wedlock because her mother would suffer so significantly from this social disgrace. Getting her divorce was painful enough; having a family out of wedlock would be more than the latter could bear. Brigit would like to "*take* [her] own way, lead [her] own life,—be [herself]." But, as she explains to her lover when she decides not to see him again, it would be "treading down part of my nature in hurting mother."[21] Therefore, she sacrifices her opportunity to have a sexually and emotionally satisfying relationship on her mother's behalf.

Ella Hepworth Dixon's Mary Erle invokes an abstract rather than a personal commitment between women in *The Story of a Modern Woman* when she refuses her lover's invitation to travel with him to Europe. "I can't, I won't deliberately injure another woman. . . . All we modern women mean to help each other now," she tells Vincent Hemming.[22] In other words, Mary refuses to injure his wife by eloping with him, not because she knows the latter personally but because modern women are determined to stand together. Thus, the modern woman's life story ends not in marriage (or a satisfying "free union") but in painful isolation, Mary's sole consolation being the idea that she has done the right thing by Hemming's wife.

The novels to be considered in this section subvert the heterosexual imperative of the traditional marriage plot still more radically than anti-naturalistic New Woman novels because they figure women supporting other women's "monstrous" ambitions to be something—anything—besides wives and mothers. While Dixon's Mary Erle remains isolated in her belief that "we modern women mean to help each other," the New Women in the following novels sustain each other as they pursue ambitions that, for whatever reason, the men in their lives cannot or will not endorse.

I mentioned in passing the subplot of *The Image-Breakers*, which focuses on the lower-middle-class young woman whose friendship with Rosalind Dangerfield predates the latter's involvement with the socialist collective. Leslie's periodic conversations with Rosalind serve to delineate the "stages" in Rosalind's life as she moves further and further away from her early life as a "lady of the manor." The two women's conversations punctuate the dramatic presentation of events in both plots as the longtime friends meet to renew their acquaintance and to share their insights into each other's current conflicts. Leslie is not, however, Rosalind's foil, the Harriet Smith in the life of this late nineteenth-century Emma Woodbury. In other words, Leslie does not act as a catalyst for Rosalind's affections because she is a potential rival for a man's affection. Instead, the two women depend upon each other to support their pursuit of activities and relationships that other people in their respective worlds would condemn.

An interesting scene in this regard is one in which Rosalind describes to Leslie her "terror" in the face of a man's sexual desire for her. Still legally married, she has been living in the socialist collective for some time. And she has been thinking of this particular man simply as her "comrade"—working extensively with him on various political campaigns, helping him coordinate the local group's activities with things happening on the national front, managing the local group's affairs. But now she confesses to Leslie that Justin is "no different from other men."[23] What she took to be his "comradely" interest in her is sexually charged. "In the silence the flimsy veil was rent; the one woman knew the truth, and the other knew that she knew. The weight of this knowledge cutting down between them was like a blighting presence, a terrible, lurid light, which made them dread to look upon each other's faces," the narrator notes (121). Rather than tearing them apart, this knowledge ultimately brings them closer together. Other women, particularly the working-class women who live in the neighborhood near the collective's office, will condemn Rosalind as a "fallen girl" and a "harlot" when she becomes sexually involved with Justin. Leslie, however, continues to stand by her. Indeed, before, during, and after Rosalind's relationship with Justin, she supports her friend's desire to "strike a blow at the foundations of poverty." She understands that Rosalind's commitment to Justin is, finally, a political one. And, as will be clearer when we discuss the relevant scene in detail, she understands Justin's ultimate rejection of Rosalind as a betrayal of the political ideals they held in common.

The point I am making here is that this novel refuses to sustain the conventional heterosexual orientation of the traditional marriage plot. As in *Red Pottage*, a friendship between two women figures more centrally than either woman's relationships with men; such friendships not only outlast the male-female relationships in both novels, they also prove more sustaining, more genuinely supportive of these women's ambitions. Thus, in spite of the fact that the plot lines in both novels follow heterosexual relationships, the high drama in these novels concerns these women's relationships to each other and to their work.

What we would now, following Adrienne Rich, term "woman-centeredness" is also figured in Edith Johnstone's *A Sunless Heart* (1894), a novel about a woman who is sexually harassed by a well-known artist while she is taking art lessons.[24] The scene of note will not make sense without the following plot summary. Leon Smith first takes an interest in Gaspardine O'Neill when he sees her work hanging in a studio at the art school. Gaspardine responds to his encouragement by fantasizing about a relationship with him. As the narrator notes, in doing this Gaspardine heads down "the old well-worn path, trodden by thousands, thousands of women since time was—treading it, too, with the bewildered feet of a savage, who has none of the benefits of civilisation" (36–37). Had Gaspardine been "civilized," she would have known that Smith was interested not in her but in "borrowing" her ideas for his own canvasses. Sensing that her work is more original than his own, yet confident of his "superior technical skill," Smith lets Gaspardine think he returns her affection. Gaining access to her studio in the art school without her knowledge, he then "modernizes" one of her paintings for a work he has been commissioned to do; he executes her painting in a more conventional style, reworking her material with reference to the current iconography of decadence.

The first time Gaspardine visits his studio, she sees his version of her painting and assumes the copy is the original, proof of her own lack of originality. When she finally realizes what Smith has done, she gives up painting altogether, disillusioned with the medium because of the conduct of one of its practitioners. Subsequently, she teaches school to support her twin brother until he dies of tuberculosis.

This is where Book One of *A Sunless Heart* ends. Johnstone then posits an alternate vision of the New Woman artist's relation to both her subject matter and her audience in her "Apology" for Book Two.

It has been, so far, the province of the novel to deal almost exclusively with lives only in their relation to the passion of love between man and woman, and the complications arising from it. . . . But this is only one side of life. There are others. In many lives such love plays but a minor part, or enters not at all. Will no one voice them, or find beauty in them?

To the readers who feel that humanity will right itself the sooner for facing *all* its wrongs, and more particularly to-day, the wrongs which, through many ages past, women have silently borne—I commend Lotus.

> Lastly, to all who feel that men and women will come closer,
> and [have] higher relationships, when they cease to wear masks
> each towards the other sex—removed when in the company of
> their own—to these I have tried to show, in all purity of intent,
> what women may be, and often are, to each other.   (148)

If, on first reading this, Johnstone's apology seems both unnecessary
and mysterious, it does not remain so for long. In Book One
Gaspardine's primary relationships are with her brother and her imagined lover/mentor, Leon Smith. Book Two finds her caught up in a love
triangle involving two women. Lotus Grace, the woman introduced by
the narrator in the "Apology," is mistress of the school where
Gaspardine teaches while mourning her brother's death. Mona Lefcadio
is one of Lotus' students. Anxious to establish an exclusive relationship
with her beloved teacher, she resents Gaspardine. Mona wants Lotus to
break all bonds to friends and family, commiting herself completely
and solely to her.

Mona does not get her way in this regard for several reasons. For one,
Lotus recognizes Mona's attachment to her as a schoolgirl's crush and
encourages her to marry a man "who will make more of you than I can"
(203). More importantly, the relationship that becomes dominant in
the closing scenes of the novel is not a strictly personal one. For the
novel ends with consideration of a portrait of Lotus that Gaspardine
paints after Lotus's death. This portrait, as the narrator notes, finally
brings her the critical acclaim she deserved twenty years before. Hailed
by one critic as " 'the finest [expression] of thought-life, of the subjective that had ever yet been given,' " Gaspardine's painting of Lotus
stands as the final proof in Johnstone's novel of "what women may be,
and often are, to each other" (220, 148).

In the previous chapter I noted the New Woman's unwillingness
to let her sexuality absorb her "character," and thereby her life.
Sexuality is still more radically decentered in scenes like this, I
think. For sexuality is not contained in private relationships. Instead, given the encouragement provided by other women, women
commit themselves—passionately—to women's rights activism, to
socialism, to art, to all manner of behavior once deemed "unwomanly"

and "sterilizing." The energy that society would have these women channel into private life is thus redirected into a wide range of cultural activities.

Three things are worth noting about *Red Pottage*, *The Image-Breakers*, and *A Sunless Heart*. For one, no male-female relationships match these relationships between women in intensity. No male-female relationship is as supportive as the bonding depicted between women in these novels. In all three, a relationship that appears to be peripheral to the main plot line eventually displaces the central male-female dynamic that had seemed to be the dominant interest in the novel. Equally significant, the bonding between women figured in these novels is homoerotic without being lesbian in the conventional sense of that term. In other words, these relationships lie somewhere along what Adrienne Rich terms "the lesbian continuum," but they do not encompass genital sexual contact between women.[25]

That these relationships are lesbian in Rich's but not in the narrower sense of the term can also be related to the third and most important feature of these scenes and these novels. Hester Gresley's fiction writing; Rosalind Dangerfield's involvement with socialism; Gaspardine O'Neill's oil painting: in different ways and for different reasons, each activity constitutes a violation of the Victorian doctrine of separate spheres. Each activity, moreover, is not endorsed by the men in these women's lives. Yet, each woman gains a new sense of the legitimacy of these activities in the scenes discussed above. It is only in their relationships with other women that they find encouragement to reject traditional gender-based divisions of labor. It is in these relationships that they learn to figure the public and private worlds not as mutually exclusive territories, not as, respectively, "male" and "female" spheres, but as a single cultural space that is theirs for the claiming.

6

Retreats

CHOLMONDELEY'S Hester Gres-
ley wants to "touch the houses and [make them] fall down." Gertrude
Dix's Rosalind Dangerfield wants to "strike a blow at the foundations
of poverty." Florence Dixie shares her protagonist's interest in instigating a "rapid Revolution" by "awaken[ing] the sluggards among
women to a sense of their Position." We might well ask, what happened to this utopian energy? What happened to the New Woman's
sense of her power to change the world? Why *wasn't* there a "Revolution of 1900?" Obviously, the houses Hester Gresley refers to are still
standing: in spite of both New Women's dreams of radical social
reorganization and conservative critics' apocalyptic warnings about
the second fall of man, the bourgeois social order survived the turn of
the twentieth century. Blows may have been struck—by New Women
and others—at "the foundations of poverty;" women were doubtless
awakened to "a sense of their Position," yet the old order did not
collapse, like a house of cards, under these various pressures. In other
words, in spite of the ambitions of writers like Florence Dixie, Mary
Cholmondeley, and Gertrude Dix, fiction about the New Woman did
not usher in a new social order. Yeats's argument notwithstanding,
the center, the hegemony of bourgeois English culture, *did* hold at
the turn of the century.

Having, in the previous chapter, highlighted the New Woman's
sense of empowerment in novels like *Gloriana*, *Red Pottage*, and *The
Image-Breakers*, I want now to focus on her disempowerment. I want to
consider how the desires figured in the novels discussed in Chapter Five

were delegitimized both by other New Woman novelists and by the culture at large in the closing years of the nineteenth century.

Boomerang Books

Iota's *A Yellow Aster*, Lucas Cleeve's *The Woman Who Wouldn't*, and Linton's *The New Woman in Haste and Leisure* were discussed in Chapter Four as novels that "boomerang" their protagonists back into conventional marriages. All end when the protagonist recovers from her New Womanly "spasms," to use Iota's term in a novel we did not consider, *A Comedy in Spasms* (1895).[1] Notably, in most of these novels, the New Woman's transgressions are sexual, not political. What concerns me here are "boomerang" characterizations of New Women's work in the public world in two capacities, as political activists and as artists. Because these two activities represent the New Woman's most radical challenges to the mid-Victorian code of womanliness, it stands to reason that these behaviors would be most carefully policed by writers who considered themselves to be either custodians of the social order or "gatekeepers" for the bourgeois literary tradition.

The novel that exemplifies the cultural politics at issue in this chapter is Rider Haggard's *She* (1887). Published approximately five years before the peak of the controversy about the New Woman, and therefore not often associated with it, *She* nonetheless anticipates all the questions to be asked of the New Woman once she makes her appearance on the socioliterary scene. Of course, Haggard's fine upstanding English narrator never offers us his observations about the English "Woman Question." Presumably, he leaves all of that mess behind when he and his young companion travel into Africa in search of the fabled "Ayesha," She Who Must Be Obeyed. Yet, his concerns about *She*'s determination to travel back to England with them are precisely those voiced about the New Woman's entrance into the public arena. "It made me absolutely shudder to think what would be the result of her arrival there," he acknowledges.

What her powers were I knew, and I could not doubt but that she would exercise them to the full. It might be possible to control her for a while, but her proud ambitious spirit would be certain to break loose and avenge itself for the long centuries of its solitude. She would, if necessary, and if the unaided power of her beauty did not prove equal to the occasion, blast her way to an end she set before her, and, as she could not die, and for aught I knew could not ever be killed, what was there to stop her? In the end she would, I had little doubt, assume absolute rule over the British dominions, and probably over the whole earth.[2]

Read the name of Haggard's terrifyingly powerful African queen generically in this passage (instead of accepting the alleged specificity of her title) and you can recognize Haggard's cultural displacement of anxieties specific to the situation in England at the turn of the century. What will follow from the New Woman's entrance into the public world? What will happen when she addresses herself to national politics rather than to domestic affairs? What will happen if "the passion [that] ha[s] kept her for so many centuries chained . . . and comparatively harmless" is released and rechanneled into political activism (245)? We have heard these questions before. Moreover, in Chapter Five we have seen New Women with political ambitions as radical as those of She—women who, like She, want to "change the order of the world." What I want to focus on here are novels that punish the New Woman for such ambitions, novels that try to keep the "Revolution of 1900" from happening through their "boomerang" plotting.

Witch-burning would not be too strong a term for Haggard's ritualistic destruction of both She's desire to "change the order of the world" and her physical being. I quote at great length because the following passage from Haggard's novel epitomizes the conservative, indeed reactionary, cultural politics of the narratives to be discussed subsequently.

[Ayesha] *was* shrivelling up; the golden snake that had encircled her gracious form slipped over her hips and to the ground. Smaller and smaller she grew; her skin changed colour, and in place of the perfect whiteness of its lustre it turned dirty brown and yellow, like to an old piece of withered parchment. She felt at her head: the delicate hand was nothing but a claw now, a human talon like that of a badly preserved Egyptian mummy, and then she seemed to realise what kind of change was passing over her, and she shrieked—ah, she shrieked!—Ayesha rolled upon the floor and shrieked.

Smaller she grew, and smaller yet, till she was no larger than a monkey. Now the skin had puckered into a million wrinkles, and on the shapeless face was the stamp of unutterable age. I never saw anything like it; nobody ever saw anything like the frightful age that was graven on that fearful countenance, no bigger now than that of a two-months' child, though the skull remained the same size, or nearly so, and let all men pray they never may, if they wish to keep their reason.

At last she lay still, or only moving feebly. She, who but two minutes before had gazed upon us the loveliest, noblest, most spendid woman the world has ever seen, she lay still before us, near the masses of her own dark hair, no larger than a big ape, and hideous—ah, too hideous for words! And yet, think of this—at that very moment I thought of it—it was the *same* woman!

She was dying: we saw it, and thanked God—for while she lived she could feel, and what must she have felt?   (279–280)

If nothing in novels like *The Strike of a Sex* (1891), *Alleyne: A Story of a Dream and a Failure* (1894), and *Clara Hopgood* (1896) quite matches the violence of this scene, the ideological valence is the same. Readers are to be discouraged from imitating the behavior of the New Women in these texts; they are to understand that the changes in the "order of the world" figured by New Women in novels like *Gloriana* and *A Sunless Heart* cannot in fact be realized without risking the social and racial devolution imaged in Haggard's text through Ayesha's physical degeneration. Perhaps the intertextuality of the novels to be discussed here with those considered in Chapter Five is not as obvious as that of *The Woman Who Didn't*, *The Woman Who Wouldn't*, and *The Woman Who Did*. Yet, it is impossible to read these narratives without thinking of the texts they answer, the utopian figurations of the New Woman's ambitions they seen determined to discredit.

Published only a year after Florence Dixie's *Gloriana*, for example, George Noyes Miller's *The Strike of a Sex* reverses the implications of the dream-vision format that Miller may well have borrowed directly from Dixie. I did not mention in the last chapter that Gloriana D'Estrange's whole life story is the dream of a young girl who falls asleep on the heath after a long walk and wakes up to find herself once again in the "stern reality" of 1890. In other words, the "Revolution of 1900" takes place only in her imagination. If Dixie's novel is a utopian dream vision, anxious to realize itself, Miller's is dystopian and admonitory at the same time. For it aims to check the ambitions of all budding Glorianas.

Set up—like *She*—as a travellogue, *The Strike of a Sex* is narrated by Rodney Carford, who plays anthropologist, observing life in an unidentified city where the female population has refused to "perform any longer those duties and functions which have hitherto been magnanimously marked out for them by man, as being the sole tasks predestined for them by the Creator."[3] Intercourse, childrearing, household maintenance: all the "duties of womanhood" have been renounced in a strike modeled after the London dockworkers' strike of 1889. This strike, as Carford notes, is even more effective than the dockworkers' strike because it unites female laborers of all ages and socioeconomic classes.

Prior to his visit to this city, Carford had assumed that women "were forever incapable of any serious, persistent contention of a principle" (46). What seems to impress him most about the present strike is not women's commitment to ratifying a new Magna Carta. Rather, he is overwhelmed by the idea that women might overcome the differences among themselves—differences in class, education, experience, and age—as they pursue their common interest in "enlarg-[ing] the category of [woman's] rights" (20). Observing the grand parade of women held in anticipation of the general referendum, he is "horrified" to see "despised old maids" and "despised courtesans" marching in step with "married menials," happily married women, and eligible "young maidens."

This procession, which offers Carford a striking visual image of united womanhood, finally convinces him of the legitimacy of their cause. Ironically enough, however, the emotional impact of this sudden conversion also makes him wake up from his dream, "sobbing with convulsive joy" (117). Is he joyous because the referendum is favorable, or because he is relieved to find himself once again in a recognizable England, an England where women have not staged a general strike? The ambiguity seems deliberate in the novel's closing. Whether or not Carford sustains his new-found sympathy for the strikers, they are *not* part of this world. All such spectacular changes in the political landscape occur safely within his dream world. While Rider Haggard displaces the "Woman Question" geographically, making an African kingdom the setting of *She*, Miller still more effectively contains the New Woman's radicalism by underscoring the fantasy element of his novel. To use both Roland Barthes's and George Egerton's phrasing again, Miller figures a social revolution that need never be represented—because it is *only* a dream. It can never be realized; it can never cross the line between fantasy and reality.

Miller does a certain violence to his readers' expectations when he exposes his whole narrative as a dream-vision. A much more common strategy for policing the New Woman's behavior is the kind of "boomerang" plotting we saw in novels like *"I Forbid the Banns!"* and *A Pliable Marriage*. In such novels, as argued in Chapter Four, the New Woman is given free rein to experiment with her sexuality. But then she is abruptly pulled back into line, educated into her "true" and "natural" roles as wife and mother. Similar strategies are used in novels like E. T. Papillon's *Alleyne: A Story of a Dream and a Failure* (1894) and Mark Rutherford's *Clara Hopgood* (1896) to curtail the New Woman's political rather than her sexual rebelliousness.

The title of E. T. Papillon's novel, *Alleyne: A Story of a Dream and a Failure*, anticipates the final outcome of his narrative. Alleyne Carlile has a dream, which she considers "an anti-dote to the false drugs" other women "were endeavouring to administer to society."[4] Other women, she notes, are "striving to cast away their natural supremacy over men by grasping at equality with them[;] leaving their own proper sphere where they may rule as they will, . . . they scorch and destroy their own peculiar nature, in which their power lies, to attain another which they never can attain, the efforts to reach which only lead them into shame and contempt" (229). In contrast, she herself has a vision of the "glorious, perfect Woman" who will make "the lives of mankind more beautiful" when she comes down from her mountaintop and enters the city of life (226). And yet, even though the book she writes describing this vision is a popular success, she finds herself in a terrible double bind. Shortly after it is published, her husband is diagnosed as an alcoholic, and she is trapped by her own idealism. If she leaves him, she discredits the ideal she figured in her book; if she stays with him, she risks her life. She decides to do the latter, and does indeed die when, in a fit of drunken fury, he pushes her down a flight of stairs. "What is the use of ideals in this world of ours?" asks a friend of hers bitterly as he scatters her ashes in the river (291). The bleakness of this ending is softened somewhat by an "envoi," which presents an allegory about storytelling; but Papillon's moral is nonetheless clear: if Alleyne had never had her dream, it never would have failed.

A similar trajectory is traced in *Clara Hopgood*, William Hale White's novel about two young middle-class sisters who find shelter in a highly politicized working-class household after one of them is disowned by their parents for being pregnant and unmarried.[5] The elderly Mrs. Caffyn's "family"—made up of herself, her daughter and son-in-law, Madge and Clara Hopgood—functions quite happily through the duration of Madge's pregnancy. While Madge settles into her new role as a mother, Clara begins her education. Having been raised on a steady diet of romance novels, she now reads history, philosophy, and the works of Marx and Engels for the first time. She argues politics with the men she meets through her job in a small second-hand bookstore; she continues such discussions at home when the "family" gathers around the fire in the evenings; and she takes pleasure in the fact that no one questions her sister Madge about the father of her child. If the two sisters have "fallen" in the world's eyes, Clara believes that they have "risen" to a community where social mores are not more highly valued than human beings. In short, Clara's new political vision sustains her in the face of the social ostracism she and Madge suffer because of Madge's sexual "disgrace."

Clara's growing faith in socialism is disrupted, however, when one of Clara's bookstore friends falls in love with Madge. A widowed Jew with a grown son, Baruch Cohen has been Clara's intellectual mentor. Through him, she has learned to value her mind and to reject the political quietism her parents demanded of her as a middle-class lady. But, having introduced Clara to radical socialist politics, Cohen now betrays her and the political ideals she thought they shared by manifesting an interest in establishing a very conventional, bourgeois relationship with Clara's sister. Cohen not only offers to marry Madge and adopt her illegitimate daughter; he also celebrates her motherhood as a symbol of her willingness to privilege a commitment to a "chosen individual" over an abstract commitment to radical politics. In other words, he invokes the Victorian ideology of womanliness as he commits himself to what he had earlier criticized as the "ferocious selfishness of love" (188). "Happy Madge! Happy Baruch!" the narrator mocks in reporting the kiss that seals their betrothal, the kiss that also makes Clara decide to join Mazzini's freedom fighters in Italy, where she dies almost immediately thereafter (291).[6]

One thinks here, too, of the very painful way in which Hardy resolves Sue Bridehead's story in *Jude the Obscure* (1896). Hardy is not satisfied simply to "boomerang" her back into her first marriage; instead, he drains her of all the unpredictable unconventionality that had made her so charming to Jude and others—and so similar to other "Protean" New Women like Schreiner's Lyndall and Brooke's Jessamine Halliday. Hardy leaves Sue with no fantasy life at the end of *Jude*; as Mary Jacobus has noted, devoid of both erotic and ambitious dreams, she vanishes into an obscurity far deeper than Jude's.[7]

Before considering "boomerang" books that feature New Women artists, let me make a general observation about the sexual economy regulating the representation of the New Woman in the novels discussed above. Undergirding the plot of these narratives is the either/or antinomy between erotic and ambitious fantasy that Freud sets up in his essay, "The Relation of the Poet to Daydreaming," as he tries to explain creativity. I quote Nancy Miller quoting Freud in her important essay, "Emphasis Added: Plots and Plausibilities in Women's Fiction," in order to suggest how the fiction at issue here both does and does not fit the model Miller develops as an alternative to Freud's.

First, Freud on the difference between male and female fantasies.

> The impelling wishes vary according to the sex, character, and circumstances of the creator; they may easily be divided, however, into two principal groups. Either they are ambitous wishes, serving to exalt the person creating them, or they are erotic. In young women erotic wishes dominate the phantasies *almost exclusively*, for their ambition is *generally comprised* in their erotic longings; in young men egoistic and ambitious wishes assert themselves plainly enough alongside their erotic desires.[8]

Now, Miller's objection to this characterization.

> Here we see that the either/or antimomy, ambitious/erotic, is immediately collapsed to make coexistence possible in masculine fantasies: "In the greater number of ambitious daydreams . . . we can discover a woman in some corner, for whom the dreamer performs all his heroic deeds and at whose feet all his triumphs are to be laid."
>
> But is this observation reversible? If, to make the logical extrapolation, romance dominates the female daydream and constitutes its primary heroine-ism, is there a *place* in which the ambitious wish of a young woman asserts itself? Has she an egoistic desire to be discovered "in some corner?" Freud elides the issue—while leaving the door open (for us) by his modifiers.   (346, emphasis in original)

If, as Miller goes on to suggest, the plausibility of a novel's plotting lies in "the structuration of its fantasy" (349), then what is interesting about *The Strike of a Sex*, *Alleyne*, *Clara Hopgood*, and *Jude the Obscure* is these male authors' inability to countenance women's ambitious fantasies. Significantly, what is figured for us in these narratives is not, as Freud has it, the coexistence of erotic and ambitious desires in masculine fantasies, but men's refusal to recognize the same combination of desires in women's fantasies. As is clearest in the final scene of *Clara Hopgood*, these male authors want their female heroines to commit themselves to "the ferocious selfishness of love" (188). For, as Rider Haggard's narrator notes in *She*, women are "comparatively harmless" when "their passion keeps them chained," that is, when romance dominates the female daydream. The male fantasy that these narrative fulfill, then, is the fantasy that women's ambitions are "implausible."

To turn from these male-authored narratives to novels like Elizabeth Robins's *George Mandeville's Husband* (1894) and Sara Jeannette Duncan's *A Daughter of Today* (1894) is to realize that the delegitimization of female ambition was effected by women as well as men in the 1890s. Although all but one of the novels to be discussed in this section were written by women, these narratives are no more tolerant of the New Woman's artistic ambitions than *The Strike of a Sex*, *Alleyne*, and *Clara Hopgood* are of her political ambitions. While there is thus an additional element of irony in these texts—we read these stories about New Woman who are punished for their ambition, knowing that they are authored by women who were highly successful public figures in their own lives—they reinforce the point made by the male-authored narratives discussed earlier: female ambition is not to be countenanced.[9]

Edith Johnstone's figuration of the love between two women that finds expression through art in *A Sunless Heart* was discussed in Chapter Five. Whether or not they had Johnstone's novel specifically in mind, Elizabeth Robins and W. S. Holnut counter Johnstone's portrait of the New Woman artist point for point in writing their cautionary tales, *George Mandeville's Husband* (1894) and *Olympia's Journal* (1895). These novels stand in the same relation to *A Sunless Heart* as *The Strike of a Sex* does to *Gloriana*. That is, they quite effectively discredit the positive modeling of the New Woman artist offered by the earlier writer. While they do not "boomerang" the New Woman artist back into a conventional life, they frame her—they accuse her of "unsexing" herself by channeling all of her energy into art, not personal relationships.

Elizabeth Robins, for example, is quite ruthless in her characterization of a woman, George Mandeville, who tyrannizes her husband and daughter by fictionalizing their lives and making "copy" of real pain, real suffering. Ironically, Robins herself enjoyed the kind of popularity she attributes to her protagonist, a woman who pretends to the greatness of the "other Georges," Sand and Eliot.[10] Yet the irony here always works against George Mandeville, whose life story concludes with Robins noting that she is now turning her daughter into an "imaginary figure" in her current work-in-progress. While Mandeville neglects her real daughter during the latter's terminal illness, she "build[s] up . . . an imaginary relation" with "an idolized only daughter" in the novel she is writing. Even as her daughter lies dying in the next room, Mandeville writes herself into the part of the adored mother, turning her daughter into one of her many heroines with eyes that are "hazel in some lights, and dark-violet in others" (155–156). As the narrator notes, this "hurts [George Mandeville's husband] as if his wife had slammed the door in the face of [their] living child." Fictionalizing their daughter "seem[s] to threaten the integrity of his own memory, and mock at all the hallowed boasts of love." Rosina, he now realizes, is "gone in a more complete sense, gone like the tear we shed last year for some sorrow we are unable to recall. Is not this death?" (156), he asks bitterly in the final paragraph of the novel. Is not George Mandeville killing even the memory of Rosina as she mothers her imaginary daughter?

Although Robins's novel ends with this question, it is not a question George Mandeville asks herself. Nor does she question in any other respect the appropriateness of her actions. As she tells an aspiring writer very early in the novel, "it's not so much the story that matters, as what *you* say and think. You must be known, and then people will read you." "The personal note is the great thing nowadays" (7), she goes on to suggest, and certainly her own work attests to the fact that recognition as a "personality" matters more to her than her relationships with her daughter and husband. Art replaces her attachments to real people. Or, as Margaret Devereux argues in *The Ascent of Woman*, "the attraction of art supersedes the attraction of actuality till it ends by absorbing the whole being. Aesthetic passion can only be indulged at the expense of human passion, and the sterilization of natural instincts follows as an inevitable result."[11]

Like George Mandeville, the protagonist of W. S. Holnut's *Olympia's*

Journal is similarly obsessed with fame. Unlike Robins, however, Holnut gives the New Woman artist a chance to redeem herself. Or rather, Holnut gives her a chance to claim her misdeeds publicly. "This is a confession, and therefore part of my punishment," writes Olympia Daw, the narrator-protagonist, in her introduction.[12] Three and a half years after the fact, Olympia describes as a "craze" her marriage to a man "whom I could neither love, honor or obey" (v–vi). As she goes on to suggest, "the singularity of [this man's] character and life" made her think that a study of him would "place [her] in the front rank of contemporary novelists" (vi, 84). Now, however, she confesses the wrongheadedness of that decision and offers her diary to the world "in the hope that my experiences may deter other women from a similar mistake" (v–vi).[13]

The mistake Olympia refers to is her assumption that she has a right to make her husband an object of study, a specimen to be dissected and analyzed from her own Olympian perspective. After their wedding, Olympia adds a "Cyril Gordon" notebook to her collection of character-study notebooks. Already full of stories that would make "strange reading," she confides: "I should not like anyone to peep into the 'Cyril Gordon' " (108).

When her notebooks disappear, Olympia cannot bring herself to accuse her husband of taking them. She asks herself: "Could I confess that it was my intention to give the world a portrait of him just as he was from my point of view? Could I further confess that it was my intention to publish the book under cover of a pseudonym and say nothing to him about it? In fact, to let him live in complete ignorance that his personality had been delivered to thousands of readers to laugh and perhaps to weep over?" (166). Admitting that her notebooks have not been "fair play," she then rationalizes her action with the following. "If I had asked, and he had granted his consent it would have been better, no doubt, but the artistic side of my work would have suffered. His singleness of mind would have gone. Conscious that all his doings and sayings were marked and noted down he would have become affected, and my portrait of him would have been a failure" (166–167).

Only after they are separated does Olympia venture to ask him about the notebooks, which he admits to having taken, not because he wanted to read them but because he wanted "to put an extinguisher on that highfalutin literary attitude of yours" (190). But it is not until he falls mysteriously ill that Olympia wonders whether he has read them. "I fancied," she admits, "that since I had left him in January, George had been studying my note-books and that my descriptions of him had had the effect of bringing on his illness" (208). Remembering in particular a "cold, cruel, minute comparison between him and my cousin Cuthbert," she wonders, "had I ever been fair—even moderately fair—to poor George? . . . Had I ever written about him without a bias—without a burning desire to show off my own cleverness at his expense?" (212, 213). Revealing his weaknesses without mentioning his strengths, she notes, she had wanted "to keep up the illusion that I was a scientific observer."

Now she asks herself:

> if I had really wanted to do the right thing in explaining many of his singularities, ought I not to have given the numberless little slights and vexations with which I had goaded him from day to day? It was there that my system had broken down. I had spared myself when it was a question of my own conduct, and said nothing. . . . A woman—another woman—with a wider sympathy than mine, what might she have done with such a man? Would she not have put her pride into the work—the work of reclaiming all that was good in him and gently opposing the rest? Would she not have been kind to him and helpful—guiding him by the hand without vainglory?
>
> Many women could have done it—women with no pretensions to genius.   (213–214, 215)

Summoned to George's deathbed, Olympia learns that he has never read her notebooks. He only took them, he tells her, because he was jealous of the time she spent with them. Now he asks that they be buried with him in a beautiful Russian leather case he has had made for them. "I love them because they are your work. They will be your parting gift," he insists (221). His last words to her sketch in the exchange he imagines at the gates of heaven when he gives St. Peter her notebooks: "Peter will read them from beginning to end, and when he has read them, he will know everything about George, because it was George's wife who wrote them. Then Peter will let George pass" (221). But of course, George's last words are no consolation to Olympia. Indeed, they are the impetus for publishing her journal. They are proof of her guilt, proof of her need to expiate her sins as a wife and an artist.

Instead of describing the coexistence of women's erotic and ambitious fantasies, Robins and Holnut view these two things in direct competition with each other, I think. They seem to have in mind something like Freud's either/or antimomy as they highlight their characters' neglect of their maternal or wifely responsibilities. We have seen other New Woman novelists equate writing with mothering in an effort to reconceptualize the relationship between public and private spheres, cultural and biological labor. Significantly, the analogy between production and reproduction works in these narratives to delegitimize women's ambitions: to ridicule women's "pretensions to genius" and their determination to create art, not babies or pleasant domestic spaces.

Any number of other novels offer similar criticisms of the New Woman artist's ambition. Theodora, the "Splendid Cousin" in Mrs. Andrew Dean's novel by the same name, for example, is introduced as someone who "will never marry. She is an artist. She does not care for men."[14] She claims to be a talented violinist, though she never practices; instead, she spends the family fortune on music lessons with a German genius, expects her cousin, Ruth Godwin, to wait on her hand and foot, charms the man Ruth loves into marrying her, and eventually ruins everyone's lives by deserting her husband and family. All in the name of a talent that would "never have been anything but an amateur['s]"—if only Theodora had spent enough time among real musicians to know the difference (166).

Like Theodora, Elfrida Bell ridicules "womanly" women in Sara Jeannette Duncan's *A Daughter of Today* (1894). "Fancy being the author of babies, when one could be the author of books!" she exclaims as she announces her intention to pursue a career in journalism.[15] When a male artist friend tries to "infli[ct] discipline upon her" by sketching her in a compromising tête à tête, this only goads her on to further "Bohemianisms." She works for six weeks in a music hall in order to write "An Adventure in Stageland." Unlike Elfrida herself, her friends are not "oblivious to the crudeness and humiliation" of exposing her legs on stage, costumed as an military officer (112). Her friend Kendal paints her portrait a second time, again trying to make her understand the scandalousness of her behavior. But this becomes clear to her only when another old friend publishes a novel that is widely acclaimed. Jealous of Janet's success, Elfrida notes spitefully that "Janet [is] a compromise; she belonged really to the British public, and the class of Academy studies from the nude, which were always draped, just a little" (124). Unlike her own studies from life, Janet's book would probably "be commended for *jeunes filles*," she mocks, trying desperately to discredit the standards that would find her own work lacking and reward Janet's (124). Finally, however, she cannot convince even herself that this is true. Thus, like so many "boomerang" books, Duncan's novel ends with Elfrida's admission that she should not have danced in the music halls or written the essay that will be published six months after she commits suicide.

The outcome of both George Paston's *A Modern Amazon* (1894) and Rita's *A Husband of No Importance* (1894) is happier, but the effect is the same. In both cases, women who consider themselves "importan[t] even in these days of Important Women" must learn humility—and subordinate their artistic ambitions to their marital responsibilities. Both protagonists consider themselves to be writers of "really clever books;"[16] both assume their husbands are "blind, foolish, witless creature[s], with no opinions worth considering, and no gifts deserving credence."[17] The denouement of *A Modern Amazon* is mild by comparison with that of *A Husband*, which ends with Mrs. Rashleigh watching her husband's play, "The New Woman, A Comedy of Modern Errors." Recognizing herself in his protagonist, she realizes that the success of his play

> swe[eps] her own feeble efforts into nothingness. He had reached a
> higher platform than she could climb, had spoken and understood
> while she had only been tolerated. He had been able to call the
> world of art and culture, society and work, to hear *him*, and had

not only won their praise, but touched their hearts. . . . [He] had
just quietly bided his time, and studied her as a doctor studies the
progress of a disease, until the time was ripe for blow. (226)

Instead of being offended by his use of her as "copy," however, she is
grateful to him for "hav[ing] taught me my lesson" (235). Trembling
"like a child in his arms," she pleads for his forgiveness—and presumably lives happily ever after not as a "writer of clever books" but as the
wife of a successful playwright. The import is as clear here as in a novel
like *Clara Hopgood*: the New Woman is hereby encouraged to renounce
her interest in being a culture-maker and satisfy herself instead with
being her husband's dependent. Infantalized, domesticated, she is to
give up her "wildness" and her "pretensions to genius" and—it seems
to be hoped—she is not be heard from again.

What is to be made of such hostile representations? For one thing,
they invite us to rethink Nancy Miller's argument about the association
between narrative plausibility and social propriety. Miller notes at the
outset of "Emphasis Added" that the notion of "plausibility" in narrative is wedded to the idea of "propriety." "The precondition of plausibility," she suggests, is "the stamp of approval affixed by public opinion."
"Critical reaction to any text is hermeneutically bound up to another
and preexistent text: the *doxa* of socialities" (346). In view of the
narratives at issue here, Miller's formulation must be altered. For,
interestingly enough, it is the very *implausibility* of these novels' "boomerang" plots that brings the narratives back into alliance with "the
doxa of socialities," more specifically, the Victorian code of womanliness. Only through implausible plotting can these authors make their
characters' actions proper. By any means necessary, it seems, the New
Woman is to be brought back into the fold.

At this point it is worth recalling not only the violent rhetoric
wielded against the New Woman by critics such as Elizabeth Linton
but also the general controversy over realism in English fiction first
discussed in Chapter Two. I mentioned in that chapter the objections
expressed by critics such as Linton and Henry James about the democratization and/or feminization of the literary marketplace. I also discussed what James Ashcroft Noble termed in his essay, "The Fiction of

Sexuality," "the problem of convincingness"—the challenge an author faces in getting readers to accept his or her representations of reality as, in fact, realistic and representational. Who has access to literature as a mode of cultural production? Whose representations of reality are to be normalized, granted the force of a standard, through the consensus that realism both implies and imposes?[18] Such questions, raised by Noble and others in the 1890s, are worth recalling as we think about the sheer number of "boomerang" books published between 1890 and 1900.

One other point deserves emphasis here. Gaye Tuchman and Nina Fortin argue that women were edged out of the literary marketplace as the novel rose to a new cultural prominence at the end of the nineteenth century. Similarly, Sandra Gilbert and Susan Gubar characterize this period in literary history as a "war between the sexes."[19] But these important feminist studies do not account for the production of "boomerang" books by women. Neither can explain women's resistance to other women's literary and political radicalism at the turn of the century. The evidence presented by the novels at issue here suggests that we need to check our tendency, as feminists, to make men the villains of the histories we (re)write. We cannot afford to deny that women as well as men were acting as cultural custodians and "gatekeepers" in the 1890s. Women as well as men were reinscribing what Christine Froula terms " 'the hysterical cultural script': the cultural text that dictates . . . the necessity of silencing women's speech when it threatens the father."[20]

Did narratives about the New Woman's political and artistic ambitions threaten "the father"? Insofar as female ambition challenges the patriarchal ideology of domesticity (which would have women channel all of their ambition, through their erotic desire, into their families); insofar as the endorsement of female ambition *and* erotic fantasies in novels like *The Image-Breakers* calls into question the either/or antimony proposed by Freud, then yes, the most radical figurations of the New Woman's desires did indeed threaten "the father," the bourgeois patriarchy. And if the "boomerang" plotting of novels like *Clara Hopgood* and *Alleyne* might serve as evidence of such a threat, further proof of this challenge is to be found in the novels I turn to now: novels that "retreat with honour" from their own radical political or artistic agendas in the face of overwhelming opposition to the New Woman's antipatriarchal and utopian energies.

"Retreat with Honour"

As in Chapter Four, I borrow the phrase "retreat with honour" from Gissing's *The Odd Women*, where it is used to describe Rhoda's decision to remain celibate once she understands that Barfoot was "never quite serious about anything [he] said" during their "perfect day" in Wales. I argued in that chapter that the New Woman's celibacy differs from the "pure" Victorian woman's because the New Woman's is anything but pure. It is wrenchingly painful; it is assumed only as a defense measure against a New Man's attempts to dominate the New Woman erotically. In this respect, it is honorable, not because it is something the New Woman desires or values in and of itself (as would a "womanly" woman) but because sexual expression continues to be predicated upon the denial of other desires the New Woman would fulfill.

I use the phrase here in reference to the New Woman's disavowal of her political and artistic ambitions. The highly self-conscious, self-reflexive novels to be considered in this section abandon their own utopian trajectories. To use Barthes's phrasing again, they continue to figure the New Woman's most radical desires—but they also represent the external conditions that curtail satisfaction of these desires. In contrast to the heroine of *Olympia's Journal*, the New Women in these novels are not made to confess and renounce their delinquency. Instead, they sustain their commitment to radical politics and "unwomanly" artistic ambitions; yet, they are also made to understand the intensity of the world's desire that these ambitions *not* be satisfied.

Consider, for example, *Marcella* (1895) and *Sir George Tressady* (1896), Mrs. Humphry Ward's pair of novels about a young upper-middle-class woman who alienates herself from her parents, first by involving herself in village politics and then by training as a nurse to work in London's notorious East End. Pursued by the local landowner's son, Marcella prefers to remain single and learn "something about the dark aspects, the crushing complexity of this world."[21] Rather than marrying this man at the earliest opportunity, Marcella wants to think her way "through the contradictions and the commonplaces" of the "present social and industrial system," a system wherein, as she notes, "this Board-School child, this man honestly out of work, this woman 'sweated' out of her life—should perish," while she herself is offered all the creature comforts provided by a large income and a doting husband. Thus far, at least, Marcella resembles other New Women who wanted to "strike a blow against poverty." Like Emma Frances Brooke's Jessamine Halliday, for example, Marcella is moved to renounce her sheltered, conventional middle-class life when she realizes that her life of luxury on her parents' estate is part of a larger economic system that depends upon the sweated labor of the London working classes in the East End. Indeed, the very matches she uses to light her candles come to symbolize the exploitativeness of that system.

Marcella may want to understand "the contradictions and the commonplaces" of capitalism; but what she eventually learns—and this is where *Marcella* differs most significantly from the other novels discussed in Chapter Five—is that she cannot change the social system in general or the relations between classes in particular simply by wishing to do so. She gets a taste of this even before she has left her parents' home. Taking up the defense of a poacher who has been shot while setting traps on the local estate, she is surprised to find that the villagers do not trust her, cannot understand her advocacy on his behalf. They suspect her motives for involving herself in this affair; moreover, they are as angry about her "unladylike" public behavior as her parents. And they make it clear to her that she is poaching on *their* territory when she invites herself into one of the cottages as their "fellow."

Mrs. Ward addresses the same issues regarding the New Woman's effectiveness as a political activist in her second novel about Marcella. *Sir George Tressady* takes up Marcella's life ten years into her marriage to Lord Maxwell, the young landowner who had unsuccessfully pursued her so many years before. As the narrator notes, Marcella had finally accepted Maxwell's marriage proposal because she had wanted "to hide herself in her own passion, to make of love her guide and shelter" from all the miseries she had observed working as a nurse in the London slums. She had fled from her life in East London "with a natural human terror" of the suffering she had witnessed in her patients' lives, only a part of which was related to their medical problems.[22] Now, however, ten years into their marriage, she maintains two households, one in the East End and one in the fashionable West End of London. While her husband has become increasingly well known for his work in Parliament, Marcella divides her energies between two activities: "converting" Sir George Tressady, a young Conservative M.P., to the Liberal party; and doing relief work out of her home in the East End.

A married woman with a considerable income at her disposal and a well-known name to wield as needed, Marcella finds she is more successful in pursuing her interest in politics than she had been as a young girl flying in the face of her parents' objections. An unforeseen event, however, shatters her confidence and leaves her questioning her efficacy as a political activist. The climax of the novel comes when Marcella attempts the unprecedented: a public speech at an East End rally. Prior to this she has worked closely with the homeless in a halfway house she set up for working girls. But she has never violated the bourgeois social code concerning a lady's appearance in public before a "promiscuous" audience. Encouraged by her political colleagues to do so now, she mounts the platform to defend the reform bill her husband is introducing into Parliament—and loses her audience within the first ten minutes of her speech. As the narrator notes, Marcella's "personal magic" deserts her in "this East End school room, before people whose lives she knows, whose griefs she carries in her heart" (313). For as Marcella senses them responding to her as a well-dressed woman, she loses her train of thought and stumbles through the prepared text of her speech, delivering "a confused mass of facts and figures, pedantic, colourless, and cold" (314). She does finally manage to collect herself, inspiring the crowd, through "that terrible second sight of hers [into] the all-environing woe and tragedy of human things," to raise their hands together in claiming their "share of the common pain" (315). But even as she turns to leave the platform, a heckler questions her capacity to share that pain, and the rally quickly dissolves into a brawl as some of the working-class members of the crowd pelt Marcella and the rest of the middle-class speakers on the platform with stones.

It might be recalled that, in a very similar situation, Florence Dixie's Gloriana had convinced a working-class audience that she could lead the "Revolution of 1900." Marcella sustains her commitment to labor politics. To some extent at least, she is satisfied by the success of her private political campaign to convert Sir George Tressady to labor's cause. But the deep scar on her forehead will always remind her of the brawl in East London. Never again will she witness in public to her faith in socialism.

Gertrude Dix's *The Image-Breakers* (1900) deserves mention here as a novel that figures the New Woman's radical political ambitions—and represents their defeat in the face of unrelenting conservative opposition. Dix, as noted earlier, shatters the cultural icon of "the good woman" when she asks her readers to identify with a protagonist who leaves her husband to join a socialist collective, then establishes herself in a common-law marriage with one of her "comrades." Rosalind Dangerfield's conceptualization of her book, her treatise on capitalism, as her "child," the product of her intellectual intimacy with her lover, also epitomizes Dix's effort to rethink the gender-based division of cultural labors. Rosalind wants "to destroy systems" and to "strike a blow at the foundations of poverty and sordid life."[23] She attempts to do this both through her writing and her activism in the socialist collective. But the Socialist party and her "comrade" betray her before the end of *The Image-Breakers*.

As the narrator notes midway through the novel, Rosalind's name has become a "byword [for socialism] through the length and breadth of England" by this point in her life. She is known to the gentry near her ex-husband's estate as a "fallen girl" and to her working-class neighbors (near the collective) as "the harlot" (210). Yet she can sustain herself in the face of such disapproval so long as she believes in the value of the work she is doing with Justin Ferrar for the party. This becomes impossible, however, when she begins to doubt the nature of Justin's feelings for her. Without really knowing why, she decides quite abruptly one day to leave both Justin and the collective. This withdrawal proves later to have been well motivated, for Justin admits to having used her for the "beautiful thoughts" which she has inspired in him (280). He has loved the idea of Rosalind's giving up everything—her husband, her comfortable income, her reputation—for "the Cause." He has desired her sexually; he has depended on her to manage his household and his political organization. But—and he tells her this straight out—he does not love her. Moreover, by the time he tells her this, he has already found another beautiful middle-class woman to play muse, lover, and housekeeper to his political genius.

The irony of this resolution is bitter: the woman who wanted to "destroy systems," the woman who has been so successful in presenting a radical critique of the Victorian political economy, still remains trapped by the bourgeois sexual economy. In other words, Rosalind has not entirely succeeded as an "image-breaker." She has crossed class lines; she has violated the social code regarding a lady's appearance in public; yet, through no fault of her own, she has not managed to upset the system of gender relations. And she knows that no truly effective blow will be struck "at the foundations of poverty and sordid life" until the patriarchal arrangement of male-female relationships has been altered radically as well.

The New Woman artists in novels such as Ella Hepworth Dixon's *The Story of a Modern Woman* (1894), George Paston's *A Writer of Books* (1899), and Mary Cholmondeley's *Red Pottage* (1899) share Rosalind Dangerfield's interest in figuring alternatives to the bourgeois social order. They conceive of their art as an act of political engagement. But, like Rosalind, they also know what they are up against. Editors, publishers, and critics remind them constantly that they will not tolerate certain kinds of innovations from these women writers.

The conflict of interest in Ella Hepworth Dixon's *The Story of a Modern Woman*, for example, is between Mary Erle and her editor. Interestingly enough, the latter refuses to let Mary pursue what was described earlier as the original agenda of the New Woman novel, the challenge to "correct" realism. Mary got her professional start under this editor writing short stories to accompany a famous artist's drawings in a monthly publication. As she built up a readership, her editor let her work on longer projects; more importantly, he also stopped assigning her topics. Now, however, their relationship deteriorates abruptly when Mary writes a novel that has "too much reality" in the final chapter. The public wants "thoroughly healthy reading," her editor insists, objecting to a scene that describes a "young man making love to his friend's wife."[24] Mary responds by noting that the "public would take anything—in a newspaper." "Not in fiction—not in fiction," he counters. "Remember you write for healthy English homes." " 'But even the people in the country parsonage must occasionally see life as it is—or do they go about with their eyes shut?' ventured Mary quietly." " 'The fact is,' he said, looking rather foolish, 'novels are-er-well-novels. The British public doesn't expect them to be like life. . . . It's really difficult now to get a thoroughly breezy book with a wedding at the end. Take my advice and stick to pretty stories. They're bound to pay best' " (222, 223).

From what little we are told in this conversation about the novel, is it clear that Mary Erle is not writing *The Woman Who Did*. When she tries to show "life as it is," she is reminded that women are supposed to write "pretty stories," "breezy book[s] with a wedding at the end." The above is the last exchange between Mary and her editor recorded in *The Story of a Modern Woman*. Shortly after this scene, Vincent Hemming reappears in her life, and, as discussed elsewhere, the rest of the novel focuses on Mary's relationship with him. We never know whether Mary rewrites her novel to fit her editor's specifications, or whether she abandons that project and starts again. We know only that when she visits her father's grave in the closing scene of the novel, she takes away with her as her own talisman the words from Tennyson's "Ulysses" etched on his tombstone: "to strive, to seek, and not to yield."

Like Dixon, George Paston highlights her protagonist's difficult relationship with an editor in *A Writer of Books*. When Cossima Chudleigh is advised to get rid of all the philosphical digressions in her first novel and add a wedding at the end, she reminds herself that "she must begin by suiting herself to the requirements of the public, or at any rate of the publishers."[25] Using the rhetoric of maternity to describe her relationship to her writing, she "compare[s] herself to the Russian mother who flung some of her children out of a sledge to the wolves in order to save the rest" when she makes the requested changes. Sacrificing "her most effective, but at the same time redundant passages," she "mutilate[s] the offspring of her brain"—and finally succeeds in getting the book accepted for publication (108).

If Mary Cholmondeley shares with both Ella Hepworth Dixon and George Paston a concern for the constraints of the literary marketplace, she also goes much further than either of them in analyzing the reasons for devaluation of the New Woman artist's work. Previously, I discussed the scene in *Red Pottage* in which Hester discovers her vocation as a New Woman artist and her power to change the world through her fiction. At the end of that chapter, Hester's first New Woman novel, published just a year after her important conversation with Rachel, is described as an overnight success. People in society may question Hester's capacity to imagine so effectively "a life [e.g., a typewriter's struggle to make a living in the East End] of which they decided she could know nothing."[26] But the novel nonetheless reaps "a harvest of astonished indignation and admiration" (38). Hester's second New Woman novel does not fare nearly so well; although it is accepted for publication, it is destroyed before it can reach a wide audience, and its destruction serves to emblematize the ill-will we have seen so many critics and writers express toward the New Woman's "revolt."

The scenes of interest here begin in Chapter Thirty-nine, which opens as Hester's clergyman brother sits down to read her manuscript. A writer of religious tracts, Mr. Gresley decides he will return the favor Hester had done for him in editing his most recent publication. When her novel "Husks" is returned to her by the publisher for final revisions, Hester is away visiting friends. Although they have had words previously about opening each other's mail, Gresley assumes the right to read the manuscript in her absence. Initially intending to skim it, he begins "correcting" his sister's prose with a red pencil almost immediately—noting first, for example, his disapproval of its dedication to Rachel West ("What an extraordinary thing! Any one, be they who they might, would naturally have thought that if the book were dedicated to any one it would be to her only brother" [237]). As Chapter Thirty-nine of Cholmondeley's novel continues, the excerpts from Hester's novel included in the text of *Red Pottage* get longer. Thus, as readers of *Cholmondeley's* text, we are allowed to witness Gresley's interaction with Hester's.

As the narrator notes, Mr. Gresley soon forgets that he had intended to skim the manuscript. "Conscious of a gift for finding the right word"; conscious, too, that "Hester did not share [this gift] with him," Gresley attacks the work's "blemishes" by changing individual words and rewriting whole sentences. The following passage brings him up short.

When we look back and see in how many characters we have lived and loved and suffered and died before we reached the character that momentarily clothes us, and from which our soul is struggling out to clothe itself anew; when we feel how the sympathy even of those who love us best is always with our last expression, never with our present feeling, always with the last dead self on which our climbing feet are set——— (258)

We never know how Hester would have completed this sentence, for Mr. Gresley stops reading the novel at this point to comment on her "hope[less] confusion." Unable to understand what Hester is saying in this passage, Mr. Gresley assumes she has muddled the classic conceit regarding the seven stages of man's life in speaking of "dead selves" rather than of the "different stages of life" (258). In other words, he imposes a conventional meaning on her unconventional text—which in fact is a rewriting of the same essentialist notion of character we have seen challenged in other New Woman novels (e.g., *A Superfluous Woman*). The Reverend Gresley assumes Hester has handled a classical allusion poorly. This then tips the scale for him against the novel, for though he is totally engrossed by it, he announces upon finishing it that it is the "worst book ever," a truly "heretical" work.

It is worth noting that the Reverend Gresley's characterization of Hester's novel is of a piece with the many adverse judgments offered in journals like the *Athenaeum*, the *Bookman*, and the *Review of Reviews* of "real" New Woman novels. An 1895 review in the *Bookman*, for example, states flatly that "a novel that mentions the New Woman deserves to remain uncut."[27] Trained as a cleric, Gresley assumes religious rather than secular standards of value. Yet he would probably concur with an *Athenaeum* reviewer's comment that it is "not the kind of book that we desire to see multiplied."[28]

Because the only way to ensure that the latter does not happen—that Hester's novel is not widely read or imitated by other writers—is by curtailing circulation, Gresley takes it upon himself to destroy Hester's manuscript. At the earliest opportunity, he confers with his archdeacon about a "most unwise letter" that has "fallen into his hands and been read by him." As he explains to the archdeacon, misrepresenting the situation so as to ensure the latter's support, "the letter, if posted, would certainly get the writer into trouble, and would cause acute humiliation to the writer's family."[29] With the archdeacon's approval, he then burns the "letter," explaining to Hester when she returns home that he has destroyed the novel "for your own sake, and for the sake of the innocent minds which might be perverted by it" (267, 276).

In their ensuing conversation, Hester attempts but fails utterly to convince Gresley he is at fault in any way for burning the manuscript. As discussed in Chapter Five, she describes her book as her child, trying to make her brother understand the magnitude of the loss she has sustained. When he learns that Hester would have received a thousand pound advance from the sale of the novel from the publisher, Gresley is sorry to lose that income. But he persists in believing Hester's reaction to the destruction of the novel is only, as he reassures his wife, "hysteria, which girls get when they are disappointed at not marrying, and are not so young as they [once] were" (373). On this very painful note the novel ends: Hester moves to Australia with her friend Rachel, but the narrator does not reassure us in the brief epigraph that she will publish other works of fiction. Hester "retreats with honour" from her confrontation with her brother; she will no longer live as a spinster in his authoritarian household. Nonetheless, she has been defeated by his defense of the social and cultural establishment. Her novel will not be lauded as a "classic" or praised as a work of "overwhelming and incontestable excellence." Indeed, it will not be read at all. It will never have a chance to voice its "heresies" in public, thereby fulfilling Hester's dream that she can "touch the houses and [make them] fall down." In this respect, if Cholmondeley's *Red Pottage* can be said to figure a revolution, it also represents its failure.

Cholmondeley's work epitomizes the utopian energy discussed in Chapter Five, but it also reflects quite self-consciously on her audience's hostility toward the New Woman's so-called "hysterical" vision.

Thus far, I have considered two kinds of retreats in this chapter, the "boomerang" plotting of novels that punish New Women for their political and artistic ambitions and the representation of honorable retreat in self-reflexive novels about the antagonism New Women encounter as they pursue their utopian visions. In closing, I want to move beyond formal textual analysis and speculate about a third kind of retreat enacted in the 1890s, the retreat of real human beings, not literary representations of writers and politicians, from the controversy over the New Woman and the New Woman novel.

Consider, for example, the following review of *Olympia's Journal*, published by the *Athenaeum* in 1895. Noting that there is "perhaps rather too much of the bludgeon" in Holnut's treatment of the New Woman artist, this critic advises Holnut not to read "any more ladies' novels. He will not cure them so long as they can sell their fifteen thousands, and he will not choke off their public by this ponderous banter. If he does not like them, he had better leave them."[30] In other words, if Holnut does not like women writers, he should not write about them, this critic is suggesting. As Nancy Fix Anderson has noted, the same advice was given to Mrs. Linton in response to her increasingly negative characterizations of New Women. Neither *The One Too Many* nor *The New Woman in Haste and Leisure* were reviewed favorably; the latter in particular was considered so "sour in tendency," so "hard in style," that it "boomeranged" on Mrs. Linton, provoking so much "reactive sympathy for her targets" that she hastened her retirement.[31]

One might wonder, too, about what lies behind Hardy's decision to concentrate on poetry after *Jude* was reviewed so scathingly in 1895. In November of 1895, the *Athenaeum* called *Jude* a "titanically bad book" and reprimanded Hardy for joining the company of "inferior writers" who "have stirred up the mud with this controversy" over the New Woman.[32] As noted in Chapter Four, Margaret Oliphant considered it more "coarsely indecent . . . than any novel ever produced by the hand of a 'Master' in English."[33] How might these harsh judgments have affected Hardy's willingness to enter the fray again with another novel? One might also wonder why Edith Johnstone published so little, even though *A Sunless Heart* was reviewed quite favorably in 1894.[34] Why, for that matter, did Mary Cholmondeley disappear into the woodwork so quickly after *Red Pottage* was touted as *the* book to read in 1899?[35] Why did Gertrude Dix publish nothing after *The Image-Breakers* in 1900? And what happened to Ella Hepworth Dixon, Menie Muriel Dowie, Dorothy Leighton, and George Paston? If these writers published nothing after their New Woman novels, were their retreats from the literary marketplace "honorable"?

Most of these questions cannot be answered, because the primary documents—the correspondence, diaries, journals, and other private papers that might enable us to answer them—either have not been saved or cannot be located. Elizabeth Linton and Hardy are the only authors mentioned above (and this is not, of course, a complete listing of authors who wrote on the New Woman) whose papers have been deposited in research libraries. In other words, Linton and Hardy are the only authors mentioned above whose papers were deemed worthy of collection at the time. Theirs are the only names on this list that are familiar to librarians at the major research institutions with holdings in this period. Would Gertrude Dix's or Edith Johnstone's letters tell us why they stopped writing or stopped trying to get their work published? Are such papers sitting uncataloged in boxes somewhere in a library or a descendant's attic? Can this history ever be recovered? Can New Woman writers' retreats from the turn-of-the-century "controversy over realism in English fiction" ever be adequately documented? I wish I could answer these questions. I wish I could do more than gesture beyond the formalist analysis of texts that feels so constraining at this point in this project. But because my letters to scholars in the field and librarians at institutions like the Fawcett Library of Women's History in London have turned up nothing but helpful suggestions about other people and other institutions to query, I can only end this chapter by acknowledging what I cannot (re)claim: the history that remains so suggestively but so elusively beyond the documentation, in literature, of her culture's antagonism to the New Woman's radical agendas in the 1890s.[36]

7

Turning the Century,
Writing New Histories

We are just beginning—thanks largely to Dora Marsden and
The Freewoman—to perceive what the New Woman actually
is, and what logically she is to be. . . . Change, except to a
fiery few, is always a doubtful good, and Ibsen's doctrine that
a woman, even though she be a mother, belongs primarily to
herself—Nora of 1879 walked out of her doll's house a
woman "new" enough to do *The Freewoman* criticisms of H.
G. Wells's latest novels!—crashed across Europe and into the
America of the early '80s as hideous, unholy, blasphemous
preachment. . . . The dance is already on; the Ann Veronicas
and Julia Frances and Olivia Lattimores and all their sisters
are springing from the spawning presses, not spontaneous
creations, however, but daughters of a normal maternal pedi-
gree, for the New Woman has been in poetry and drama and
fiction for close to sixty years; at her worst portrayed according to her decade's definition of her; at her best that real sort
to whom neither society's attitude nor her creator's conscious
or unconscious point of view matters, whose only concern is
her own attitude toward life and herself.

Edna Kenton, "A Study of the Old 'New Woman' " *Bookman* (1913)[1]

Finished reading *Modern Women* by Laura Hans[s]on this morn-
ing. It has interested me very much but I think it is biased and
sometimes even cruel. It seems to me to be small and show
narrow sympathies when a writer can speak of George Eliot as a
"moralising old maid." I do not agree with L. Hans[s]on that
marriage (love) is the supreme end of a woman's life—it is

most certainly one of the great fundamentals of life, without which one is the poorer, but I think it is a morbid and unhealthy view to take that a woman's life is a failure because she never experiences love and marriage.

Ruth came this evening, and we sat at needlework. . . . Her affairs are in abeyance just now; Francoise is very worried—she wishes to form another free union, this time with Mr Hoffmeyer, and fears the effect of the news upon her Mother.

Eva Slawson, *Dear Girl* (1914)[2]

As THIS PASSAGE from the *Bookman* suggests, even if a considerable number of New Woman writers published nothing after 1900, the history of the New Woman and the New Woman novel did not end at the end of the nineteenth century. While the New Woman appeared less frequently in reviews written after 1900 than she did in the 1890s, she continued to be applauded and reviled in journals such as the *Westminster Review*, the *Bookman*, and *Arena*; additionally, she was featured in new publications such as *The Vote* and the *Freewoman*. And as the passage from *Dear Girl* (an anthology of letters and diaries written by two lower-middle-class women living in London between 1897 and 1916) suggests, the English public was still reading about her in 1914—still reading works like Hansson's that were published in the 1890s, still appropriating the literary discourse about the New Woman to deal with issues and situations in their own lives.

It should also be noted that although the writers mentioned at the end of Chapter Six withdrew from the literary and social debate on the New Woman, others continued to produce fiction about her. After working exclusively for almost five years in children's theater, for example, Netta Syrett began writing novels again in 1902, publishing four in quick succession between then and 1916.[3] While Florence

Dixie, Jane Hume Clapperton, Mona Caird, and George Paston championed other causes after 1900, Annie Holdsworth, Arabella Kenealy, John Strange Winter, and Sara Jeannette Duncan continued to publish New Woman fiction, whether or not they labeled their female characters specifically in that manner.[4] Moreover, as Edna Kenton notes, the twentieth century ushered in a new generation of writers who became involved in this now old controversy over the New Woman. Arnold Bennett, Joseph Conrad, H. G. Wells, Virginia Woolf, and D. H. Lawrence (to name only the writers who are still familiar to us): all wrote novels about New Women between 1900 and 1920. In works like *Anna of the Five Towns*, *Ann Veronica*, *The Secret Agent*, *Chance*, *The Voyage Out*, *Night and Day*, *The White Peacock*, and *The Lost Girl*, they addressed the various issues associated with the New Woman during the 1890s.

It is worth emphasizing that twentieth-century writers did not always invoke the same legacy as they produced new riffs on the theme of the New Woman. Their work was as heterogeneous as that written in the 1880s and 1890s; their characterization of new cultural pressures attending upon figuration of the New Woman after the turn of the century—the increasing militancy of both the suffrage campaign and the eugenics movement, for example, and the impact of World War I on British culture—are as diverse as those from the 1880s and 1890s we have examined in detail.[5] Rather than discussing Edwardian and modernist presentations of the New Woman in the same kind of detail, however, I simply want to suggest two things in this chapter: first, that the ongoing controversy over the New Woman and the New Woman novel needs to be factored into our genealogies of high modernism; and second, that the erasure of this turn-of-the-century history is particularly poignant in light of some of the tensions dividing contemporary American culture today.

On the one hand, the fact that issues of female identity fueled tremendous experimentation with narrative form in the 1890s suggests that now-forgotten turn-of-the-century women writers are "as responsible for 'originating' modernism" as better-known figures such as Joseph Conrad, Henry James, Kate Chopin, and Charlotte Perkins Gilman.[6] Emma Frances Brooke, Mona Caird, Mary Cholmondeley,

Gertrude Dix, Ella Hepworth Dixon, Florence Dixie, Arabella Kenealy, Edith Johnstone, Dorothy Leighton, George Paston, Olive Schreiner, Netta Syrett: all were both using and transforming nineteenth-century modes of representation at the same time as the customarily accredited proto-modernists and modernist originators. While their novels are rarely "associated with either proto-modernism or the high modernist canon," their narratives nonetheless feature the decentered subjectivity and disrupted linearity that we have come to associate with high modernism.[7]

But on the other hand, a genealogy of modernism cannot encompass the most radical feminist texts discussed in this book. Experimentation with the form of the novel is one legacy of the writers of the 1890s to high modernism; it is one way in which the controversy over realism in English fiction at the turn of the century both anticipated and contributed to the production of modernist form. But there were other legacies the modernists might have claimed from the New Woman novelists—for example, the legacy of socialist politics or of "woman-centered" artistic production we have seen in *Gloriana*, *Dear Faustina*, *Sir George Tressady*, *The Image-Breakers*, *A Sunless Heart*, and *Red Pottage*. Significantly, these New Woman novels highlight *not* women's ambivalence toward a radical reordering of both gender and class relations, *not* self-repression, but rather the culture's interest in curtailing or containing such socioliterary anarchy. These writers do not use form to obscure, repress, or mute their controversial feminist content. They flaunt their anger. They proclaim their heresies in loud voices. They document the efforts made to silence them. And they produce an aesthetic of political engagement that is quite different from the (ostensibly) apolitical formalism of high modernism. Notably, these are the novels that are getting written out of literary history again as contemporary critics valorize modernist formalism by arguing that a straightforward presentation of feminist content "would have been too threatening" in the 1890s.[8] These are the novels that are getting written out of history again as critics assume that the rise of high modernism was somehow inevitable, that modernism was the only aesthetic paradigm available in the early twentieth century.[9]

This study contributes to the characterization of a "gendered modernity,"[10] yet it also differs from many of the revisionary histories of modernism now being produced because the New Woman novel invites us to decenter the modernist aesthetic. Familiarity with the gynocentric writing of the 1890s encourages us, I think, to acknowledge that modernism succeeded in making itself *seem* like the only way to "make it new." If many New Woman novels do not fit the aesthetic paradigm of high modernism; if so much literature produced at the turn of the century is rendered invisible by the modernists' oppositions between either high art and popular culture, aesthetics and politics, this invisibility might make us question the usefulness of these oppositions.

New Woman novelists such as Gertrude Dix, Florence Dixie, Mary Cholmondeley, and Ella Hepworth Dixon conceived of art as an act of political engagement. The modernists—if not initially, then certainly by 1922—presented their reactionary politics as apolitical formalism, insisting upon the dissociation of art from the rest of culture. The New Woman novels were known to be "for" as well as about women; they were said to be written "from the Standpoint of Woman."[11] The modernist blasts of Wyndham Lewis, Ezra Pound, T. E. Hulme, and T. S. Eliot, on the other hand, create chasms between the "male" avant-garde and the oozy "femaleness" of mass culture.[12] Severing the Futurist "moment" from the Victorian past, Wyndham Lewis writes in the first issue of *Blast* in 1914:

BLAST—
years 1837 to 1900
CURSE Abysmal inexcusable middle-class
(also Aristocracy and Proletariat)[13]

"We have to hate our immediate predecessors, to get free of their authority," D. H. Lawrence confesses in a letter to Edward Garnett in 1913.[14] Is such hatred a sign of unvoiced competition and unacknowledged ancestry? Is the strident "maleness" of modernism a way of marking turf and engendering difference from the novels written about and "for" women at the turn of the century?

By answering such questions, we uncover the cultural politics that are repressed as the modernists establish the authority of their work.[15]

We might, for example, note how Lewis's characterization of the nineteenth century in the above allows him to claim all antibourgeois energy and all socioliterary radicalism as the property of the twentieth-century literary avant-garde. Lewis asserts the cultural centrality of his own aesthetic movement not simply by marginalizing but by grossly misrepresenting the history that precedes it. He can "make it new" by suggesting that the "old" was so flat and uninteresting and conventional. He can "make it new" by refusing to acknowledge that this phrase has been the rallying cry for artists at least since George Moore attacked the circulating libraries in 1885. He can "make it new" in a novel like *Tarr* by stylizing a male artist's violent objectification of his female subject in a rape.

Similarly, we might explore the anxiety of influence Lawrence acknowledges in his letter to Garnett by narrating what Gayatri Spivak terms a shifting limit between the 1890s debate about "the fiction of sexuality" and Lawrence's characterization of the "new" novel. "I want carbon," Lawrence growls in 1913, declaring both his impatience with social realism and his determination to affront his bourgeois readers with deep truths about human sexuality.[16] But how different is this from Grant Allen's or Iota's determination to tell "the truth" about female sexuality in *The Woman Who Did* or *A Yellow Aster*? To what extent is Lawrence simply appropriating the naturalistic New Woman novelists' project: claiming it as his own, counting on his audience's short-term cultural memory?

In the same vein, we might question Virginia Woolf's strategic devaluation of novelistic realism in "Mr. Bennett and Mrs. Brown," interrogating both her need to feminize realism and her willingness to disavow her own earliest novels, as she allies herself with and against James Joyce at this point in her career.[17] Or we might ask the more general question: why is there a place for the New Woman and the New Woman novel in histories of modernism written before World War I but no mention of them in the histories written subsequently? Writing for *The Vote* in 1911, Ford Madox Ford echoed Hardy and other 1890s writers in his essays on "The Woman of the Novelist," as he described his objections to nineteenth-century novelists' idealization of feminine purity.[18] Lawrence focused on the same issues in "Surgery for the

Novel—Or a Bomb," *without*, however, acknowledging the predecent set by the 1890s writers in challenging the "socio-literary" conventions of classic realism.[19] But in "Tradition and the Individual Talent" (1922), T. S. Eliot—who superceded both Ford and Lawrence as the most influential historian of modernism[20]—wrote this whole chapter of English literary and social history into oblivion when he not only defined a tradition that excludes women writers but also discredited the efforts made by women writers in the 1890s to associate "the mind that creates" with "the [wo]man who suffers."[21] How did the politics of the literary avant-garde change between 1911 and 1922 such that Eliot's version of literary history was more "useful" than either Ford's or Lawrence's?

The kind of detailed readings that would allow us to answer the questions outlined above remain beyond the scope of this study. Rather than closing down this history of the New Woman novel, I prefer to open it up—to emphasize the work that still lies ahead. I would emphasize something else as well: namely, that mine is a history, not the history of the New Woman novel, and the still-unwritten history of modernism to which this work points must be equally disinvested from all claims of universality and completeness. If "the making of the modern has become a critical preoccupation in recent works, both as a *subject* (how modernism was made by its practitioners) and as an *ideology* (how modernism has been and will be made by literary historians)"; if recent critics have "focus[ed] on different writers, isolate[d] different texts, and as a result, construct[ed] divergent explanations for the engendering of literary modernism,"[22] then what should matter to us is not whose version of literary history is "true" but rather what is at stake for ourselves in writing culture.[23]

To this end, I close with my characteristic response—a thumbnail autobiography of this project, in effect—to the question I am always asked about this fiction: "have you discovered any great novels?"[24] This book had its beginnings in a study of D. H. Lawrence's *The Lost Girl* (1920). I wanted to know why Lawrence resuscitated what I assumed was an outmoded character type, the New Woman, in this novel. And I wanted to know why this novel won a literary prize, given that it subsequently dropped so quickly out of both Lawrence's canon and the canon of high modernism. The dissertation I wrote was to have had a single chapter on the New Woman novel and the 1890s controversy over realism in English fiction; subsequent chapters on Woolf, Lawrence, and H. D. were to focus on the very different ways these early twentieth-century writers used the New Woman in their experimentations with narrative form.

But the grand plan collapsed once I started researching that first chapter, that is, once I had worked through the bibliographies of other critics and was tracking down leads in the British Museum—scanning the *Athenaeum*, the *Academy,* and the *Bookman* for reviews of novels that never made it into bibliographies, hunting down works cited in other primary texts about the New Woman. I surprised myself by producing a two-hundred-page draft of that first chapter. The strength of my identification with this material and these issues surprised me as well. I worried that I would be skewing the dissertation's focus on canonical figures like Woolf, Lawrence, and H. D. if I devoted more than a single chapter to the New Woman novel. I feared I would be jeopardizing my marketability as a job candidate if I dealt exclusively with noncanonical writers. Nonetheless, the pleasure of these texts, for me, was undeniable. The difficulty of conceptualizing an alternative to the traditional modeling of cultural and biological labor as antithetical activities; the anxiety associated with having internalized bourgeois culture's devaluation of women's intellectual and professional work; the struggle not to limit female sexuality to "the models and laws devised by the male subject;"[25] the need to move beyond the class-ism of bourgeois feminism: these were—and are—my issues, not simply the subject of my historical research. These are today's issues, not the concerns of turn-of-the-century feminists alone. I stand by my contention that reading the gynocentric writing of the 1890s in conjunction with the masterworks of high modernism makes modernism's reactionary cultural politics stand out in high relief—makes it possible to see how the female subject, not mass culture, functions as modernism's Other.[26] But, equally importantly, I think, familiarity with the turn-of-the-century debate on the New Woman also sheds light on the cultural dynamic of the 1980s whereby the feminist serves as the dominant culture's scapegoat.

On December 6, 1989, fourteen women were killed and another thirteen were injured when a gunman, later identified as Marc Lepinc, went on a rampage at the University of Montreal.[27] Blaming feminism for his lack of success in life, he ordered male students out of the way, lined the women up against the wall of a classroom, and executed them. At the turn-of-the-century, the New Woman was accused of instigating the second fall of man. The novels about her were referred to as "socio-literary portents" of anarchy and total cultural degeneration.[28] As Teresa deLauretis has argued, there *is* a connection between the rhetoric of violence and real violence.[29] Thus, one might well wonder: if there is a historical precedent, in the turn-of-the-century debate on the New Woman, for the increasingly strong current of antifeminism in contemporary culture, are we doomed to repeat this history because we have forgotten it?

When asked if I have found any great works in all my reading of "second-," "third-," and" fourth-rate" literature, I usually respond by invoking Barbara Smith's "Contingencies of Value" and turning the question back on my interlocutor: does your interest in aesthetic value disguise anxiety about the feminist politics of these novels? What cultural values are you defending through an emphasis on the formal rather than the ideological pleasures of these texts? When push comes to shove in such discussions, I qualify Smith's argument. I grant her claim, first, that literary value is constituted by a text's cultural distribution, rather than being an inherent property of the work itself, and second, that critics mystify the production of literary value when they want to preserve the illusion of objectivity, of ahistorical universality, regarding their agendas. But I also stop short of arguing that aesthetics are only a strategy for disguising bourgeois politics. At least for me, novels such as Mary Cholmondeley's *Red Pottage*, Gertrude Dix's *The Image-Breakers*, Ella Hepworth Dixon's *The Story of a Modern Woman*, and Dorothy Leighton's *Disillusion* offer a more satisfying reading experience than, say, Edith Johnstone's *A Sunless Heart*, Florence Dixie's *Gloriana*, or Rhoda Broughton's *Dear Faustina*. I concede that the latter are as awkwardly written as they are interesting, as explorations of woman's relationships with women and, in the case of *A Sunless Heart*, as a fantasy about a future in which gender does not obtain in aesthetic evaluations. In other words, if I take equal pleasure, as a feminist, in the politics of both groups of novels, I still recognize a difference in quality of writing.

But the last thing I want to do here is reinstate a model of literary hierarchies, thereby steering readers away from the texts that might be taken as my own topos of disvalue. Whether or not this is what Smith had in mind, I think that what she terms a "noncanonical theory of value" can be articulated only by acknowledging the "positionality" of a reading.[30] In the 1970s feminist critics made strong truth-claims in their revisionary histories.[31] More recently, postmodern ethnographers and literary theorists have suggested that we might be better served by bracketing such truth-claims and interrogating the construction of cultural "otherness" in our own narratives, as well as in the cultural texts we study. It is imperative for us "to confront the present with periods from the past," Holly Laird writes.[32] It is imperative for us to confront the differences between the past and the present, I would add, for how else can we imagine a future that is different from either?[33] I choose not to reinforce either a nostalgic configuration of sexual difference or a negative stereotyping of the feminist as a sexless spinster, a woman "terrified by childbirth and disgusted by sex."[34] I choose not to endorse the new histories of modernism that turn a historically specific construction of gender into a tranhistorical phenomenon. I prefer a history of modernism that includes the dreams of fictional New Women like Mary Cholmondeley's Hester Gresley, who want "to touch the houses and [make them] fall down" but also know how violent patriarchal culture's reactions to such desires can be.[35]

NOTES

Introduction.
Attending to Marginality

1. "The Apple and the Ego of Woman," *Westminster Review* 131 (1889): 374–382, 377.

2. See Penny Boumelha, *Thomas Hardy and Women: Sexual Ideology and Narrative Form* (Totowa, N.J.: Barnes and Noble, 1982), 8–93; Vineta Colby, " 'Devoted Amateur': Mary Cholmondeley and *Red Pottage*," *Essays in Criticism* 20 (1970): 213–228; A. R. Cunningham, "The 'New Woman Fiction' of the 1890s," *Victorian Studies* 17 (1973): 177–186; Gail Cunningham, *The New Woman and the Victorian Novel* (New York: Macmillan, 1978), Lloyd Fernando, "The Radical Ideology of the 'New Woman,' " *Southern Review* 2 (1967): 206–222; and *"New Women" in the Late Victorian Novel* (State College, Pa.: Pennsylvania State University Press, 1977); Leone Scanlon, "New Women in the Literature of 1883–1909," *University of Michigan Papers in Women's Studies* 2 (1976):133–158. Critics who view this material in a more positive light include Gerd Bjorhovde, *Rebellious Structures: Women Writers and the Crisis of the Novel, 1880–1900* (Oxford: Norwegian University Press, 1987); Diva Daims, "A Criticism of Their Own: Turn-of-the-Century Feminist Writers," *Turn-of-the-Century Women* 2, 2 (1985): 22–31; Linda Dowling, "The Decadent and the New Woman in the 1890s," *Nineteenth-Century Fiction* 33 (1979): 434–454; Katherine Ellis, "Paradise Lost: The Limits of Domesticity in the Nineteenth-Century Novel," *Feminist Studies* 2, 2/3 (1975): 55–63; Paul Eporn, *"Demos*: Late Victorian Values and the Replacement of Conjugal Love," *Studies in the Novel* 1, 3 (1969): 334–346; Susan Gorsky, "Old Maids and New Women: Alternatives to Marriage in the English Woman's Novel 1847–1915," *Journal of Popular Culture* 7 (1973): 68–85; Wendell V. Harris, "Egerton: Forgotten Realist," *Victorian Newsletter* 33 (1968): 31–35; Margaret Stetz, "Odd Woman, Half Woman, Superfluous Woman: What Was the New Woman?" *Iris, a*

Journal about Women 11 (1984): 20–21. Interestingly enough, the most negative
judgments of this material are made in the book-length studies (the one exception
being Bjorhovde's recent study); furthermore, essays in journals do not seem to
have dislodged those judgments.

3. Elaine Showalter, *A Literature of Their Own* (Princeton: Princeton University Press, 1977); Patricia Stubbs, *Feminism and the Novel: Women and Fiction,
1880- 1920* (Totowa, N.J.: Barnes and Noble, 1979). For a very different interpretation of Olive Schreiner's work, see Rachel Blau DuPlessis, *Writing Beyond the
Ending: Narrative Strategies of Twentieth-Century Women Writers* (Bloomington: Indiana University Press, 1985). In "Home Rule: The Colonies of the New Woman,"
Sandra Gilbert and Susan Gubar reiterate Showalter's view of the limitations of
late-nineteenth-century feminist writers; see *No Man's Land 2: Sex Changes* (New
Haven: Yale University Press, 1989), 47–62.

4. George Gissing, *The Odd Women* (New York: New American Library,
1983), 59.

5. [H. S. Scott and E. B. Hall], "Character Note. The New Woman," *Cornhill*
23 n.s. (1894): 365–368, 367.

6. See the Selected Bibliography for listings of New Woman novels and turn-
of-the-century criticism on this work.

7. Gayatri Spivak, *In Other Worlds: Essays in Cultural Politics* (New York and
London: Methuen, 1987), 103–117.

8. For interesting arguments about modernism's roots in the late nineteenth
century, see Bjorhovde, *Rebellious Structures*; Joseph Boone, "Modernist Maneuver-
ings of the Marriage Plot," *PMLA* 101, 3 (1986): 374–388; DuPlessis, *Writing
Beyond the Ending*; Marianne DeKoven, "Gendered Doubleness and the 'Origins'
of Modernist Form," *Tulsa Studies in Women's Literature* 8 (Spring 1989): 19–42;
Fredric Jameson, *The Political Unconscious: Narrative as a Socially Symbolic Act*
(Ithaca: Cornell University Press, 1981), 207–280; and Allon White, *The Uses of
Obscurity: The Fiction of Early Modernism* (London: Routledge & Kegan Paul,
1981).

9. Sheila Jeffreys, *The Spinster and Her Enemies: Feminism and Sexuality 1880–
1930* (London: Pandora Press, 1987), 2–16; David Rubenstein, *Before the Suffragettes: Women's Emancipation in the 1890s* (New York: St. Martin's Press, 1986), 3.

10. Showalter, *Literature*, quoting E. P. Thompson, 11.

11. Showalter defines the term "gynocriticism" in "Feminist Criticism in the
Wilderness," in *Writing and Sexual Difference*, ed. Elizabeth Abel (Chicago: University of Chicago Press, 1982), 14.

12. Stubbs, *Feminism and the Novel*, xiii.

13. Barbara Herrnstein Smith, "Contingencies of Value," *Critical Inquiry* 10
(1983): 1–33, 7. For an important defense of American sociohistorical feminist

criticism, see Janet Todd, *Feminist Literary History* (New York: Routledge, 1988), 1–4.

14. See, respectively, Stubbs, *Feminism and the Novel*, xv; and Showalter, *Literature*, 308–313.

15. See Bruce Robbins, "Modernism in History, Modernism in Power," in *Modernism Reconsidered*, ed. Robert Kiely (Cambridge: Harvard University Press, 1983), 229–245; Edward Said, "Reflections on Recent American 'Left' Criticism," *boundary 2* 8, 1 (Fall 1979): 11–30; Francis Mulhern, *The Moment of "Scrutiny"* (London, 1979); and Michael Levenson, *A Genealogy of Modernism: A Study of English Literary Doctrine, 1908–1922* (Cambridge: Cambridge University Press, 1984).

16. Barbara Christian, "The Race for Theory," *Cultural Critique* 6 (Spring 1987): 51–63. The shoe metaphor is Nancy K. Miller's; see "The Text's Heroine: A Feminist Critic and her Fictions," *Diacritics* 12 (Summer 1982): 53, and the cover of *The Poetics of Gender* (New York: Columbia University Press, 1986).

17. Janice Doane and Devon Hodges, *Nostalgia and Sexual Difference: The Resistance to Contemporary Feminism* (New York and London: Methuen, 1987), 3.

1. Preliminaries:
Naming the New Woman

1. Ellen Jordan, "The Christening of the New Woman: May 1894," *Victorian Newsletter* 48 (Spring 1983): 19. David Rubenstein traces a slightly different genealogy in the chapter entitled "The Revolt of the Daughters and the New Woman," in *Before the Suffragettes*, 16–23. He views Sarah Grand's March 1894 essay as itself a response to the four articles published still earlier that year in the *Nineteenth Century* on "The Revolt of the Daughters" (35 [1894]: 424–450).

2. See, respectively, Scott and Hall, "Character Note. The New Woman"; Gissing, *The Odd Women*; Elizabeth Lynn Linton, "The Wild Women as Politicians," *Nineteenth Century* 30 (1891): 79–88; and Emma Frances Brooke, *A Superfluous Woman* (New York: Cassell, 1894).

3. Jordan, citing Ouida in *North American Review* 158 (1894), 610.

4. Sigmund Freud, *Jokes and the Relation to the Unconscious* (New York and London: W. W. Norton, 1960).

5. Jordan, citing *Punch*, 26 May 1894, 252. In *Before the Suffragettes*, Rubenstein notes that *Punch* was either "so pleased with this verse, or so short of copy, that it repeated it little changed on 21 September 1895, p. 136" (22).

6. "The Apple and the Ego of Woman," 337.

7. See, respectively, Arthur Waugh, "Reticence in Literature," *Yellow Book* 1 (1894): 210–219; D. F. Hannigan, "Sex in Fiction," *Westminster Review* 143 (1895): 616–625; and James Ashcroft Noble, "The Fiction of Sexuality," *Contemporary Review* 67 (1895): 490–498.

8. Mrs. Eastwood, "The New Woman in Fiction and in Fact," *Humanitarian* 5 (1894): 375–379, 375.

9. *Athenaeum*, 23 March 1895, 375.

10. Mrs. Morgan-Dockrell, "Is the New Woman a Myth?" *Humanitarian* 8 (1896): 339–350, 340.

11. Elizabeth R. Chapman, *Marriage Questions in Modern Fiction, and Other Essays on Kindred Subjects* (London: George Redway, 1897), xiii.

12. "Socio-Literary Portents," *Speaker* 10 (1894): 683–685.

13. Nancy Cott, "Passionlessness: An Interpretation of Victorian Sexual Ideology, 1790–1850," *Signs* 4, 2 (1979): 219–236. See also Nancy Armstrong, *Desire and Domestic Fiction: A Political History of the Novel* (Oxford: Oxford University Press, 1987), 3–27; Nina Auerbach, *Woman and the Demon: The Life of a Victorian Myth* (Cambridge: Harvard University Press, 1982), 1–6; Carol Christ, "Victorian Masculinity and the Angel in the House," in *A Widening Sphere: Changing Roles for Victorian Women*, ed. Martha Vicinus (Bloomington: Indiana University Press, 1977), 146–162; Deidre David, "Ideologies of Patriarchy, Feminism and Fiction in *The Odd Women*," *Feminist Studies* 10 (Spring 1984): 117–139; Judith Newton, *Women, Power, and Subversion: Social Strategies in British Fiction, 1778–1886* (London and New York: Methuen, 1981); and Mary Poovey, *Uneven Developments: The Ideological Work of Gender in Mid-Victorian England* (Chicago: University of Chicago Press, 1988).

14. Grant Allen, *The Woman Who Did* (London: John Lane, 1895).

15. Vicinus models historical change more disruptively in her important review essay, "Sexuality and Power: A Review of Current Work on the History of Sexuality," *Feminist Studies* 8 (Spring 1982): 134–156. See also Judith Newton's "Making—and Remaking—History, Another Look at 'Patriarchy,' " in *Feminist Issues in Literary Scholarship*, ed. Shari Benstock (Bloomington: Indiana University Press, 1987), 124–140; and Mary Poovey's *Uneven Developments* for very important arguments about the need to recognize the instability of "dominant" ideologies.

16. Judith Walkowitz, *Prostitution and Victorian Society: Women, Class, and the State* (Cambridge and New York: Cambridge University Press, 1980); Coral Lansbury, *The Old Brown Dog: Women, Workers, and Vivisection in Edwardian England* (Madison: University of Wisconsin Press, 1985).

17. John Goode, "Women and the Literary Text," in *The Rights and Wrongs of Women*, ed. Juliet Mitchell and Ann Oakley (New York: Penguin, 1976), 230.

18. Margaret Devereux, *The Ascent of Woman* (London: John Lane, 1896), 58, 59.

19. Martha Vicinus, *Independent Women: Work and Community for Single Women, 1850–1920* (London: Virago, 1985).

20. See Deborah Epstein Nord, *The Apprenticeship of Beatrice Webb* (London: Macmillan, 1985); Stanley Pierson, *British Socialists, the Journey from Fantasy to Politics* (Cambridge and London: Harvard University Press, 1979), especially Chapters 1–3; Patricia Pugh, *Educate, Agitate, Organize: One Hundred Years of Fabian Socialism* (New York and London: Methuen, 1984); Lianne Radice, *Beatrice Webb and Sidney Webb, Fabian Socialists* (London: Macmillan, 1984); Sheila Rowbotham and Jeffrey Weeks, *Socialism and the New Life: The Personal and Sexual Politics of Edward Carpenter and Havelock Ellis* (London: Pluto Press, 1977); and Willard Wolfe, *From Radicalism to Socialism: Men and Ideas in the Formation of Fabian Socialist Doctrine, 1881–1890* (New York and London: Yale University Press, 1975).

21. August Bebel, *Women in the Past, Present, and Future*, trans. H. B. Adams Walter (London: The Modern Press, 1885), 90, 76.

22. Alys Pearsall Smith, "A Reply from the Daughters, II," *Nineteenth Century* 35 (1894): 446–450, 446, 450. Smith's is the last of a series of four essays entitled, respectively, "The Revolt of the Daughters," "Mothers and Daughters," "A Reply from the Daughters," I and II; see 424–450.

23. Mona Caird, *The Wing of Azrael* (London: Trubner & Co., 1889); *The Daughters of Danaus* (London: Bliss, Sands & Foster, 1894); "A Defense of the So-Called Wild Women," *Nineteenth Century* 31 (1892): 811–829, 815. For more recent feminist work on the inadequacy of traditional Marxism's approach to gender, see Rosalind Coward, "The Concept of the Family in Marxist Theory," in *Patriarchal Precedents* (London: Routledge & Kegan Paul, 1983), 141–187; Lise Vogel, *Marxism and the Oppression of Women Today* (Rutgers: Rutgers University Press, 1983); and Linda Nicholson, "Feminism and Marx: Integrating Kinship with the Economic," in *Feminism As Critique: On the Politics of Gender*, ed. Seyla Benhabib and Drucilla Cornell (Minneapolis: University of Minnesota Press, 1987), 16–30.

24. Teresa DeLauretis, *Technologies of Gender: Essays on Theory, Film, and Fiction* (Bloomington: Indiana University Press, 1987), 31–50.

25. Linton, "The Discontented Woman," in *The Girl of the Period*, 2 vols. (London: R. Bentley, 1883), 2:290, 285. See Nancy Fix Anderson, *Woman Against Women in Victorian England: A Life of Elizabeth Lynn Linton, 1822–1899* (Bloomington: Indiana University Press, 1987) for a discussion of Linton's status as the "Grundyometer" at the turn of the century (197).

26. W. T. Stead, "The Novel of the Modern Woman," *Review of Reviews* 10 (1894): 64–74, 74.

27. "The Apple and the Ego of Woman," 377.

28. See, respectively, G. S. Layard, ed., *Mrs. Lynn Linton, Her Life, Letters, and Opinions* (London 1901), 292, as quoted by Showalter in *Literature*, 205; Stead, "The Novel of the Modern Woman," 65; "A Century of Feminine Fiction," *All The Year Round* 12 (1894): 537–540, 538; Noble, "The Fiction of Sexuality," 490–498; Hugh E. M. Stutfield, "Tommyrotics," *Blackwood's* 157 (1895): 833–845; Linton, "The Wild Women as Politicians," 80; "The Strike of a Sex," *Quarterly Review* 179 (1894): 289–318; Caird, "A Defense of the So-Called Wild Women," 813.

29. Janet E. Hogarth, "The Monstrous Regiment of Women," *Fortnightly Review* 68 (1897): 926–936, 926.

30. Walter Besant, "Candour in English Fiction," *New Review* 2 (1890): 6–9, 7–8.

31. Linton, "Womanliness," in *The Girl of the Period*, 2: 113.

32. Grant Allen, "Plain Words on the Woman Question," *Fortnightly Review* 52 (1889): 448–458, 455.

33. Linton, "Womanliness," in *The Girl of the Period*, 2: 113.

34. Neil Hertz, "The Medusa's Head: Male Hysteria Under Political Pressure," *Representations* 4 (Fall 1983): 27–54.

35. Linton, "The Wild Women as Politicians," 80; "The Wild Women as Social Insurgents," *Nineteenth Century* 30 (1891): 596–605, 597.

36. For more detailed discussion of the analogy Victorians drew between the sexual "otherness" of (white) women and the racial or cultural otherness of non-Europeans, see Gilbert and Gubar, *No Man's Land 2: Sex Changes*, 3–46; and Sander Gilman, "Black Bodies, White Bodies: Toward an Iconography of Female Sexuality in Late Nineteenth-Century Art, Medicine, and Literature," *Critical Inquiry* 12 (Autumn 1985): 201–242.

37. See also Charles Harper, *Revolted Woman, Past, Present, and To Come* (London: Elkin Mathews, 1894), 48; and Devereux, *Ascent of Woman*, 22–23. Virginia Woolf describes this concept in detail in *Three Guineas* (New York: Penguin, 1977), 147–157.

38. In *Before the Suffragettes*, Rubenstein notes that smoking was a "curiously potent symbol of emancipation" (19) and cites two additional articles focusing on this gesture of rebellion: E. B. Harrison, "Smoke," *Nineteenth Century* 36 (1894): 389–396, and "Should Ladies Smoke," *Lady's Realm* 7 (1900): 513–518.

39. Auerbach, *Woman and the Demon*, 186.

40. Smith, "The Reply of the Daughters," 450. See Alice Jardine's "Spaces for Further Research," in *Gynesis: Configurations of Woman and Modernity* (Ithaca: Cornell University Press, 1985) for further discussion of the way in which women's discourse disrupts the discourse on "Woman."

41. The more primary anxiety, in other words, is not about gender in particular but about a more generally defined ability to name reality. For interesting discussions of connections often made between sexual and linguistic "deviancy" or disruptiveness, see Doane and Hodges, *Nostaligia and Sexual Difference*, 12–14, and Thais Morgan, "Mixed Gender, Mixed Metaphor: Swinburne and the Victorian Critics," *Victorian Newsletter* 73 (Spring 1988): 16–29.

2. The Controversy over Realism

1. Chapman, *Marriage Questions*, xiii.

2. Jane Tompkins, *Sensational Designs: The Cultural Work of American Fiction, 1790–1860* (New York: Oxford University Press, 1985), xi, xviii.

3. William Frierson, "The English Controversy over Realism in Fiction, 1885–1895," *PMLA* 43 (1928): 533–550.

4. Carla L. Peterson, *The Determined Reader: Gender and Culture in the Novel from Napoleon to Victoria* (New Brunswick and London: Rutgers University Press, 1987), 227.

5. See, respectively, Stutfield, "Tommyrotics," 840; Max Beerbohm, as quoted by John Mark Longaker in *Ernest Dowson* (Philadelphia: University of Pennsylvania Press, 1945), 135; and Stead, "The Novel of the Modern Woman," 65.

6. Thomas Hardy, *Jude the Obscure*, ed. Norman Page (New York: W.W. Norton, 1978), 7–8.

7. Cunningham, *The New Woman*, 107–108; see also Boumelha, *Thomas Hardy*, 132.

8. George Moore, *Literature at Nurse, or Circulating Morals*, ed. Pierre Coustillas (Sussex: Harvester Press, 1976), 32. As Allon White notes in *The Uses of Obscurity*, "we still have no standard, detailed history of the publication and reception of fiction after the collapse of the three-decker" (31). Gaye Tuchman and Nina Fortin's study, *Edging Women Out: Victorian Novelists, Publishers, and Social Change* (New Haven and London: Yale University Press, 1989) begins to fill in the gap left by the work of Richard Altick (*The English Common Reader: A Social History of the Mass Reading Public, 1800–1900* [Chicago: University of Chicago Press, 1957]), Q. D. Leavis (*Fiction and the Reading Public* [London: Chatto & Windus, 1932]), and Guinevere Griest (*Mudie's Circulating Library and the Victorian Novel* [Bloomington: Indiana University Press, 1970]). But the fact that Tuchman and Fortin base their research on Macmillan's records does not allow

them to consider how the introduction of new publishing houses would have affected the marketplace in the 1890s. See both Chapter Two of White's study, "Obscure Writing and Private Life, 1880–1914," and Margaret Stetz's " 'Life's Half-Profits': Writers and their Readers in Fiction of the 1890s" (*Nineteenth-Century Lives*, ed. Lawrence Lockridge, John Maynard, and Donald Stone [Cambridge: Cambridge University Press, 1989]), for interesting speculations about how the relationship between authors, readers, and publishers was changing at the end of the century. The autobiographies of the writers and publishers are also of interest, though often less helpful than one might hope. See Gertrude Atherton, *Adventures of a Novelist* (New York: Liverwright, 1932); Helen Black, *Notable Women Authors of the Day* (Glasgow: David Bryce & Son, 1893); E. F. Benson, *As We Were: A Victorian Peepshow* (London: Longman Green & Co., 1930); Ella Hepworth Dixon, *As I Knew Them* (London: Hutchinson, 1929); William Heinemann, *The Hardships of Publishing* (1893); George Paston [Emily Morse Symonds], *At John Murray's: A Record of a Literary Circle, 1843–1942* (London: John Murray, 1932); Grant Richards, *Author Hunting, by an Old Literary Sports Man* (New York: McCann, 1934); William Pett Ridge, *I Like to Remember* (London: Hodder & Stoughton, 1925); Percy Russell, *The Author's Manual*, 4th ed. (London: Digby & Long, 1891), and *A Guide to British and American Novels* (London: Digby & Long, 1894); Evelyn Sharpe, *Unfinished Adventures: Selected Reminiscences from an English Woman's Life* (London: John Lane, 1933); Netta Syrett, *The Sheltering Tree* (London, G. Blest, 1939); Helen Thomas [daughter of James Ashcroft Noble], *As It Was* (New York: Harper, 1927); *The Life of John Oliver Hobbes, As Told in Her Correspondence*, ed. Rev. Weldon (London: John Murray, 1911).

9. See, in particular, the *New Review*'s follow-up to the symposium on "Candour," entitled "The Tree of Knowledge" (*New Review* 10 [1891]: 675–690). Many of the same writers who participated in the earlier debate voiced their opinions again, arguing variously that the "new" realism either had or had not brought about both the "fall" of the novel and the corruption of the reading public.

10. Linton, "Candour in English Fiction," *New Review*, 2 (1890): 10–14, 14.

11. Hardy, "Candour in English Fiction," *New Review* 2 (1890): 15–21, 17.

12. Havelock Ellis, "Concerning 'Jude the Obscure,' " *Savoy* 6 (1896): 35–49, 46.

13. W. S. Holnut, *Olympia's Journal* (London: George Bell, 1895), 36–37.

14. Edmund Gosse, *Questions at Issue* (London: W. Heinemann, 1893).

15. Michel Foucault, *The History of Sexuality, I* (New York: Vintage Books, 1980), 11. See Boumelha, *Thomas Hardy*, 9–26, for a Foucauldian analysis of the discourse on sexuality in New Woman novels.

16. See, in particular, Stephen Marcus, "Freud and Dora: Story, History, Case History," in *In Dora's Case: Freud—Hysteria—Feminism*, ed. Charles Bernheimer and Claire Kahane (New York: Columbia University Press, 1985), 56–91.

17. It is worth remembering that Freud's work was not translated into English until the 1910s. During the 1890s, a very lively discourse on sexuality was produced in England quite independent of developments in European clinics. The English "sexologists," Edward Carpenter and Havelock Ellis, were not only on the cutting edge of scientific research in England; they were also well connected in literary and radical socialist circles. Though their work has proven much less influential in the long run than Freud's or his followers, at the turn of the century their circle of influence included as many literary figures as scientists. See Paul Robinson, *The Modernization of Sex* (New York: Harper & Row, 1976), 4–40; Sheila Rowbotham and Jeffrey Weeks, *Socialism and the New Life*; and Samuel Hynes, *The Edwardian Turn of Mind* (Princeton: Princeton University Press, 1968), 138–174.

18. Oliphant, "The Anti-Marriage League," *Blackwood's* 159 (1896): 135–149, 136.

19. It is also worth noting the facility of the New Woman novelists' dismissal of "old" realism, the imprecision of their allusions not only to French but also to English literature. Nowhere do the New Woman novelists name their disdained precursors. Nowhere do they stipulate exactly to whom their criticisms apply. If it is impossible to know who they had in mind as "old" realists, it is nonetheless clear that this sense of both the old regime's and their foreign competitors' failings empowered this new generation of novelists and gave them a sense of vocation and direction.

20. Richards, *Author Hunting*, 8.

21. Mark Samuels Lasner notes that the two-volume format remained uncommon. My thanks go to both him and Margaret Stetz for reading and correcting details in this chapter.

22. Showalter, *Literature*, 158–159.

23. For an important discussion of publishers' attempts to market personality, see Margaret Stez, " 'Life's Half-Profits': Writers and Their Readers in Fiction of the 1890s," in *Nineteenth-Century Lives*, ed. Lawrence Lockridge, John Maynard, and Donald Stone (Cambridge: Cambridge University Press, 1989), 172–174.

24. George Egerton [Mary Chavelita Bright], *Kyenotes* (London: John Lane, 1893), 29.

25. As noted by Margaret Stez, " 'Life's Half-Profits,' " 174.

26. See Chris Baldick, *The Social Mission of English Criticism* (Oxford: Oxford University Press, 1985); and Terry Eagleton, *Literary Theory* (Minneapolis: University of Minnesota Press, 1983), 17–53. See also Nigel Cross, *The Common Writer:*

Life in Nineteenth-Century Grub Street (Cambridge: Cambridge University Press, 1985), 205.

27. George Gissing, *New Grub Street* (London: Penguin, 1985), 43.

28. Linton, "Literature: Then and Now," *Fortnightly Review* 52 (1890): 517–531, 527. For similar arguments about the adverse effect of democratization, see Percy Russell, *The Author's Manual* (4th ed., 1891), 252–260; *A Guide to British and American Novels*, 228–230; and *The Literary Manual. A Complete Guide to Authorship* (London: London Literary Society, 1886), 32–49; and *"John Strange Winter." A Volume of Personal Record*, ed. Oliver Bainbridge (London: East & West, 1916), 157. For arguments focusing on the feminization of the literary world, see A.G.P. Sykes, "The Evolution of the Sex," *Westminster Review* 143 (1895): 396–400; Hubert Crackanthorpe, "Reticence in Literature: Some Roundabout Remarks," *Yellow Book* 2 (1894): 259–269; and the *Athenaeum*, 23 March 1895, 375.

29. See Boumelha, *Thomas Hardy*, 63. Tuchman and Fortin's model of the "empty field phenomenon" in *Edging Women Out*—whereby men discredit their female precursors in any profession prior to claiming that field as a "male" (and therefore, culturally respected) occupation—leaves them wedded to the idea of women's victimization by male institutions, an idea that is not entirely supported by the history of the New Woman novel. For similar reasons, I have trouble with Gilbert and Gubar's glib characterization of the "war between the sexes" at the turn of the century in *No Man's Land 1: The War of the Words* (New Haven and London: Yale University Press, 1987). (See, in particular, "The Men's Case" and "The Women's Case," 3–64, 65–124.) A more supple model needs to be developed, one that would explain two things: first, how writing by men was feminized and thereby devalued at the turn of the century (e.g., the way Grant Allen's work was dismissed along with all the other New Woman novels); and second, why women participated in the devaluation of female writing (e.g., Linton's or Oliphant's obsession with discrediting New Woman fiction).

30. Laura Marholm Hansson, *Six Modern Women*, trans. Hermione Ramsden (London: John Lane, 1896), 70.

31. Devereux, *Ascent of Woman*, 7.

32. Stead, "The Novel of the Modern Woman," 64. Hansson and Devereux are cited in Stutfield, "Tommyrotics," 104; and William Courtney, *The Feminine Note in Fiction* (London: Chapman & Hall, 1904), xv–xvi. See also an unsigned review in the *Academy*, 17 February 1894, 143–144, on the "new dispensation" of women novelists, and H. E. Harvey's "The Voice of Woman," 193–194; both of these critics view the feminization of the literary marketplace quite favorably. On the other hand, A.G.P. Sykes mocks the "temporar[y] . . . succes[s"] of "women's pictures, women's plays, [and] women's books" in "The Evolution of the Sex (397). And the reviewer for the *Speaker* (as quoted in "Some Modern Ideas on Marriage,"

Westminster Review 143 [1895]: 520—537) argues that "it would save the public machinery of emotion a great deal of fatigue if the ladies who have been freezing our blood, young and middle-aged, with stories of the inconvenience found by their sex in associating with ours, would put their heads together and formulate their demands. The time for definition has come, and, the demands being once defined, we might be allowed a spell of quiet in which to study them and find out exactly what these ladies want" (530).

33. An advertisement in the *Athenaeum*, 27 July 1895, for Heinemann's new fiction series is of particular interest in this context. Acknowledging a "slight reaction against a recent tendency in literary criticism," the ad goes on to suggest that "we are in danger of obscuring the central features of literature, and the beauty of the greatest writing in each country, by an exaggerated attention to points which are rather scientific than literary" (117). In the new series that Heinemann is proposing, "Literature will be interpreted as the most perfect utterance of the ripest thought of the finest minds"; moreover, "the classics of each country rather than its oddities and . . . obsolete features" will be given "particular attention," the ad promises. Given all of the public controversy regarding both the New Woman novel and Wilde's trial, I read this promulgation of a transhistorical, universal standard of aesthetic excellence as a defensive move on Heinemann's part—an attempt to reassure readers that his firm will no longer be associated with such risqué matters.

34. Linton, "Candour," 14.

35. Note, however, that her essay for *Fortnightly Review*, "Literature: Then and Now," contradicts her argument in "Candour."

36. As quoted by Katherine Lyon Mix in *A Study in Yellow: The Yellow Book and Its Contributors* (Lawrence: University of Kansas Press, 1960), 173.

37. Henry James, "The Future of the Novel," in *The Future of the Novel*, ed. Leon Edel (New York: Vintage, 1956), 40—41. Edel notes that James's essay was first published in 1900.

38. Waugh, "Reticence," 209.

39. See, respectively, Stutfield, "Tommyrotics"; B. A. Crackanthorpe, "Sex in Modern Literature," *Nineteenth Century* 218 (1895): 607—616; Hannigan, "Sex in Fiction"; and Janet E. Hogarth, "Literary Degenerates," *Fortnightly Review* 63 (1895): 586—592. See also Grant Allen, "The New Hedonism," *Fortnightly Review* 61 (1894): 377—392; Thomas Bradfield, "A Dominant Note of Some Recent Fiction," *Westminster Review* 142 (1894): 537—545; "A Century of Feminine Fiction," 537—540; Hubert Crackanthorpe, "Reticence in Literature: Some Roundabout Remarks," 259—269; "Borgia Smudgiton," "She-Notes," *Punch* 106 (1894): 109, 129; "Socio-Literary Portents," 683—685; and "Recent Novels," *Spectator* 483 (1895): 431—433.

40. See Showalter, *Literature*, 184–185.

41. W. T. Stead, "The Book of the Month. 'The Woman Who Did,' by G. Allen," *Review of Reviews* 11 (1895), 177–190, 177. As Stead puts it, "the net effect of [Allen's] story is to convince the most casual reader that the sheer anchor of all morality in sexual relations is the sense of parenthood" (178). Thus, Stead argues, Allen ultimately redeems rather than eradicates marriage as a social institution.

42. Millicent Garrett Fawcett, " 'The Woman Who Did,' " *Contemporary Review* 67 (1895), 625–631, 626. See also Percy Addleshaw's " 'The Woman Who Did,' " *Academy* 47 (1895): 186–187.

43. Lucas Cleeve [Adelina G. I. Kingscote], *The Woman Who Wouldn't* (London: Simpkin, Marshall, & Co., 1895); Victoria Cross [Vivian Cory], *The Woman Who Didn't* (London: John Lane, 1895).

44. Cleeve, *The Woman Who Wouldn't*, vi.

45. In the first of these Wilde provides an update on the life of the governess after whom Thackeray modeled Becky Sharpe. According to Wilde, this woman's unhappiness as a companion to a "very selfish and rich old woman" had been the original inspiration for an episode in Becky's life. After reading *Vanity Fair*, however, Becky's real-life counterpart ran way with her employer's son. It is said, Wilde notes with glee, that "for a short time [she] made a great splash in society, quite in Mrs. Rawdon Crawley's style, and entirely by Mrs. Rawdon Crawley's methods" ("The Decay of Lying," in *Literary Criticism of Oscar Wilde*, ed. Stanley Weintraub [Lincoln: University of Nebraska Press, 1968], 186. First published in *Nineteenth Century* 25 [1889]: 35–56, the essay was reprinted in revised form in *Intentions*, [1891], 3–53). A second story, ostensibly from Wilde's own life, has a similar punch line. Wilde describes his fascination with a woman whose beauty and "entire vagueness of character" are exceptional. She is the prototypical New Woman: a "kind of Proteus, and as much a failure in all her transformations as that wondrous sea-god" (185). "She seem[s] to have no personality at all, but simply the possibility of many types." Reading a serialized story "in one of the French magazines," Wilde is shocked to recognize the heroine's similarity to his friend. When he reads the final installment of the story several months later, he writes to his friend, noting that "her double in the story had behaved in a very silly manner" by "running away with a man absolutely inferior to her, not merely in social station, but in character and intellect also." But before she receives his letter, he hears word that she has run away with a man who will desert her within six months. Years later, when Wilde meets her again, he asks her "whether the story had had anything to do with her action." "She told me that she had felt an absolutely irresistible impulse to follow the heroine step by step in her strange and fatal progress, and that it was with a

feeling of real terror that she had looked forward to the last few chapters of the story. When they appeared, it seemed to her that she was compelled to reproduce them in life, and she did so" (186). "Life imitates Art far more than Art imitates Life," Wilde concludes, refuting the reflection theory of art by inverting the Platonic formulation of the relation between the two. It is precisely because Life imitates Art that so many critics responded so violently to the success of New Woman novels. A considerable amount of work has been done recently on gender in reader-response criticism. Discussions of women's identificatory reading experience that seem particularly germaine here include: Dale Bauer, "Identificatory Reading," *Perigraph* 2 (Fall 1988): 7–21; Rachel Brownstein, *Becoming a Heroine* (New York: Viking Press, 1982); and Helene Cixous and Catherine Clement, "The Untenable," in *The Newly Born Woman* (Minneapolis: University of Minnesota Press, 1987), 147–160.

46. Tompkins, *Sensational Designs*, xi.

47. *Athenaeum*, 12 May 1894, 392.

48. Ibid., 6 January 1894, 145.

49. Courtney, *Feminine Note*, xii. Courtney was a reviewer for the *Daily Telegraph* in the 1890s.

50. Notably, Courtney does not discredit *all* women writers; when he argues that "artistry is a masculine mode," he does concede that the work of a "masculine genius" like George Eliot meets his standard for the novel as a "work of art" (xii). But of course Eliot is no longer writing fiction by this point in time—therefore, she represents the standard that contemporary women writers have not achieved.

51. Smith, "Contingencies of Value," 1–33; Christine Froula, "The Daughter's Seduction: Sexual Violence and Literary History," in *Feminist Theory in Practise and Process*, ed. Micheline R. Malson, Jean F. O'Barr, Sarah Westphal-Wihl, and Mary Wyer (Chicago and London: University of Chicago Press, 1989), 139–162.

52. Linton anticipates the argument on aesthetics in her 1894 novel, *The One Too Many* (Chicago and New York: F. Tennyson Neely). In spite of having taken Beatrice Harraden under her wing in person, Linton has one of her characters object to another character's reading Harraden's first novel, *Ships That Pass in The Night*, because "it is not a classic, and cannot be a masterpiece" (262–263). "There are not wanting signs that the present outburst of sexual hysteric (for which, to their disgrace, women have been chiefly responsible) has spent its fury, and will give place before long to the recognized masters of English fiction," suggests a critic writing for the *Athenaeum* in a review of George Egerton's *Discords* (23 March 1895, 375). "For the first one or two romantic expositions of the sex-problem in its sharpest form there was something like an adequate reason," notes another critic reviewing *The Woman Who Didn't* for the *Athenaeum* in 1895 (2 September 1895, 382). "Almost every human problem may, at least once,

demand literary expression as a right, or may obtain it without very serious protest. But indefinite repetition of the same thing will have to be judged *according to a different standard*," he then warns (382, emphasis added). See also Boyd Winchester, "The Eternal Feminine—I. The New Woman," *Arena* 27 (1902): 367–373. Winchester shares Courtney's belief that "thought is masculine; sentiment is feminine" (369).

3. The Romance Plot

1. George Eliot, *Daniel Deronda* (New York: New American Library, 1979), 573, 576.

2. Edith Slater, "Men's Women in Fiction," *Westminster Review* 149 (1898): 571–577, 575.

3. Oliphant, "The Anti-Marriage League," 136.

4. The term is Nancy K. Miller's in, "Emphasis Added: Plots and Plausibilities in Women's Fiction," *PMLA* 96, 1 (1981): 36–47.

5. Hardy, "Candour," 17.

6. Tony Tanner, *Adultery in the Novel: Contract and Transgression* (Baltimore and London: Johns Hopkins Press, 1979), 15.

7. Eliot, of course, presents the "pattern" of the good woman as a Jewish ideal, not a Judeo-Christian English one, in this speech by Daniel's mother; that should not keep us from recognizing this as Eliot's exotic recasting of the "native" English "Woman Question."

8. Leslie Rabine, *Reading the Romantic Heroine: Text, History, Ideology* (Ann Arbor: University of Michigan Press, 1987), viii.

9. Olive Schreiner, *The Story of an African Farm* (London: Chapman & Hall, 1883; rept. Penguin, 1971), 183.

10. Stead, "The Novel of the Modern Woman," 65.

11. The stage conventions referred to are those of nineteenth-century theater: if the audience can see three walls of a room on stage, they sit behind the fourth, which functions like a one-way mirror—letting them observe events on stage without being seen themselves.

12. Armstrong, *Desire and Domestic Fiction*, 24.

13. Ibid., quoting Mrs. Gaskell's *Mary Barton*, 45.

14. Showalter offers the most negative evaluation of Schreiner's work, arguing that she was "sadly underambitious" and motivated by a "perverse will to fail," even though she "made an important contribution to the female tradition" (*Litera-*

ture, 203, 198). Gilbert and Gubar seem to be following Showalter's example in *No Man's Land 2,* as they conclude their chapter entitled "Home Rule" by underscoring the same claustrophia Showalter finds in her work. Schreiner, they argue "forged a tradition that, by identifying the woman primarily with the womb, continued to deny women either tactical strategies for resistance to male domination or psychological strategies for coming to terms with female eroticism" (82). In *Writing Beyond the Ending* and *Rebellious Structures,* DuPlessis and Bjorhovde offer more positive readings of Schreiner's work (20–30, and 25–49, respectively). But I think both DuPlessis and Bjorhovde go too far in the other direction by suggesting that Schreiner is the key transition figure in the move beyond realism at the turn of the century—*the* writer (according to DuPlessis) who sets the stage for modernist renovations of the novel. Too many other writers were doing this to warrant giving any one author this kind of acclaim, I think. Other important recent work on Schreiner includes Carol Barash, ed., *An Olive Schreiner Reader: Writings on Women and South Africa* (New York: Pandora Press, 1987); Ruth First, *Olive Schreiner* (New York: Schocken Books, 1980); and Joyce Berkman, *The Healing Imagination of Olive Schreiner* (Amherst: University of Massachusetts Press, 1989).

15. For a similar reading of other women writer's refiguration of the "dysphoric" ending, see Dale Bauer,"Kate Chopin: *The Awakening,*" in *Feminist Dialogics: A Theory of Failed Community* (Albany: State University of New York Press, 1988), 129–138; and Margaret Higonnet, "Speaking Silences," in *The Female Body in Western Culture,* ed. Susan Rubin Suleiman (Cambridge: Harvard University Press, 1986).

16. Mikhail Bakhtin, "Discourse in the Novel," *The Dialogic Imagination,* trans. Caryl Emerson and Michael Holquist (Austin: University of Texas Press, 1981), 259–422.

17. Caird, *The Wing of Azrael,* vii. See also Boumelha's discussion of this novel, *Thomas Hardy,* 79–81.

18. Gilbert and Gubar argue in *No Man's Land 2* that "no Jill the Ripper [myth] . . . emerg[ed] to retaliate for her sex either in fact or fiction during the *fin de siècle*" (48). Yet, a number of narratives are written during this period about female violence as an assertion of agency, including *The Wing of Azrael,* Hardy's *Tess of the D'Urbervilles,* and George Egerton's short story, "Wedlock," published in *Discords* (1894). The same motif appears in Sarah Grand's *The Heavenly Twins* when one of Grand's protagonists dreams of murdering her husband; as in Eliot's *Daniel Deronda,* which prefigures all of these novels, the murder in *The Heavenly Twins* remains imagined, not literal. Both the American writer Susan Glaspell's newly anthologized short story, "A Jury of Her Peers" and Joseph Conrad's *The Secret Agent* are worth mentioning in this context as well.

19. Joseph Boone, *Tradition Counter Tradition* (Chicago: University of Chicago Press, 1987), 7.

20. For a similar emphasis on the community's—not the individual's—failures, see Bauer, *Feminist Dialogics*, and Scanlon's reading of *Story of an African Farm* in "New Women in the Literature of 1883–1909," 154.

21. Hardy, "Candour," 16–17, 19.

22. Hardy, *Tess of the D'Urbervilles*, ed. P. N. Furbank (London: Macmillan, 1976).

23. The term is Ian Watt's, as used in *The Rise of the Novel: Studies in Defoe, Richardson, and Fielding* (Berkeley: University of California Press, 1967) to talk about the importance of graphic description in the history of the novel.

24. See Elizabeth Ermarth, *Realism and Consensus in the English Novel* (Princeton: Princeton University Press, 1983).

25. Boumelha, *Thomas Hardy*, 132.

26. Mary Jacobus, "Sue the Obscure," *Essays in Criticism* 25 (1975): 304–328.

27. I am grateful to Margaret Stetz for first pointing this out to me.

28. Roland Barthes, *A Lover's Discourse: Fragments* (New York: Hill and Wang, 1978).

29. For a similarly tragic (and wrong-headed, I think) modeling of the "doomed encounter between the female self and the middle-class world," see Myra Jehlen, "Archimedes and the Paradox of Feminist Criticism," *Signs* 6 (1981): 575–610, 597; and Stubbs, *Feminism and the Novel*, xi.

30. See Hardy, *Tess*, 408.

31. While acknowledging that Tess provokes "an unusually overt maleness in the narrative voice," Boumelha also assumes that narrative omniscience is an "androgynous" mode (*Thomas Hardy,* 120). I am arguing instead that the tension between female characters and male narrators in novels like *Tess* at the turn of the century exposes the gendered power dynamic that remains implicit and unchallenged in the convention of narrative omniscience. In *This Sex Which Is Not One*, Luce Irigaray argues that psychoanalysis thematizes sexuality but "has not lead to an interpretation of the *sexualization of discourse*" ("The Power of Discourse," *This Sex Which Is Not One*, trans. Catherine Porter [Ithaca: Cornell University Press, 1985], 73). Freud, she goes on to suggest, does not fully analyze the presuppositions of the production of discourse. . . . The questions that Freud's theory and practise address to the scene of representation do not include the question of the sexualized determination of that scene" (73). If Freud does not address this issue, it is nonetheless one that contemporary novelists were dealing with in their fiction. See, for example, the unusually overt maleness of the narrator's voice in Gissing's *The Odd Women* and George Moore's *A Mummer's Wife* (London: Vizetelly, 1885) and *Esther Waters* (London: W. Scott, 1894).

32. Boone, *Tradition*, 129; see also Boumelha, *Thomas Hardy*, 132.

33. John Strange Winter [Henrietta Stannard], *A Blameless Woman* (New York: International News Co., 1894).

4. Erotomania

1. Oliphant, "The Anti-Marriage League," 138.

2. Most of the criticism written to date on the New Woman novel focuses on the first of the four groupings of novels mentioned here, what Gail Cunningham terms the "purity school" fiction (*New Women*, 64). See also Fernando, *"New Women" in the Late Victorian Novel*, 131–133; Showalter, *Literature*, 182–189. Because so much has already been said about the novels that idealize female virtue, I want to turn my attention elsewhere and concentrate on the New Woman novels that explore alternatives to the Victorian ideology of womanliness.

3. Armstrong, *Desire*, 11.

4. Charlotte Brontë, *Shirley* (New York and London: Penguin, 1985), 462. In "A Study of the Old 'New Woman,' Part I," Edna Kenton identifies Jane Eyre as the first New Woman and then traces a lineage from Brontë, through Tennyson's *Princess*, Meredith's *Diana of the Crossways* and *The Amazing Marriage* to the late-century works we have been discussing (*Bookman* 37 [1913]: 154–158).

5. Peter Cominos, in *Suffer and Be Still: Women in the Victorian Age*, ed. Martha Vicinus (Bloomington: Indiana University Press, 1972), 155–172. See also Cora Kaplan's "Wild Nights: Pleasure, Sexuality, Feminism," in *The Ideology of Conduct: Essays in Literature and the History of Sexuality*, ed. Nancy Armstrong and Leonard Tennenhouse (London and New York: Methuen, 1987), 160–184, for a more recent discussion of this central contradiction in Victorian sexual ideology.

6. H. E. Harvey, "The Voice of Woman," *Westminster Review* 145 (1896): 193.

7. Cott, "Passionlessness," quoting Rebecca Harding Davis, 236.

8. Hansson, *Six Modern Women*, 72.

9. "The Year in Review," *Athenaeum*, 6 January 1894, 17–18.

10. Foucault, *The History of Sexuality I*, 56.

11. Boumelha, *Thomas Hardy*, 28–29.

12. Gissing, *The Odd Women*, 131.

13. Emile Zola, "The Experimental Novel," in *The Modern Tradition*, ed. Richard Ellmann and Charles Fiedelson (New York: Oxford University Press, 1965), 274.

14. Allen, "Plain Words on the Woman Question," 452.

15. See Jessica Benjamin, *The Bonds of Love: Psychoanalysis, Feminism and the Problem of Domination* (New York: Pantheon Books, 1988).

16. Newton, "Making—and Remaking—History," 135–136.

17. Arabella Kenealy, *A Semi-Detached Marriage* (London: Hutchinson, 1899); Frank Frankfurt Moore, *"I Forbid the Banns!" The Story of a Comedy Which Was Played Seriously* (London: Hutchinson, 1893); George Moore, "Mildred Lawson," in *Celibates* (London: Walter Scott, 1895); Percival Pickering, *A Pliable Marriage* (London: Osgood, McIlvaine & Co., 1895); and John Smith, *Platonic Affections* (London: John Lane, 1895). See also Beatrice Harraden, *Ships That Pass in the Night* (London and New York: G. P. Putnam, 1894); Violet Hunt, *The Maiden's Progress* (New York: Harper & Brothers, 1894); Mary E. Mann, *Susannah* (London: Henry & Co., 1895); George Moore, *A Mummer's Wife* and *Esther Waters*. A male character in George Paston's *The Career of Candida* (London: Chapman & Hall, 1896) argues that he is doing the New Woman "a favour in providing her with such an unparalleled opportunity for the self-immolation that all true women are supposed to love" (289). Paston's *A Modern Amazon* (London: Osgood, McIlvaine & Co., 1894) ends when the female protagonist renounces her career as a journalist and confesses to her estranged husband that "I have wanted you all the time" (286). Elizabeth Robins's *The New Moon* (London: Heinemann, 1895) ends with the death of the New Woman who has missed her opportunity to have a satisfying sexual relationship; in a later novel, *The Dark Lantern*, however, her protagonist learns to live by "the dark lantern" of her physician-husband's sexuality.

18. Allen, "Plain Words on the Woman Question," 452.

19. Allen, *The Woman Who Did*, 138.

20. Boumelha, *Thomas Hardy*, 85.

21. Iota [Kathleen Mannington Caffyn], *A Yellow Aster* (Leipzig: B. Tauchnitz, 1894), 161. In George Paston's *The Career of Candida*, the protagonist awakens to "the joy and pride of motherhood" (203). See also Smith, *Platonic Affections*; Netta Syrett, *The Tree of Life* (London: John Lane, 1897); Beatrice Whitby, *Mary Fenwick's Daughter* (London: Hurst & Blackett, 1894).

22. Waugh, "Reticence," 218.

23. Cleeve, *The Woman Who Wouldn't*, 225.

24. Caird, "A Defense," 818.

25. Cleeve, *The Woman Who Wouldn't*, 86.

26. Linton, *The New Woman in Haste and Leisure* (New York: Merriam, 1895), 41.

27. Stead, "The Book of the Month. 'The Woman Who Did,' " 187.

28. Linton, *The Rebel of the Family* (London: Chatto & Windus, 1880), 243.

29. Lucas Malet, "The Threatened Re-Subjection of Women," *Fortnightly Review* 83 (1905): 806–819, 816.

30. "The Year In Review," *Athenaeum*, 6 January 1894, 18.

31. "A Century of Feminine Fiction," 539.

32. Egerton, "A Cross Line," *Keynotes*, 19—20.

33. For an interesting argument about the multivocality of women's narratives, see Maria Childers, "Narrating Structures of Opportunity," *Genre* 19 (Winter 1986): 447—469.

34. Gosse, *Questions at Issue*, 22.

35. Annie E. Holdsworth, *Joanna Trail, Spinster* (London: W. Heinemann, 1894), 75.

36. Mona Caird, *The Daughters of Danaus* (London: Bliss, Sands & Foster, 1894), 190.

37. Netta Syrett, *Roseanne* (London: Hurst & Blackett, 1902). Interestingly enough, the view of genetics presented in *Roseanne* directly counters its thematization in *The Tree of Life*, where the female protagonist asserts her connection with a mother she has never known because her father denied the latter's existence after she had run away with a lover. "I am glad to be her child," Christine announces, after also accusing both her husband and her father of valuing her skills as a political speaker over the child they have just lost (387). For an account of Syrett's relationship with Allen, see Mix, *A Study in Yellow*, 77—80. Syrett herself has very little to say about the first ten years of her career as a novelist; she expresses her gratitude toward Allen for his patronage, but offers no discussion of either the controversy over New Woman fiction or her own very varied contributions to it. See her autobiography, *The Sheltering Tree* 10—45.

38. George Paston [Emily Morse Symonds], *A Study in Prejudices* (London: Hutchinson, 1895), 96.

39. Hogarth, "Literary Degenerates," 591.

40. Emma Frances Brooke, *A Superfluous Woman* (New York: Cassell, 1894), 121.

41. Ella Hepworth Dixon, *The Story of a Modern Woman* (New York: Cassell, 1894), 308.

42. Netta Syrett, *Nobody's Fault* (London: John Lane, 1896), 79.

43. George Egerton, *Keynotes*, 29.

44. In *The Wing of Azrael*, the narrator refers to Philip Dendraith as "a Perseus to [Viola's] Andromeda" (I: 200). Henry Lancaster also uses this allusion to explain how she has sacrificed herself to save her parents' home: "Andromeda has been chained to the rock, for the gods are angry, and must be appeased by sacrifice. And the monster is about to devour her, so that Andromeda is having a rather bad time of it just now" (2: 32). Caird refers to the myth in "A Defense of the So-Called Wild Women" as well; see 815.

45. Showalter, *Literature*, 190. See also Gail Cunningham, *New Woman*, 64; Fernando, *"New Women" in the Late Victorian Novel*, 24; and Stubbs, *Feminism and the Novel*, 126. My argument parallels Hazel Carby's objection to the common characterization of late-nineteenth-century black American feminists "prudishness:" see " 'On the Threshold of Woman's Empire': Lynching, Empire, and Sexuality in Black Feminist Theory," *Critical Inquiry* 12 (Autumn 1985): 262–277.

46. Linton, "Womanliness," in *The Girl of the Period,* 2: 113.

47. Gissing, *The Odd Women*, 262.

48. Boumelha, *Thomas Hardy*, 73.

49. Irigaray, *This Sex Which Is Not One*, 86. Catherine Clement and Helene Cixous's discussion of hysteria—specifically, their disagreement regarding the hysteric's disruptiveness or her reabsorption by the patriarchy—at the end of *The Newly Born Woman* (135–160) is also worth mentioning in this context.

50. See also Dorothy Leighton's *Disillusion: A Story with a Preface* (London: Henry & Co., 1894), which highlights the New Woman's disillusionment regarding the capacity of the man she loves to view her as something other than either a "fallen" woman or a sexless spinster.

51. The reference is to John 9:7, where Jesus tells a blind man to go wash himself in the pool of Siloam after Jesus had smeared the man's eyes with mud. The man does as he is told—and returns, able to see.

52. See also the scene in Mrs. Humphry Ward's *Marcella* (London: Macmillan, 1895), in which the protagonist objects to the "doctrine of identity," a doctrine that asserts the continuity of identity over time: "I must be the same person I was then" (218). A similar critique of this doctrine figures significantly in Mary Cholmondeley's *Red Pottage* (London: Edward Arnold, 1899), a novel to be discussed in detail in the next two chapters. Also worth recalling here is Oscar Wilde's characterization of the New Woman's "Protean" nature in "The Decay of Lying" (185). Nina Auerbach discusses "the death" of Victorian character in *Woman and the Demon*, 185–229.

5.   *Crossing the Line*

1. For a discussion of the social construction of "nature," see Alison Jaggar, *Feminist Politics and Human Nature* (Sussex: Rowman and Allanheld, 1983), 126; for a discussion of women's relationship to both nature and culture, see Sherry B. Ortner's classic essay, "Is Female to Male as Nature Is to Culture?" in *Woman,*

Culture, and Society, ed. Michelle Rosaldo and Louise Lamphere (Stanford: Stanford University Press, 1974), 67–87.

2. See, respectively, Hardy, "Candour," 18; Linton, "Candour," 14, 11, 14.

3. Hardy, "Candour," 17.

4. Lady Florence Dixie, *Gloriana; Or, The Revolution of 1900* (London: Henry & Co., 1890), vii.

5. Cleeve, *The Woman Who Wouldn't*, vi.

6. Gosse, *Questions at Issue*, 22.

7. Roland Barthes, *The Pleasure of the Text* (New York: Hill and Wang, 1975), 56.

8. See, respectively, "The Apple and the Ego of Woman," 382; Linton, "The Wild Women as Politicians," 80; and "The Strike of a Sex," 289–290.

9. Jane Hume Clapperton, *Margaret Dunmore; or, A Socialist Home* (London: Swan Sonnenschein, Lowry & Co., 1888). For important new work on the tradition of socialist realism in Britain, see Gustav Klaus, ed., *The Socialist Novel in Britain: Toward the Recovery of a Tradition* (New York: St. Martin's Press, 1982) and Klaus, *The Literature of Labour: Two Hundred Years of Working-Class Writing* (New York: St. Martin's Press, 1988). Klaus views this as a tradition quite separate from the tradition of bourgeois realism. I am arguing instead that writers like Clapperton and Dixie push the bourgeois novel in new directions, test its capacity to engage new interests.

10. See Heidi Hartmann, "The Unhappy Marriage of Marxism and Feminism: Toward a More Progressive Union," in *Women and Revolution*, ed. Lydia Sargent (Boston: South End Press, 1981), and Rowbotham and Weeks, *Socialism and the New Life*.

11. See Showalter, *Literature*, 189; Vicinus, *Independent Women*.

12. George Eliot, *Adam Bede* (New York: New American Library, 1961); for a discussion of the gender code governing Victorian women's appearance in public, see Robyn Warhol, "Towards a Theory of the Engaging Narrator: Earnest Interventions in Gaskell, Stowe, and Eliot," *PMLA* 101 (October 1986): 811–818.

13. Gissing, *The Odd Women*, 139.

14. Rhoda Broughton, *Dear Faustina* (London: Richard Bentley & Son, 1897), 16.

15. Gertrude Dix, *The Image-Breakers* (London: W. Heinemann, 1900).

16. Helena Michie, *The Flesh Made Word: Female Figures and Women's Bodies* (New York and Oxford: Oxford University Press, 1987), 63.

17. See recent interpretations of the relation between writing and mothering, in Nina Auerbach, "Artists and Mothers: A False Alliance," *Women and Literature* 6 (Spring 1978): 1–17; Margaret Homans, *Bearing the Word: Language and Female*

Experience in Nineteenth-Century Women's Writing (Chicago: University of Chicago Press, 1986); Susan Rubin Suleiman, "Writing and Motherhood," in *The (M)other Tongue: Essays in Feminist Psychoanalytic Interpretation*, ed. Shirley Nelson Garner, Claire Kahane, and Madelon Sprengnether (Ithaca and London: Cornell University Press, 1985), 352–377.

18. Mary Cholmondeley, *Red Pottage* (London: Edward Arnold, 1899; rept. Penguin, 1985), 276. For readings of *Red Pottage*, see Colby, " 'Devoted Amateur,' " 213–228; Showalter's introduction to the Penguin reprint, vii–xv; and Gilbert and Gubar, *No Man's Land 1*, 176–178.

19. See in particular Sigmund Freud, *Civilization and Its Discontents* (New York: W.W. Norton, 1961).

20. By way of contrast, recall Hardy's struggle in *Tess of the D'Urbervilles* to maintain some semblance of objectivity in his presentation of Tess, while at the same time expressing his desire *for* her.

21. Syrett, *Nobody's Fault*, 243. Other "woman-centered" New Woman novels include Ethel Arnold, *Platonics: A Study* (London: Osgood, McIlvaine & Co., 1894); William Francis Barry, *The Two Standards* (London: T. Fisher Unwin, 1898); Dorothy Leighton, *As a Man Is Able: A Study in Human Relationships* (London: W. Heinemann, 1893); and Rita [Eliza Humphreys], *A Woman in It; A Sketch of Feminine Misadventure* (Philadelphia: Lippincott, 1895).

22. Dixon, *Modern Woman*, 304.

23. Dix, *Image-Breakers*, 122.

24. [Edith Johnstone], *A Sunless Heart* (London: Ward, Lock & Bowden, 1894); see Adrienne Rich, "Compulsory Heterosexuality," in *Powers of Desire: The Politics of Sexuality*, ed. Ann Snitow, Christine Stansell, and Sharon Thompson (New York: Monthly Review Press, 1983), 177–205.

25. Significantly, lesbian relationships are characterized very negatively in the handful of New Woman novels that present such relationships at all. In Mrs. Linton's *The Rebel of the Family* and Rhoda Broughton's *Dear Faustina*, as well as in *A Sunless Heart*, lesbian partnerships simply reproduce the pattern of sexual, intellectual, and economic domination that New Women were objecting to in the practice of Victorian heterosexuality. In other words, lesbian pairings do not represent any kind of alternative to patriarchal (hetero)sexuality in these novels; women "invert" their sexuality, to use Havelock Ellis's phrasing, but they sustain the active/passive dichotomy associated with male/female partnerings. If Radclyffe Hall's *The Well of Loneliness* (1928) represents a later manifestation of this conceptualization of lesbianism, the kind of homoerotic bonding I am highlighting in *The Image-Breakers*, *The Odd Women*, and *Red Pottage* points ahead to Virginia Woolf's figuration of female relationships in works like *Night and Day* and *To the Lighthouse*.

6. Retreats

1. Iota [Kathleen Mannington Caffyn], *A Comedy in Spasms* (London: Hutchinson, 1895).

2. Rider Haggard, *She* (London and New York: Penguin, 1982), 245. See Gilbert and Gubar's discussion of this text and its cultural significance, *No Man's Land 2*, 3–22.

3. George Noyes Miller, *The Strike of a Sex* (London: William Reeves, 1891), 46.

4. Edward Thomas Papillon, *Alleyne: A Story of a Dream and a Failure* (London: T. Fisher Unwin, 1894), 223.

5. Mark Rutherford [William Hale White], *Clara Hopgood* (London: T. Fisher Unwin, 1896).

6. Note the temporal displacement White enacts by setting this story in the 1840s, not the 1880s or 1890s.

7. Mary Jacobus, "Sue the Obscure," 304.

8. Miller, "Emphasis Added," 345–346.

9. Besides Edith Johnstone, Sarah Grand is the only New Woman novelist to provide an optimistic account of a New Woman artist's success. In *The Beth-Book* (London: W. Heinemann, 1897), Beth fails as a writer, but she does discover her talent as an orator in the closing scenes of the novel.

10. Elizabeth Robins, *George Mandeville's Husband* (London: W. Heinemann, 1894), 7.

11. Devereux, *Ascent of Woman*, 23.

12. W. S. Holnut, *Olympia's Journal*, v–vi.

13. Recall Lucas Cleeve's comments in the preface to *The Woman Who Wouldn't* about wanting her narrative to have a similar affect on readers.

14. Mrs. Andrew Dean, *A Splendid Cousin* (London: T. Fisher Unwin, 1892), 22.

15. Sara Jeannette Duncan [Mrs. Everard Cotes], *A Daughter of Today* (London: Chatto & Windus, 1894), 28. Similarly mocking uses of the child:book analogy are to be found in plays produced during the 1890s as well. See, for example, J. M. Barrie's *Ibsen's Ghost*, in which Tia, the Hedda Gabler character, burns old letters (not a manuscript), complaining all the while, "It breaks my heart, for I look upon each of them as a little child, George's children and mine. There are a hundred and twenty-seven"; and Miss Prism's confusion regarding the baby and the "abandoned" novel she wrote years before in Oscar Wilde's *The Importance of Being Earnest*.

16. Rita [Eliza Humphreys], *A Husband of No Importance* (London: T. Fisher Unwin, 1894), 13.

17. George Paston [Emily Morse Symonds], *A Modern Amazon* (London: Osgood, McIlvaine & Co., 1894), 226.

18. See Ermarth, *Realism and Consensus.*

19. Tuchman and Fortin, *Edging Women Out*; Gilbert and Gubar, *No Man's Land 1: The War of the Words.* For an important discussion of conservative turn-of-the-century women's resistance to feminism, see Brian Harrison, *Separate Spheres: The Opposition to Women's Suffrage* (London: Croom & Helm, 1979).

20. Froula, "The Daughter's Seduction," 141.

21. Mrs. Humphry Ward, *Marcella* (London: Macmillan, 1895; rept. Penguin, 1984).

22. Ward, *Sir George Tressady* (London: Smith, Elder & Co., 1896), 313.

23. Dix, *Image-Breakers*, 155.

24. Dixon, *Modern Woman*, 221.

25. George Paston [Emily Morse Symonds], *A Writer of Books* (New York: D. Appleton, 1899), 108.

26. Cholmondeley, *Red Pottage*, 38.

27. *Bookman*, April 1895, 55.

28. *Athenaeum*, 12 May 1894, 392.

29. For more recent discussions of the privatization of women's writing, see Susan Lanser, "Towards a Feminist Narratology," *Style* 20 (1986): 341–363; and Jane Gallop, "Annie Leclerc Writing a Letter, with Vermeer," in *The Poetics of Gender*, 137–156.

30. *Athenaeum*, 16 March 1895, 342.

31. Anderson, *Woman Against Women*, 212.

32. *Athenaeum*, 23 November 1895, 709.

33. Oliphant, "The Anti-Marriage League," 136.

34. Johnstone published two novels in 1896, *The Girleen* (London: Blackie & Son) and *The Douce Family* (London: T. Fisher Unwin) but never seems to have written anything else.

35. See Showalter's introduction to the Penguin edition of *Red Pottage*, vii–xv.

7.   *Turning the Century,*
Writing New Histories

1. Edna Kenton, "A Study of the Old 'New Woman,' " *Bookman* 37 (1913), 154.

2. Eva Slawson's diary entry, 22 January 1914, in *Dear Girl*, ed. Tierl Thompson (London: The Women's Press, 1987), 191.

3. As noted earlier, Syrett's autobiography offers no explanation of her changing interests and generic preoccupations; the novels published after 1900 include *Roseanne* (1902), *Olivia Carew* (London: Chatto & Windus, 1910), *Rose Cottingham* (London: G. P. Putnam, 1915), and *Rose Cottingham Married* (London: T. Fisher Unwin, 1916).

4. Florence Dixie wrote about fox hunting (*The Horrors of Sport* [1892; 1895]), horse racing (*Little Cherie; Or, The Trainer's Daughter* [1901]), and the treatment of gypsies (*Isola; Or, the Disinherited* [1903]; and *Izra, A Child of Solitude* [1906]). Jane Hume Clapperton published nothing in the 1890s, but finished a socialist tract, *A Vision of the Future Based on the Application of Ethical Principles*, in 1904. Mona Caird spent the last few years of the nineteenth century writing antivivisection materials (*A Sentimental View of Vivisection* [1895] and *Beyond the Pale. An Appeal on Behalf of the Victims of Vivisection* [1897]), while George Paston worked mainly in eighteenth-century studies (*Little Memoirs of the Eighteenth Century* [1901], *Side-Lights of the Georgian Period* [1902], *Lady Mary Worley Montague and her Times* [1907], *Mr. Pope; His Life and Times* [1909]) before turning her hand to drama (*Feed the Brute* [1909], *The Parents' Progress* [1910], *Doubt or Quits* [1919], *Nobody's Daughter* [1924]). Kenealy, Winter, and Holdsworth published fiction well into the 1910s.

5. See, for example, Jeffreys, *The Spinster and Her Enemies*; Michael Freeden, "Eugenics and Progressive Thought: A Study in Ideological Affinity," *Historical Journal* 22 (1979): 645–672; Gilbert and Gubar, *No Man's Land 2*, "Soldier's Heart: Literary Men, Literary Women, and the Great War," 258–323, and Margaret Stetz, "Planting Corpses in Our Mother's Gardens: Feminist Criticism and World War I," *Iris* 14 (1985): 24–27.

6. DeKoven, "Gendered Doubleness and the 'Origins' of Modernist Form," 20.

7. Ibid. I am both argreeing and disagreeing with DeKoven: agreeing with her claim that women are as responsible for modernizing the novel as the better-known male writers; disagreeing with her neglect of other women writers through her exclusive focus on Chopin and Gilman; disagreeing, too, with her defense of the indirect expression or the muting of feminist content through modernist form.

8. Ibid., 36.

9. For important discussions of modernism's cultural hegemony in the early twentieth century, its delegitimization of other aesthetics, see Andreas Huyssens, "Mass Culture as Woman: Modernism's Other," in *After the Great Divide* (Bloomington: Indiana University Press, 1986), 44–64; and Deborah Fried, "Andromeda Unbound: Gender and Genre in Millay's Sonnets," *Twentieth-Century Literature* 32 (1986): 1–22.

10. Holly Laird's term, *Tulsa Studies in Women's Literature* 8 (Spring 1989): 14.

11. Stead, "The Novel of the Modern Woman," 65.

12. T. E. Hulme, "Romanticism and Classicism," in *Speculations*, ed. Herbert Read (New York: Harcourt, Brace, 1924), 126–127.

13. Wyndham Lewis, *Blast* 1 (1914): 46.

14. Lawrence, *Collected Letters*, ed. George Zytank and James Boulton (Cambridge: Cambridge University Press, 1981), 2: 165.

15. See Spivak, "Explanation and Culture: Marginalia," 104.

16. Lawrence, *Collected Letters*, 183.

17. Virginia Woolf, "Mr. Bennett and Mrs. Brown," *The Captain's Death Bed* (New York and London: Harcourt Brace Jovanovich, 1950), 94–121 (read first to the Heretics Club at Cambridge on 18 May 1924).

18. Ford Madox Ford, "The Woman of the Novelist," *The Critical Attitude* (London: Duckworth, 1914), 159.

19. D. H. Lawrence, "Surgery for the Novel—Or a Bomb," *Phoenix I* (London: Penguin, 1958), 227.

20. See "Epilogue. The editor and the loathed disturber," in Levenson, *A Genealogy of Modernism*, 213–220.

21. T. S. Eliot, "Tradition and the Individual Talent," *Selected Essays* (New York: Harcourt, Brace & World, 1964), 8.

22. Pamela Caughie, "The (En)gendering of Literary History," *Tulsa Studies in Women's Literature* 8 (Spring 1989): 111.

23. See James Clifford's introduction to *Writing Culture* (Berkeley: University of California Press, 1986) and Joan Scott's *Gender and History* (New York: Columbia University Press, 1988).

24. See Jane Tompkins, "But Is It Any Good?" in *Sensational Designs*.

25. Irigaray, *This Sex Which Is Not One*, 86.

26. Huyssens argues in "Mass Culture as Woman" that modernists viewed mass culture as its feminized other, the cultural formation it sought both to define and protect itself against. With Gilbert and Gubar, I would argue that modernism's antagonism toward mass culture is itself motivated by an antagonism to the feminization of all culture.

27. The story made most major newspapers and weekly news journals. See *New York Times,* 8 December 1989, I, 9:1.

28. "Socio-Literary Portents," 683–685.

29. DeLauretis, "The Violence of Rhetoric," in *Technologies of Gender,* 46.

30. Linda Alcoff introdes the term "positionality" in "Cultural Feminism versus Post-Structuralism: The Identity Crisis in Feminist Theory," *Signs* 13 (1987): 405–436.

31. Specifically, I'm thinking of the emphasis on recovering and reclaiming lost texts—restoring something to its original state.

32. Laird, "Editor's Introduction," *Tulsa Studies in Women's Literature* 8 (Spring 1989): 11.

33. See also Donna Haraway, "A Manifesto for Cyborgs," *Socialist Review* 15 (1985): 65–108.

34. Showalter, *Literature*, 186.

35. Cholmondeley, *Red Pottage*, 36.

SELECTED
BIBLIOGRAPHY

New Woman Fiction, 1880–1920

Allen, Grant. *The Woman Who Did*. London: John Lane, 1895.

Arnold, Ethel. *Platonics*. London: Osgood, McIlvaine & Co., 1894.

Barry, Rev. William Frances. *The New Antigone; A Romance*. London and New York: Macmillan, 1887.

———. *The Two Standards*. London: T. Fisher Unwin, 1898.

Beaumont, Mary. *Two New Women and Other Stories*. London: James Clark & Co., 1899.

Benson, E. F. *Dodo*. New York: Appleton, 1893.

Brooke, Emma Frances. *A Superfluous Woman*. New York: Cassell, 1894.

Broughton, Rhoda. *Dear Faustina*. London: Richard Bentley & Son, 1897.

Caird, Mona. *The Daughters of Danaus*. London: Bliss, Sands & Foster, 1894.

———. *The Wing of Azrael*. London: Trubner & Co., 1889.

Cholmondeley, Mary. *Red Pottage*. London: Edward Arnold, 1899. Rept. with an introduction by Elaine Showalter, Penguin, 1985.

Clapperton, Jane Hume. *Margaret Dunmore; or, A Socialist Home*. London: Swan Sonnenschein, Lowry & Co., 1888.

Cleeve, Lucas [Adelina G. I. Kingscote]. *The Woman Who Wouldn't*. London: Simpkin, Marshall & Co., 1895.

Clifford, Mrs. W. K. *A Flash of Summer: The Story of a Simple Woman's Life*. London: Methuen, 1895.

Crommelin, May. *Dust Before the Wind*. London: Bliss, Sands & Foster, 1894.

Cross, Victoria [Vivian Cory]. *The Woman Who Didn't*. London: John Lane, 1895.

Dalton, Henry Robert S. *Lesbia Newman*. London: George Redway, 1889.

D'Arcy, Ella. *Monochromes*. London: John Lane, 1895.

Dean, Mrs. Andrew. *A Splendid Cousin*. London: T. Fisher Unwin, 1892.

Dix, Gertrude. *The Image-Breakers*. London: W. Heinemann, 1900.

Dixie, Lady Florence. *Gloriana; Or, The Revolution of 1900*. London: Henry & Co., 1890.

Dixon, Ella Hepworth. *The Story of a Modern Woman*. New York: Cassell, 1894.

Dowie, Menie Muriel. *Gallia*. London: Methuen & Co., 1895.

Duncan, Sara Jeannette [Mrs. Everard Cotes]. *An American Girl in London*. London: Chatto & Windus, 1891.

———. *A Daughter of Today*. London: Chatto & Windus, 1894.

Edwardes, Annie. *A Blue-stocking*. Leipzig: B. Tauchnitz, 1877.

———. *A Girton Girl*. Leipzig: B. Tauchnitz, 1885.

Egerton, George [Mary Chavelita Bright]. *Discords*. London: John Lane, 1894.

———. *Keynotes*. London: John Lane, 1893.

George, W. L. *A Bed of Roses*. London: Frank Palmer, 1911.

Gissing, George. "The Foolish Virgin," *Yellow Book* 8 (1896): 201–225.

———. *The Odd Women*. London: W. Heinemann, 1893. Rept. New American Library, 1983.

Grand, Sarah [Frances Elizabeth McFall]. *The Beth-Book*. London: W. Heinemann, 1897. Rept. Penguin, 1979.

———. *A Domestic Experiment*. Edinburgh: Blackwoods, 1891.

———. *The Heavenly Twins*. London: W. Heinemann, 1893.

———. *Ideala: A Study from Life*. London: E. W. Allen, 1888.

Hardy, Thomas. *Jude the Obscure*. London: Osgood, McIlvaine & Co., 1896.

———. *Tess of the D'Urbervilles*. London: Osgood, McIlvaine & Co., 1891.

Harraden, Beatrice. *In Varying Moods*. Edinburgh: Blackwoods, 1894.

———. *Ships That Pass in the Night*. London and New York: Putnam, 1894.

Harrison, Mrs. Burton. *A Bachelor Maid*. London: T. Fisher Unwin, 1895.

Holdsworth, Annie E. *Joanna Trail, Spinster*. London: W. Heinemann, 1894.

Holnut, W. S. *Olympia's Journal*. London: George Bell, 1895.

Hunt, Violet. *A Hard Woman. A Story in Scenes*. New York: Appleton, 1895.

———. *The Human Interest: A Study in Incompatibilities*. London: Methuen, 1899.

———. *The Maiden's Progress*. New York: Harper, 1894.

———. *The Way of Marriage*. London: Chapman & Hall, 1896.

Iota [Kathleen Mannington Caffyn]. *A Comedy in Spasms*. London: Hutchinson, 1895.

———. *A Yellow Aster*. Leipzig: B. Tauchnitz, 1894.

Johnstone, Edith. *A Sunless Heart*. London: Ward, Lock & Bowden, 1894.

Kendall, May. *White Poppies*. London: Ward, Lock & Bowden, 1893.

Kenealy, Arabella. *Dr. Janet of Harley Street*. London: Digby, Long & Co., 1893.

————. *The Honourable Mrs. Spoor*. London: Digby, Long & Co., 1895.

————. *A Semi-Detached Marriage*. London: Hutchinson, 1899.

Kinross, Albert. *A Game of Consequences*. London: T. Fisher Unwin, 1895.

Lawrence, D. H. *The Lost Girl*. London: W. Heinemann, 1920.

Leighton, Dorothy. *As a Man Is Able: A Study in Human Relationships*. London: W. Heinemann, 1893.

————. *Disillusion: A Story with a Preface*. London: Henry & Co., 1894.

Linton, Elizabeth Lynn. *The New Woman in Haste and Leisure*. New York: Merriam, 1895.

————. *The Rebel of the Family*. London: Chatto & Windus, 1880.

Mann, Mary E. *Susannah*. London: Henry & Co., 1895.

Marsh, Richard. *Mrs. Musgrave and Her Husband*. London: W. Heinemann, 1895.

Miller, George Noyes. *The Strike of a Sex*. London: William Reeves, 1891.

Moore, Frank Frankfurt. *"I Forbid the Banns!" The Story of a Comedy Which Was Played Seriously*. London: Hutchinson, 1893.

————. *The Marriage Lease*. London: Hutchinson, 1907.

Moore, George. *Celibates*. London: W. Scott, 1895.

————. *Esther Waters*. London: W. Scott, 1894.

————. *A Mummer's Wife*. London: Vizetelly, 1885.

Papillon, Edward Thomas. *Alleyne: A Story of a Dream and a Failure*. London: T. Fisher Unwin, 1894.

Paston, George [Emily Morse Symonds]. *The Career of Candida*. London: Chapman & Hall, 1896.

————. *A Modern Amazon*. London: Osgood, McIlvaine & Co., 1894.

————. *A Study in Prejudices*. London: Hutchinson, 1895.

————. *A Writer of Books*. New York: D. Appleton, 1899.

Pickering, Percival. *A Pliable Marriage*. London: Osgood, McIlvaine & Co., 1895.

Raimond, C. E. [Elizabeth Robins]. *George Mandeville's Husband*. London: W. Heinemann, 1894.

————. *The New Moon*. London: W. Heinemann, 1895.

Rita [Eliza Humphreys]. *A Husband of No Importance*. London: T. Fisher Unwin, 1894.

————. *A Woman in It*. Philadelphia: Lippincott, 1895.

Russell, Percy. *A Husband's Ordeal; Or, the Confessions of Gerald Brownson*. London: Bellair & Co., 1896.

Rutherford, Mark [William Hale White]. *Clara Hopgood*. London: T. Fisher Unwin, 1896.

Schreiner, Olive. *The Story of an African Farm*. London: Chapman & Hall, 1883.

Sharp, Evelyn. *At the Relton Arms*. London: John Lane, 1895.

Simcox, Edith. *Episodes in the Lives of Men, Women, and Lovers*. London: Trubner & Co., 1882.

Smith, John. *Platonic Affections*. London: John Lane, 1896.

Syrett, Netta. *Nobody's Fault*. London: John Lane, 1896.

―――. *Olivia Carew*. London: Chatto & Windus, 1910.

―――. *Roseanne*, London: Hurst & Blackett, 1902.

―――. *Rose Cottingham*. London: G. P. Putnam, 1915.

―――. *Rose Cottingham Married*. London: T. Fisher Unwin, 1916.

―――. *Three Women*. London: Chatto & Windus, 1912.

Ward, Mrs. Humphry. *Marcella*. London: Macmillan, 1895. Rept. with an introduction by Amie Watters, Penguin, 1984.

―――. *Sir George Tressady*. London: Smith, Elder & Co., 1896.

Warden, Gertrude. *The Sentimental Sex*. London: John Lane, 1897.

Waterloo, Stanley. *A Man and a Woman*. London: George Redway, 1896.

Wells, H. G. *Ann Veronica*. London: T. Fisher Unwin, 1909.

Whitby, Beatrice. *The Awakening of Mary Fenwick*. New York: George Munro, 1890.

―――. *Mary Fenwick's Daughter*. London: Hurst & Blackett, 1894.

Winter, John Strange [Henrietta Stannard]. *A Blameless Woman*. New York: International News Co., 1894.

Woolf, Virginia. *Night and Day*. London: Hogarth Press, 1919.

―――. *The Voyage Out*. London: Hogarth Press, 1915.

Wotton, Mabel *A Pretty Radical and Other Stories*. London: David Scott, 1890.

Prose Writings on
the New Woman
and Related Subjects

Adam, Juliette. "Woman's Place in Modern Life," *Fortnightly Review* 57 (1892): 522–529.

Addleshaw, Rev. Percy. " 'The Woman Who Did,' " *Academy* 47 (1895): 186–187.

Allen, Grant. "The New Hedonism," *Fortnightly Review* 61 (1894): 377–392.

―――. "Plain Words on the Woman Question," *Fortnightly Review* 52 (1889): 448–458.

Anthony, Susan B. "The Status of Woman, Past, Present, and Future," *Arena* 17 (1896): 901–908.

"The Apple and the Ego of Woman," *Westminster Review*, 131 (1889): 374–382.

Arling, Nat. "What Is the Role of the 'New Woman'?" *Westminster Review* 150 (1898): 576–587.

Bebel, August. *Woman in the Past, Present, and Future.* H. B. Adams Walther, trans., London: The Modern Press, 1885.

Besant, Walter, Elizabeth Lynn Linton, Thomas Hardy, et al. "Candour in English Fiction," *New Review* 2 (1890): 6–21.

Besant, Walter, Sarah Grand, Thomas Hardy, Max Nordau, Elizabeth Linton, et al. "The Tree of Knowledge," *New Review* 10 (1894): 675–690.

Billington-Greig, Teresa. "Feminism and Politics," *Contemporary Review* 100 (1911): 693–703.

Black, Helen C. *Notable Women Authors of the Day.* London: MacLaren, 1906.

Bradfield, Thomas. "A Dominant Note of Some Recent Fiction," *Westminster Review* 142 (1894): 537–545.

Bulley, Amy. "The Political Evolution of Women," *Westminister Review* 84 (1890): 1–8.

Caird, Mona. "A Defense of the So-Called Wild Women," *Nineteeth Century* 31 (1892): 811–829.

———. "The Emancipation of the Family, Part I," *North American Review* 150 (1890): 692–705.

———. "The Emancipation of the Family, Part II," *North American Review* 151 (1890): 22–37.

———. "The Lot of Women," *Westminster Review* 174 (1910): 52–59.

———. *The Morality of Marriage and Other Essays on the Status of Women.* London: George Redway, 1897.

———. "The Phases of Human Development, I," *Westminster Review* 141 (1894): 37–51.

———. "The Phases of Human Development, II," *Westminster Review* 141 (1894): 162–179.

Carpenter, Edward. "The Return to Nature," *Humanitarian* 8 (1896): 193–195.

"A Century of Feminine Fiction," *All The Year Round* 12 (1894): 537–540.

Chant, L. Ormiston. "Woman as an Athlete," *Nineteenth Century* 45 (1899): 745–754.

Chapman, Elizabeth R. *Marriage Questions in Modern Fiction, and Other Essays on Kindred Subjects.* London: George Redway, 1897.

Courtney, William L. *The Feminine Note in Fiction.* London: Chapman & Hall, 1904.

Crackanthorpe, B. A. "Sex in Modern Literature," *Nineteenth Century* 218 (1895): 607–616.

Crackanthorpe, Hubert. "Reticence in Literature: Some Roundabout Remarks," *Yellow Book* 2 (1894): 259–269.

Crawford, Virginia M. "Feminism in France," *Fortnightly Review* 67 (1897): 524–534.

Davidson, Mrs. Hugh Coleman. *What Our Daughters Can Do For Themselves.* London: Smith, Elder & Co., 1894.

DeCleyre, Voltairine. "They Who Marry Do Ill," *Mother Earth* 2 (1908): 500–511.

Deland, Margaret. "The Change in the Feminine Ideal," *Atlantic Monthly* 105 (1910): 289–302.

Devereux, Mrs. Roy. *The Ascent of Woman.* London: John Lane, 1896.

Dorr, Rheta Childe. *What Eight Million Women Want.* Boston: Small, Maynard, 1910.

Eastwood, Mrs. "The New Woman in Fiction and in Fact," *Humanitarian* 5 (1894): 375–379.

Ellis, Havelock. "Concerning 'Jude the Obscure,' " *Savoy* 6 (1896): 35–49.

———. *The New Spirit.* London: G. Bell, 1890.

Ethelmer, Ellis. "Feminism," *Westminster Review* 149 (1898): 50–62.

Fawcett, Millicent Garrett. " 'The Woman Who Did,' " *Contemporary Review* 67 (1895): 625–631.

"The Future of Single Women," *Westminster Review* 121 (1884): 151–162.

Gaskell, C. M. "Women of Today, What Is Expected of Them?" *Nineteenth Century* 26 (1889): 776–784.

Gerould, Katharine Fullerton. "The Newest Woman," *Atlantic Monthly* 109 (1912): 606–611.

Gosse, Edmund. *Questions at Issue.* London: W. Heinemann, 1893.

Grand, Sarah [Frances Elizabeth McFall]. "The Modern Girl," *North American Review* 158 (1894): 706–714.

———. "The New Aspects of the Woman Question," *North American Review* 158 (1894): 270–276.

Greville, Violet. *The Gentlewoman in Society,* London: Henry & Co., 1892.

Grossman, Edith Searle. "The New Sex Psychology," *Westminster Review* 172 (1899): 497–510.

Haggard, Rider. "About Fiction," *Contemporary Review* 51 (1887): 172–180.

Hallyar, Florence. "The Superfluity of Women," *Westminster Review* 171 (1909): 171–181.

Hannigan, D. F. "Sex in Fiction," *Westminster Review* 143 (1895): 616–625.

Hansson, Laura Marholm. *Six Modern Women.* Hermione Ramsden, trans. London: John Lane, 1896.

Harper, Charles. *Revolted Women: Past, Present, and To Come.* London: Elkin Mathews, 1894.

Harrison, Frederick. "The Emancipation of Women," *Fortnightly Review* 56 (1891): 437–452.

Harvey, H. E. "The Voice of Woman," *Westminster Review* 145 (1896): 193–196.

Hewitt, Emma Churchman. "The 'New Woman' in her Relation to the 'New Man,' " *Westminster Review* 147 (1897): 335–337.

Hogarth, Janet E. "Literary Degenerates," *Fortnightly Review* 63 (1895): 586–592.

————. "The Monstrous Regiment of Women," *Fortnightly Review* 68 (1897): 926–936.

Kenton, Edna. "How Women Propose," *Bookman* 33 (1911): 274–279.

————. "The Militant Women—and Women," *Century* 87 (1913): 13–20.

————."The Pap We Have Been Fed On," *Bookman* 39 (1914): 467–471.

————. "A Study of the Old 'New Woman,' Part I," *Bookman* 37 (1913): 154–158.

————. "A Study of the Old 'New Woman,' Part II," *Bookman* 37 (1913): 261–264.

Layard, Florence. "What Women Write and Read," *National and English Review* 10 (1887–1888): 376–381.

Leppington, Blanche. "Debrutalisation of Man," *Contemporary Review* 67 (1895): 725–743.

Linton, Elizabeth Lynn. *The Girl of the Period.* 2 vols. London: R. Bentley, 1883.

————. "Literature: Then and Now," *Fortnightly Review* 53 (1890): 517–531.

————. "Partisans of Wild Women," *Nineteenth Century* 31 (1892): 455–464.

————. "The Wild Women as Politicians," *Nineteenth Century* 30 (1891): 79–88.

————. "The Wild Women as Social Insurgents," *Nineteenth Century* 30 (1891): 596–605.

Malet, Lucas. "The Threatened Re Subjection of Women," *Fortnightly Review* 83 (1905): 806–819.

March-Phillipps, Evelyn. "The Working-Lady in London," *Fortnightly Review* 58 (1892): 193–203.

Moore, George. *Literature at Nurse, or Circulating Morals.* London: Vizetelly, 1885.

Morgan-Dockrell, Mrs. "Is the New Woman a Myth?" *Humanitarian* 8 (1896): 339–350.

"Mothers and Daughters;" "The Revolt of the Daughters;" and " A Reply from the Daughters," *Nineteenth Century* 35 (1894): 424–450.

Noble, James Ashcroft. "The Fiction of Sexuality," *Contemporary Review* 67 (1895): 490–498.

Nordau, Max. *Degeneration.* London: W. Heinemann, 1895.

"Novel Notes," *Bookman* 6 (1894): 24–25.

Oliphant, Mrs. Margaret. "The Anti-Marriage League," *Blackwood's* 159 (1896): 135–149.

————. "New Novels," *Blackwood's* 128 (1880): 378–404.

Peyton, J. "The Modern Malignant, II," *Humanitarian* 8 (1896): 52–58.

Pimenoff, Lydia Lvovna. "Science and the Woman's Question," *North American Review* 156 (1893): 248–251.

"Recent Novels," *Spectator* 483 (1895): 431–433.

Repplier, Agnes. "Marriage in Fiction," *Harper's Bazaar* 38 (1904): 451–455.

————. "The Spinster," *Harper's Bazaar* 38 (1904): 115–120.

Roberton, William. *The Novel-Reader's Handbook: A Brief Guide to Recent Novels and Novelists*. Birmingham: Holland Co., 1899.

Salmon, Edward. "What Girls Read," *Nineteenth Century* 20 (1886): 515–529.

[Scott, H. S., and E. B. Hall]. "Character Note. The New Woman," *Cornhill*, ns 23 (1894): 365–368.

Schreiner, Olive. *Women and Labour*. Leipzig: B. Tauchnitz, 1911.

Slater, Edith. "Men's Women in Fiction," *Westminster Review* 149 (1898): 571–577.

Smedley, Constance. "The Hedda Gabler of To-day," *Fortnightly Review* 88, ns 82 (1907): 77–90.

"Smudgiton, Borgia." "She-Notes," *Punch* 106 (1894): 109, 129.

"Socio-Literary Portents," *Speaker* 10 (1894): 683–685.

Somerset, Lady Henry, Harriet Prescott Spoffard, and Marian Harland. "Nagging Women," *North American Review* 160 (1895): 311–312.

Stead, W. T. "The Book of the Month. 'The Woman Who Did' by G. Allen," *Review of Reviews* 11 (1895): 177–190.

————. "The Novel of the Modern Woman," *Review of Reviews* 10 (1894): 64–74.

"The Strike of a Sex," *Quarterly Review* 179 (1894): 289–318.

Stutfield, Hugh E. "The Psychology of Feminism," *Blackwood's* 161 (1897): 104–117.

————. "Tommyrotics," *Blackwood's* 157 (1895): 833–845.

Sykes, A.G.P. "The Evolution of the Sex," *Westminster Review* 143 (1895): 396–400.

Tooley, Sarah, "The Woman's Question," *Humanitarian* 8 (1896): 161–169.

Waugh, Arthur. "Reticence in Literature," *Yellow Book* 1 (1894): 201–219.

Williams, Harold. *Modern English Writers, 1890–1914*. London: Sedgewick & Jackson, 1925.

Winchester, Boyd. "The Eternal Feminine—I. The New Woman," *Arena* 27 (1902): 367–373.

INDEX